A TRANSFORMED MIND AND HEART

# *A Transformed Mind and Heart*

## Becoming Vulnerable and Compassionate

*Joseph L. Breault*

Servant Books
Ann Arbor, Michigan

248
Br T



Published by: Servant Books
Box 8617
Ann Arbor, Michigan 48107

Available From: Servant Publications
Distribution Center
237 North Michigan
South Bend, Indiana 46601



Printed in the United States of America

ISBN 0-89283-057-3

*To*
*the other founders of the vision*
*in the Community of God's Love*
*Tom, Lyn & Bill*

*"My dear children, I love you and I call you to this vision. As my Son has laid down his life for you, so I empower you with my Spirit to daily lay down your lives in radical love for one another. As I have loved him so do I love you. I want you to experience my love as I draw you into the unity I have with him. Commit your lives to me in living this vision that you may be a sign of my love, of my kingdom, to all my children."*

*Prophetic Vision for*
*Community of God's Love*

# CONTENTS

# FOREWORD

The day one decides to be a Christian is the day one decides to relate in a new way toward others. Love of neighbor and love of God are inseparable (Matthew 22:37-38). In the first fervor of conversion one may think it easy to love even one's enemies. But as one continues to journey, one finds that it is not so easy to love even one's brothers and sisters in the Christian community. Perhaps for that reason, the final gospel to be written, that of John, does not speak any more of love of enemies, but only of fraternal love. Not that the former has been forgotten. But it is called forth only rarely in the Christian life, whereas fraternal love is tested daily. And if one cannot love those of one's own household, how will one ever love one's enemies?

In order to grow as a Christian I need roots. My roots are my relationships—with the Lord and with others. And the roots that really feed me and hold me in the storm are those relationships sealed by commitment. They are precious. They are life-giving. They are saving relationships. The quality of our living the gospel depends on the quality of our relationships.

Those who accept such premises will find in Joseph Breault's book a penetrating light on the growth of relationships, especially in community. How does a community live the gospel that forbids us to judge one another, yet calls us to fraternal correction? What is the Lord's plan concerning judgments in relationships and in community? These are the questions to which the author seeks an answer.

The book is experiential. It comes out of the challenge of one called to be a leader for a large Christian community, one who has reflected on his experience and that of his community in the light of scripture, Christian tradition, and insights offered by contemporary theology and psychology. And so it is more than experiential. It is wisdom. I have found much of what Joe has written here enlightening for myself and my own community.

"By this will all men know that you are my disciples, if you have love for one another" (Jn 13:35). Prayerfully read, this book can help us learn how to do just that.

George T. Montague S.M.

# PREFACE

Writing this book has been an opportunity for me to experience a deeper renewal of my mind and heart, for the book's subject is becoming vulnerable and compassionate, especially in the revealing areas of judgments, expectations, and fraternal correction.

These are crucial areas. Yet in eight years of working in a developing Christian community, I have met many people who have been confused about them. Some are scrupulous; others are too eager to judge and correct. This confusion, along with the wisdom our community has gained, has motivated me to undertake this work. It can aid in transforming our relationships regardless of our life situation.

I am aware of the dangers of writing on such sensitive topics when so many people need affirmation and encouragement. Yet these topics can and ought to go together with affirmation and encouragement, for love is strong and involves the truth. I hope that no one, by glancing through this book, misapplies its advice to justify harsh criticism of others. The book is meant to be prayerfully read as a catalyst for our own personal transformation.

I would like to thank the many people who have helped in the preparation of this book. To my family and the brothers and sisters of the Community of God's Love for their love and patience during the times these past few years when the book absorbed my time. It is from my relationships in the community that this book flows. To those who have helped me with their valuable criticisms, especially Rev. Chris Aridas, Jim Manney from Servant Books, and Rev. George Montague, S.M. To many who have helped with much typing, particularly Patrice Amatrudi, Stephanie Barresi, and Marge Pasko; and to Ellen Tejral who has gone over the notes and did the bulk of the index preparation with Kathy Dempsey's help. And most special thanks to God, for his mercy.

Joseph Breault

CHAPTER ONE

# FREEDOM TO BE VULNERABLE

Our Lord's final commandment—to love one another as he has loved us—is lived out in our relationships with others. God's love is not a functional service of others that happens in a superficial relationship. The context of his love is the depth of relationship and unity he calls us to: "Father, may they be one in us, as you are in me and I am in you" (Jn 17:21). Jesus is praying us into a very deep relationship with other brothers and sisters in the Lord. The heart of the gospel—loving others as God has loved us—can only be lived out in our relationships with others.

Our relationships are of many kinds, on many levels and of varied intensity. We have relationships with brothers and sisters in the Lord, our spouse, parents, children, co-workers, and friends. We have a relationship with the Lord himself. Some relationships are new, and we might find them exciting or confusing and threatening. Others are old; perhaps old problems trouble these relationships or perhaps they are simply stale. We might even be getting a little sick of the word "relationship" because so many of them are vaguely unsatisfying.

The question naturally arises, where do we turn for wisdom in our relationships with others? Do we turn to the Bible, to Church tradition, to modern psychology and theology? As good as those sources are, they remain merely theoretical until we can see how transformed relationships with others are being lived out in practice through the power of the Holy Spirit. We can see how this happens in small communities which have grown up in recent years in the Church. Those who are part of these communities are experiencing transformed relationships with others and have acquired wisdom on how to enter into deeper life-giving relationships in the Lord where we can love one another as he has loved us. The wisdom taps scripture, Church tradition, modern psychology and theology, and will be sketched out below.

First though, I will briefly describe the community out of whose experience this book is being written, Community of God's Love in Rutherford, New Jersey.[1] The community had its origins in 1969 when a number of us in the New York metropolitan area who were involved in the charismatic renewal gathered together to pray.[2] We heard the Lord gradually speaking to us about giving up our individual plans for our lives and coming to live together in Rutherford. In the summer of 1970, we moved together in a community living situation. Since then the Lord has been teaching us, often through our mistakes, about entering into deeper relationships in the Lord. This has truly been a death-resurrection experience. We believe that what God is doing among us goes far beyond the scope of a small community. The renewal and transformation of our relationships in the Lord is a charism for the Church and a witness to what all are called to.

How does one go about sharing what God has been teaching us in relationships, drawing on the different sources of wisdom which have been tapped? We felt it would be best for the purpose of this book to concentrate on a pivotal and normally difficult aspect of deeper relationships in the Lord—namely, the judgments and expectations involved in fraternal correction.

"Judgments" and "expectations" are problem words. Most Christians think they should avoid making judgments. However, while scripture says we should not condemn others, it encourages making right judgments in relationships in specific situations. While we will have to wait for later chapters to clarify the meaning of such judgments in our relationships, experience shows that deeper relationships do not occur without them. Refusing to judge at all leads to either superficial or unsatisfying relationships, where we repress what is really going on inside of us. The question of judgment boils down to an effort to achieve a posture in relationships that allows us to make right judgments instead of wrong ones.

"Expectations" is another problem word, similar to "judgments." Whose expectations do we mean? Our expectations of someone else? Their expectations of us? God's expectations? If, for example, I expect someone to love me by being available and sensitive when I am experiencing difficulties, I will make a judgment that something is wrong in the relationship if this is not happening. To live in the make-believe land of "no expectations and judgments" means we will either have superficial relationships or we will accumulate negative feelings that damage relationships. Right judgments and expectations are essential to loving one another as Jesus loves us.

In the following chapters, we will discuss in depth our posture for judgments, expectations, and fraternal correction. If relationships with others are to continually deepen and be empowered by the Holy Spirit, we will sooner or later confront questions like these. What does it mean to be pure of heart as we call one another to holiness? How should I approach my brother or sister when there is a fault to be pointed out? What should my posture be in such situations? How can I authentically support instead of condemn or discourage? What judgments and expectations need to be brought out into the light in relationships so we can draw closer together in unity? These questions become germane as our relationships with other Christians deepen and as we take seriously the call we have to love one another as Christ Jesus has loved us.

## *A Vulnerable Posture*

What we have learned in our community experience is that the "how to's" are of secondary importance. The most important aspect of judgments and expectations in relationships is our posture in approaching them.

As we reflect on our community experience, scripture, tradition, and some modern sources, a clarity emerges regarding our posture toward our brothers and sisters. Our Christian stance in relationships is one of having compassion with others and openly exposing our hearts to them, trusting in their compassion for us. This is true throughout our relationships, yet this truth emerges even more sharply in the area of expectations and judgments. We find that our judgments and expectations of others become the ideal laboratory in which to test and discern whether we are loving as Jesus does, and to determine how we can yield more fully to his grace. It is here that we have a heightened awareness of the presence or absence of vulnerability and compassion. Reflection on these matters gives us wisdom, not just about isolated judgments we make, but about the way we live full Christian lives. Freedom to surrender in trust is God's gift of grace to us. This gift comes only through him.

Unless we are secure in God's personal love for us, knowing as St. Paul did that Jesus Christ died for me (Gal 2:20), we will never be able to expose our hearts to one another. "Perfect love casts out all fear" (1 Jn 4:18) and to live in such love frees us to risk. Loving, entering into deeper relationships of unity, bringing judgments and expectations into the light, is a risk well worth taking, as scripture says in Psalm 133:1, "Behold, how good it is, and how pleasant, where brethren dwell as one."

However, living this way costs us our protections. This is exemplified in nature when the male albatross courts the female. He reveals his intentions by raising one wing in such a manner that he makes himself vulnerable to attack. He is communicating trust by an act which removes his protections.[3] In loving as Jesus does, we freely choose to make ourselves vulnerable; it is the posture for loving which refuses to be determined by the fear of being overwhelmed, demolished, attacked.

The meaning of vulnerability is beautifully expressed in a poem by Robert Fox.

> Vulnerability is that quality in a man that enables
> him to be:
> defenseless, unfettered by ties of fear; unchained
> by ideologies; uncharted by predetermined goals;
> powerless, lacking the will to impose or manipulate;
> open, capable of being affected and shaped, reachable,
> gateless, wall-less;
> receptive, able to be reached or penetrated, unlocked,
> unblocked, open-armed;
> growing, undefined in any final way, in constant process
> of definition;
> wanton, foolishly exposed to life and its crashing impact,
> free.[4]

The struggle for freedom to be vulnerable, to be open to risking our protections in order to love, to relinquish control of others and to call them forth, is a life-long journey. It is an exciting journey, a painful journey, for as we begin to taste the freedom to surrender in trust on one level, new vistas appear where we are still locked in, closed, rigid, fearful, isolated, and doing everything we can to protect ourselves from others, including God. He who is faithful in the struggle will prove victorious, and God promises to "give him a white stone upon which is inscribed a new name, to be known only by him who receives it" (Rv 2:17). We become increasingly secure in our identities, in our Father's love for us, in who we are in the light of the Lord's love. We become more able to absorb both God's love and the love of our brothers and sisters. It is undeniably worth trading our protections for all of this.

The story of the rich young man in scripture is a warning against such self-protections. He comes to Jesus asking how to enter eternal life. When Jesus tells him to keep the commandments—the structures—he responds that he has done all this. Jesus says there is one more thing to do—to sell everything and follow him. Jesus asks him to dispose of all his protections, to become vulnerable, and to live as Jesus himself does. This is too much for the rich young man; he is fearful of what it might mean, and he goes away sad. He does not see the life available if he trusts in God for protection.

We are rich in things that protect us—money, possessions, defense mechanisms, false identities, barriers, illusions of status and acceptability, predetermined goals that rule out the uncharted leadings of the Spirit. Jesus asks us to get rid of it all, to strip ourselves and to follow him. "Foxes have lairs, the birds of the sky have nests, but the Son of Man has nowhere to lay his head" (Lk 9:58).

Jesus is saddened when we refuse to open ourselves more deeply to others, and cling to the protections we are rich in. "I assure you, only with difficulty will a rich man enter into the Kingdom of God" (Mt 19:23). It costs to enter life, to be free, to surrender in trust. Yet we gain more than it ever costs. When we attempt to save our life by protecting ourselves, we lose it. When we lose our lives by letting go of our protections, we find it by trusting God. If we persist in maintaining all our protections so we can safely be in control, then each new thing is only one more burden to cope with instead of a doorway to the exciting possibilities of God's miracles and his guidance. "Moreover, everyone who has given up home, brothers or sisters, father or mother, wife or children or property for my sake will receive many times as much and inherit eternal life" (Mt 19:29).

Vulnerability is a decisive posture for our relationships, and is noticeably absent or present in our judgments and expectations of others.

## *Struggling With Our Posture*

We can experience the struggle of becoming vulnerable especially in our gifts. Our gifts can get in our way. I know this from my own life as I experience the struggle for freedom to be vulnerable in the very gifts that I have.

As the community has developed over the years, the shepherds—the overall leaders of the community—come together to pray and care for the community's life and vision. We have realized that God has gifted each of us in a unique way and that our ministry becomes life-giving and effective as each of us and our gifts are linked together. This fundamental lesson—that spiritual power flows from unity—has led us to put the highest priority on our relationships together in the Lord. We are committed to deal immediately with any static, resistance, distancing, or temptations that undermine our unity. In the process, we have become more aware of our gifts.

The other shepherds tell me I have a gift to govern, to organize, and to draw people together in a way that facilitates the Spirit's work. I am able to help people see how to live the Christian life in a practical, daily way. We have also discovered that every gift can be used poorly. In my case, I have a tendency to structure things too soon. Rather than letting relationships develop, I can succumb to a proclivity to be in control. At times, when people do not fit into the planned or existing structure, I am tempted to squeeze them in. At times I perceive as an interference anything that might involve change or re-orientation.

Because of this, when a person speaks a word to me which seems to interfere with the way things are going, I am often closed without my realizing it. Frequently I would simply reject such a word and ignore it. Perhaps I will tolerate it, intellectually analyze it, but still not let it penetrate my mind and heart. Yet true discernment can begin only when such a word can enter.

Usually the other person realizes he or she is not getting through, that I am not allowing myself to be really touched, truly vulnerable to the word. The other person is then in a dilemma. He can either insist and press the matter, or give up, in which case we grow more and more distant.

I resist others at times because I fear that if I let their word penetrate, I will no longer be on top of the situation and it will overwhelm me. Before I am willing to accept their comment, I unrealistically want a whole new understanding of things that integrates the new word. I am tempted to find security in the predictable status quo instead of in God's love. I find it uncomfortable if things are messy, if plans are changed, or if different ideas linger without a clear resolution of them.

Yet that is real life; my understanding cannot be perfect. It is not possible to be in control in that kind of way. We know that things—and people—are not all that neat. Real people never fit in perfectly. My tendency to be on top, to be in control, reflects a lack of vulnerability. It is a way of protecting myself from brothers and sisters, and even from God himself.

It is good to critically reflect on the words people give us and to think things through. Yet God wants us to place first priority on accepting one another and being in a close unity in our relationships. Letting a disquieting word deeply enter into us is not to be gullible; it is the requirement for true discernment. A seeming interference might turn out to be a surprise of the Holy Spirit.

In the scriptures, Mary is a beautiful example of vulnerability. When the angel came to announce that she was to be the mother of God, she opened herself without structures to protect her. If I were in a situation like hers, I think I would have asked the angel to arrange for a media blitz and official approval from the Sanhedrin before consenting. I would have looked ahead to all the complications, changes, implications. Instead of just accepting the word, I would have wanted God to present a detailed, comprehensive plan to implement it. I would be more than willing to serve and give myself as long as I was protected from getting in trouble and was able to have it my way.

But Mary was vulnerable and trusted God's plan totally. She knew she did not fit into anyone's plan but God's, not even Joseph's. She realized that God's plan was scandalous in terms of her time; it put her in great jeopardy and had seemingly impossible complications. She resisted proving herself to Joseph and trusted God to protect her. "Her husband Joseph, being a man of honor and wanting to spare her publicity, decided to divorce her informally. He had made up his mind to do this when the angel of the Lord appeared to him in a dream and said, 'Joseph son of David, do not be afraid to take Mary home as your wife.' When Joseph woke up he did what the angel of the Lord had told him to do: he took his wife to his home" (Mt 1:19, 20, 24 JB). God always provides when we trust in him.

Mary's focus was on rejoicing in God, in his exciting miracles and leadings. A lack of structural protection or intellectual understanding were not obstacles to her. She was capable of being affected and shaped by the Holy Spirit, reachable, gateless, wall-less. She was undefined in any final way in terms of her own plan for her life or else she would have rejected God's word. She was open to finding out God's plan for her life step-by-step, never having the whole picture and never locking out what God might do next. She was free to be vulnerable to God.

I recall an experience a few years ago that was a breakthrough to being more vulnerable. It occurred during a month's retreat at a Trappist monastery. My daily job was to feed the cattle. One day, after filling the trailer with silage and driving the tractor to the feed bin, I noticed how hungry the cattle were. As soon as they saw me driving toward the gate, they all came running. They were not concerned with manners or politeness; their single-hearted desire was to eat. It struck me how much more inhibited I was in my hunger for God.

After feeding the cattle I went to the Shenandoah River nearby and reflected on my inhibitions. I wanted God, I desired him, but it had to be within respectable limits; it had to stop short of embarrassment. I was not free; I was fearful of lowering my defenses. Only God's mercy could help me, so I went to chapel to pray.

It was winter and the way to chapel was covered with a sheet of icy snow. Seeing this I thought of how cold and hard my own heart was; how I resisted being a fool and professing before men my desire for God.

When I arrived at the chapel I knelt to pray. Suddenly, out of nowhere, I experienced Mary's presence. Without seeing or hearing a thing I felt my heart softening and melting, and experienced a freedom to surrender in trust, to be less self-conscious in my desire for God than ever before. In experiencing this precious gift of freedom, I knew there was no way in the world I could ever produce it or deserve it. I was filled with thanks to the Lord for this experience with Mary which softened and opened my heart. I was very conscious of my need for God's ongoing help in order to give myself to this grace of freedom, and yield to it afresh day by day.

## *This Book's Goal: Transformation*

Our goal in this book is to help you to experience a transformation in your relationships with others and to acquire wisdom about how to enter into deeper life-giving relationships in the Lord where we can love one another as he has loved us. To achieve this goal, we will zero in on one of the touchiest, yet most important aspects of deeper personal relationships—the expectations and judgments involved in fraternal correction. It is an area of strongly conflicting emotions. We both desire yet fear others telling us their perceptions and judgments about us. On the one hand, we want that kind of honest communication with others so that we may grow from it and that our relationship may deepen. Yet we fear and resist communication on that deeper level.

This book is coming out of our community's experience. We have learned that a transformed relationship life with others depends more on our posture or approach than on the "how-to's," even though many of the practical "how-to's" become clear along the way. This book is not a text to study how to correct other people, or to adjust our expectations and judgments. Neither is it a subjective journal account of our community experiences in becoming more vulnerable and compassionate. It is something in between: a collection of wisdom, focused on judgments and expectations, which has been accumulated as the fruit of our community's experience of deeper relationships of love. It is practical wisdom reflected upon in the light of scripture, Christian tradition, and contemporary psychology and theology.

I have written this book in the expectation that it will help you make your relationships work better. You are going to be less confused about how to act in tough interpersonal situations. You will have a better idea of the way God works in your life through other people. It might be presumptuous to say this, except that we have experienced the power of the Holy Spirit that is available to empower our relationships; we are confident that it can happen to you too. This book should be read prayerfully with an eye toward contrasting it section-by-section to your own relationships, expecting the Holy Spirit to be speaking to you about them. The wisdom shared here is meant for all your relationships and is in no way limited to relationships among those who are in a closer community together.

We are drawing wisdom about deeper personal relationships transformed by the Lord from many sources: our community's experience, scripture, the Desert Fathers, a modern psychologist, Thomas Aquinas, Bernard Lonergan, a recent paper from the American bishops, and a study of Psalm 51. Such a diversity of material warrants a map through the book at its beginning, so that the theme of posturing fraternal correction, becoming vulnerable and compassionate, can be seen in an overview right away.

The Introduction, "Freedom to be Vulnerable," and the Conclusion, "Freedom for Compassion," set the stage and close the curtain for the discussion on the posture for judgments and expectations in our relationships. The experience of our life together in community has taught us that the vital qualities in a Christian's posture are the qualities of being vulnerable and compassionate. While the community's experience underlies the entire book, these two major insights from our life together underlie and surround the rest of the material in the book.

Part One of the book discusses scripture and deals with our thought patterns (Chapter Two), expectations (Chapter Three), and judgments (Chapter Four). A call to child-like vulnerability emerges. Our scriptural identity gives us a new way of thinking and a new security in God's love. The practical aids of actively praising and apocalyptic thinking are discussed, and their potential for changing our posture is explained.

Chapter Three—Scriptural Expectations: Completing or Competing?—examines the tensions between divergent expectations in scripture. In our limited view they appear to compete but in God's larger vision they complete each other. We first consider how to apply the teaching of the Old Testament wisdom books on correcting others. Next we consider the balanced New Testament approach to judging others and examine in detail the key passage on fraternal correction, Matthew 18, and its practical advice about encouragement, care for others, and desiring unity and forgiveness.

Part Two of the book focuses on Christian tradition and goes from the Desert Fathers (Chapter Five) to Aquinas (Chapter Six) to the Church (Chapter Seven). The Desert Fathers clarify the practical discipline needed to preserve purity of heart in the midst of our judgments and expectations.

Aquinas helps clarify exactly what judging others means and deals with such common questions as rash judgments, giving people the benefit of the doubt, and the value of agreements and authority. In Church decisions concerning inner and outer forums we see the need to vulnerably share in freedom. Vatican II teaches us the centrality of respecting persons in the process. The recent papers of the National Conference of Catholic Bishops on due process highlight this point more practically by giving us some criteria to discern whether we are respecting people in the process of expectations and judgments.

Part Three contains some reflections from modern psychology (Chapter Eight) and theology (Chapter Nine) and an application of this knowledge to transformed relationships in light of our community experience (Chapter Ten). From these modern sources we gain deeper insight into what prevents vulnerability and how to counteract obstacles. Finally, Chapter Twelve has a prayer for purity of heart that helps us enter into the posture for hope in judgments.

We do not want to miss the forest because of the trees. Our topic throughout is judgments and expectations and the main point of our reflections is our posture—the state of our heart—with respect to the topic. The transformation that the Lord wants to do in us as we read this book is a transformation of our thought patterns and posture out of which come our expectations and judgments. Letting the Lord speak to us about the topic of fraternal correction is an ideal way to let him transform our relationships with others.

# *Part One*

# *Scripture*

CHAPTER TWO

# OUR SCRIPTURAL IDENTITY

Approaching fraternal correction in a life-giving way requires a new way of thinking, a new mind-set, a revolutionary thought pattern. Our thoughts reveal our beliefs and affect our posture and emotional life. When we interpret a difficulty or another's wrongdoing as catastrophic because it interferes with our plans (a worldly way of thinking), then we are bound by condemnation, fear, bitterness, and resistance. When we interpret a difficulty or wrongdoing as an opportunity for grace to abound even more as God's plan unfolds (a spiritual way of thinking), then we are freed for compassion, faith, peaceful joy, and vulnerability. Either the worldly way of thinking or the spiritual way of thinking forms our posture and determines the emotions surrounding our expectations and judgments.

Part One of this book focuses on three successive levels of approaching fraternal correction in scripture. The first level, presented here in Chapter Two, is the foundation of our thought patterns. The transformed mind opens up to us the meaning of our scriptural identity. Who are we as sons and daughters of God, and how do God's children think? We discuss the importance of acknowledging God's plan, a task which exposes the struggle inherent in being faithful to a spiritual way of thinking. Two practical helps are explained which root us in a spiritual way of thinking more deeply: actively praising and apocalyptic thinking. A concrete example of the posture shift that results from knowing our scriptural identity is then given.

Later in Chapter Three we delve into the second level of scriptural expectations. This is not a separate topic but flows organically from our scriptural identity. Only in light of a spiritual way of thinking can we see the tensions and contrasts of different expectations in scripture as instructions which complete instead of compete. In Chapter Four, the third level of fraternal correction in scripture is examined. In both the wisdom literature of the Old Testament and New Testament passages on fraternal correction, especially Matthew 18, we see that our posture is the most important aspect of our judgments. This insight takes on a noon-time clarity only in the light of our scriptural identity which frees us to complete instead of compete.

As we enter into the progression of Part One of this book—from thought patterns, to the understanding of expectations, to the judgments involved in relationships—let us journey with a consciousness that God wants to speak to our hearts about ourselves, our posture, and our relationships. The topic of expectations and judgments in the background of our thought patterns is the scaffolding God can use to rebuild us, transform us, and change our relationships.

## *A Transformed Mind*

What does scripture say about our identity? Who are we? What is the appropriate way to think about ourselves? In Galatians we read, "You are no longer a slave but a son! And the fact that you are a son makes you an heir, by God's design" (4:7). Our scriptural identity as sons becomes clearer as we consider Jesus who prayed "Abba," for we have received "a spirit of adoption through which we cry out, 'Abba!' (that is, 'Father')" (Rom 8:15).

Jesus liked to be away from the crowds, alone in the desert or on a mountain, praying to his Father and being with him.[5] Jesus' emotions and faith found their clearest expression in the word "Abba." The Hebrew concept of fatherhood is a relationship of care and authority on the one side and of love and obedience on the other. "Abba," ("Father") holds the meaning of absolute authority and tenderness. It is a language of experience, not doctrine. It was the expression of a warm intimacy and trust. As Dunn puts it:

> Jesus experienced an intimate relation of sonship in prayer: he found God characteristically to be "Father;" and this sense of God was so real, so loving, so compelling, that whenever he turned to God it was the cry "Abba" that came most naturally to his lips.[6]

Out of the identity of sonship comes not only a security in his Father's love, but a responsibility and a mission. His Father has a plan that must be followed and obeyed, no matter what the cost. This, combined with the deep security in his Father's love, creates a spiritual way of thinking. When worldly ways of thinking emerge—for example, Satan's temptations in the wilderness and Peter's resistance to Jesus' death—Jesus resisted them as incompatible with experienced sonship. Jesus' experience of sonship opens the way for ours, as he is "the first-born of many brothers" (Rom 8:29). Our identity is in being sons and daughters of God. Do our thought patterns reflect it?

Insight into the answer can be gained by reflecting on how St. Paul writes of the worldly mind in Chapter one of Romans. The pagans refuse to glorify God or thank him (v. 21) even though God's power and divinity is visible (v. 20). Because of this refusal, their hearts were darkened (v. 21) and they began to get involved in all sorts of disastrous things (v. 22 f). "And since they did not see fit to acknowledge God, God gave them up to a base mind and to improper conduct" (RSV, v. 29). Their mind—meaning their way of thinking, attitude, or thought pattern[7]—was base because it refused to recognize and acknowledge God's power at work. The fruit of this worldly way of thinking was to take on the wrong posture of ill-will, envy, deceit (v. 29) and unmercifulness (v. 31).

In light of the prevailing worldly mind-set, Paul urges the Romans, "Do not conform yourselves to this age but be transformed by the renewal of your mind . . ." (12:2). This spiritual thought pattern is sensitive to God's working in our daily life and so enables us to "judge what is God's will, what is good, pleasing and perfect" (12:2). In the following verses Paul describes the fruit of this spiritual way of thinking as taking on the posture of humility (v. 3), unity (v. 4-8), respecting the brethern (v. 10), rejoicing in hope, and being patient under trial (v. 12).

In these passages "mind" means our way of thinking or thought patterns. An old mind involves a worldly way of thinking that ignores God and creates a bitter, self-centered posture. A transformed mind involves a spiritual way of thinking which acknowledges God and creates a loving, open posture in us. For Paul, "mind" does not mean our intelligence as measured in I.Q. tests or how quickly we can experience insights.[8] He is talking about how we approach life and respond to it. What do we do, for example, when we experience a relationship that is difficult to work out? Is our response characterized by thought patterns of What am I going to do? What a mess this is. How can I avoid having this person interfere with my life? Why did this have to happen? If so, Paul would say that our mind is a worldly one which will lead to a posture that is bitter, angry, depressed, overwhelmed. For Paul, our way of thinking is an ever-evolving pattern, not a static mind that we are locked into. Our mind needs constant renewal, constant transformation.

The need for a transformed mind which recognizes God's working in our daily lives and relationships also comes out clearly in Ephesians. "I declare and solemnly attest in the Lord that you must no longer live as the pagans do—their minds empty, their understanding darkened. They are estranged from a life in God because of their ignorance and their resistance" (4:17-18). The worldly way of thinking cannot see how God is working in everything that happens in one's daily life. The reason they are out of touch with God is their ignorance of how the Spirit is leading and guiding them through everything that happens, an ignorance founded on hardness of heart and resistance to God which refuses to accept their identity as sons.

Paul urges the Ephesians to lay aside the old self (4:22) now that they have "learned Christ" (4:20), and to "acquire a fresh spiritual way of thinking" (4:23). This putting on of the transformed mind is an active unlearning and re-education process about which Paul gives practical advice in 4:25-5:21. As Paul describes the practicalities involved in this "mind transplant," you can sense how a person's posture changes. "Get rid of all bitterness, all passion and anger, harsh words, slander, and malice of every kind. In place of these, be kind to one another, compassionate, and mutually forgiving, just as God has forgiven you in Christ" (4:31-32).

A transformed mind is founded upon our experience of sonship and evokes our acknowledging and responding to God's presence and direction in the everyday circumstances of our lives. It is a question of our identity, of who we say we are. The effect of this new creation mind-set on us is the development of a childlike posture of vulnerability and compassion, a change in our whole emotional tone. It is not a magic transformation. Though being done under the power of the Spirit, it requires an active vigilance in putting off the old and yielding to the new. Let us reflect on each of these elements in turn.

## *Acknowledging God's Plan*

A transformed mind opens up to us our scriptural identity as sons and daughters of God. Who we say we are forms our way of thinking, our thought patterns. These in turn form a basis for our expectations and judgments. In this section we want to continue to explore a transformed mind as a relationship with God and expose the struggle inherent in being faithful to a spiritual way of thinking.

The transformed mind which acknowledges God is the work of the Spirit in us; it is not simply the self-discipline of positive thinking. The continual transformation and renewal of our minds is synonymous with an ever-deepening relationship with God. An ideal means to discern whether we are opening ourselves more deeply to God is whether we are opening ourselves more deeply to others. "If anyone says, 'My love is fixed on God,' yet hates his brother, he is a liar" (1 Jn 4:20). Our posture in receiving God is no different than our posture in receiving our brothers and sisters. The transformed mind is brought about by our experience of God as our Father and of Jesus as the first of many brothers. Our relationship with God allows us to acknowledge and respond to his presence and direction in the everyday circumstances of our lives. This heightened awareness of God's presence and guidance is our experience of the Holy Spirit, a divine person who can have a direct and startling effect on our experience of God.

Christians have been given the gift of the Holy Spirit in Baptism. Many of us, however, put the gift on the shelf, unaware that the gift needed to be opened. For many of us the Spirit's presence was never activated or released in a way that makes a startling experiential difference. Today in the charismatic renewal many are experiencing what is called the baptism of the Spirit, the opening of the gift received in Baptism and the opening of ourselves to a personal relationship with the Holy Spirit.

My own experience of the baptism of the Holy Spirit brought my relationship with God from a theoretical realm focused on what ought to be done to the practical and personal realm of knowing God. I experienced God's love as my Father and became secure in it. I had a new realization that Jesus was the center of my life; everything now revolved around him. I experienced being called by God for a purpose and left empowered by the Spirit through the gifts he had given to me. Scripture and prayer became opportunities for a deeper personal relationship with God, Father and Son. Service became an opportunity for a deeper relationship with the Holy Spirit as I experienced him working through me. My mind was transformed so that I was focused on God and his plan instead of on me and my plans. This happened in a way that freed me and brought the real desires of my heart to fulfillment.

In receiving the gift of the Holy Spirit, our minds are transformed and we are a new creation. Yet we must actively receive and open ourselves to the Holy Spirit, not just once but as a continuing lifetime process. It is similar to deeply receiving and opening ourselves to any other person—allowing them to enter in and affect us, being fully present to them. The power of the Spirit that raised Jesus from the dead is the power that transforms our minds and floods our hearts with God's love (Rom 5:5). Our minds, in a sense, are encompassed by a spiritual zone which is sensitive to and resonant with the Spirit. It senses whether God is giving a green light or a red one; where he is leading and which path to take. Our hearts are flooded with God's personal love for us as our Father as we fall in love with God. Being in love with God becomes the grounding principle of our thoughts, actions, and desires and helps us be faithfully present to his Spirit, who through our trust and openness can touch and change us.

The Spirit empowers us to "put on the new man, one who grows in knowledge as he is formed anew in the image of his

Creator" (Col 3:10). This is not the willpower drudgery of trying to think the right thoughts, but the Spirit through whom "the love of God has been poured out in our hearts" (Rom 5:5). As Lucien Cerfaux writes, in considering theories on the immanence of the Spirit:

> St. Paul, however, speaks boldly of the creation, in ourselves, of a new mind capable of assimilating the mystery of God and of realizing our rank as sons. I felt justified in continuing his thought by suggesting that there is a sort of spiritual zone, connatural with the Holy Spirit, which encompasses our human minds. Thus we shall become once again what God desired us to be, in the likeness of himself, created anew 'in knowledge.'[9]

The gift of the Spirit is given to us through Baptism. The Spirit is present to us. But are we present to the Spirit? The Spirit is a person, and, as with any person, both parties need to be present to one another for a personal relationship to flower. Receiving another person means much more than simply being physically together. It involves an active faith and trust where we are vulnerably present to the other person, allowing him to enter into us and affect us. We grow in this trust; being present to the other person is ever-evolving. As more of our fear is cast out by his love, we have the faith to let him enter more deeply, to enter into more sensitive areas. As he enters, we discover with him new things about ourselves. However, being present to the other person is precarious; we need to continually and actively lean forward to give ourselves to him more deeply or else we will wake up one morning and realize how separated we have become.

Obstacles to our fully receiving another human person are the same obstacles to receiving the person of the Spirit. They largely boil down to fears and insecurities which are unique to each person yet not so different that we cannot understand them and have compassion for one another.

A personal example from my own life might illustrate the point that the obstacles to receiving others are the same as the obstacles to receiving God. A few years ago the four shepherds of our community, the four of us who are the overall leaders, went away for a week to pray and talk about what God was doing in the community and what ought to happen in several situations. At one point we sensed that we needed to come into a deeper unity ourselves before we could continue with the business at hand. There was some kind of static or resistance in our relationships which did not allow us to clearly hear God's word to us about the business we needed to discuss.

We stopped and for three days prayed to be more open. God confirmed in our prayer that he wanted to do a significant thing in our hearts but he said there were obstacles to our hearing him and absorbing his love. As we continued to pray and ask him what these obstacles were, we strongly sensed him saying that the obstacles which blocked his voice and his love were the same obstacles which kept us from hearing one another and absorbing one another's love. We began to discuss what these obstacles were and prayed over one another to be freed from them.

I talked about my tendency to be in control, and the other shepherds prayed over me to be freed from it. As they prayed, I suddenly felt closed, resistant, tight. I felt afraid of being freed. I told this to the others and we talked about it. It seemed that God was giving me a deeper awareness than I had had before about an obstacle to receiving the other shepherds and him. I had always thought I was open, but now I was able to see that I wasn't.

We continued to pray and asked the Lord to reveal the source of the resistance I felt. An image came to my mind. I stood in front of a large dam. There were thousands of tons of water on the other side of the dam. I was on the side the water would come out, exactly at the center of it. On my right hand was a lever which would open the dam. The sense I had was that to be open to other people was the same as being asked to pull the lever. I was afraid of drowning, of being overwhelmed.

Tom, one of the other shepherds, received another image while we were praying. It was almost identical except that he saw what was behind the dam: a life-giving stream of water which would refresh me, not drown me. I began to see the source of the obstacles to really receiving the others, and was increasingly free. I also experienced a freedom to be with God and to absorb his love. After the days of praying with one another for freedom, we went back to the business items. We experienced a grace of unity and love to be fully present to one another. As we shared about different items, a huge number of questions seemed to be answered in a few hours. In the remaining four days of our week together, we wondered what the Lord wanted to do. We asked him and we received a prophecy about the vision he had for the community and the direction he wanted it to go in. We spent the days discerning the prophecy and coming to understand its implications. That word has turned out to be the directional foundation for the entire community. We would never have been present enough to the Lord and his love to hear him speaking it if we hadn't been present enough to one another.

The core of our fears is thinking that we will be overwhelmed and destroyed by the other person—not physically, but in terms of our identity, our person, our feelings, and our plans. We fear we will not be respected or understood, that if we vulnerably reveal ourselves, our openness will be used against us to thwart our very hopes and plans. Each of us could spell out this fear more completely for ourselves.

However, letting other people enter in and *receiving* them means a decision to trust, to have faith. This is not a blind decision, for unless there were some evidence for the other's love, the decision would be silly. Yet we act in faith nevertheless, and this involves risking ourselves with no absolute assurance of the outcome. And so if we do let another person enter, then something will die: a false self-image will gradually be undermined. Something will also be born of the Spirit: a transformed mind, and freedom.

This lack of trust, wanting to have hold of our lives instead of giving our lives to others, shows up acutely in our "hidden plans." If a friend does something for us we like, we are grateful and presume he is acting out of love. However, if a friend does something for us which interferes with our plans, which perhaps touches a sore spot, or questions an illusion we are living in, then we tend to be upset. The only way to grow in that relationship is to make a decision to trust, to choose unity with that person over our own plan. Choosing authentic unity means choosing to be formed by the Spirit instead of being led by our plans. It means choosing to receive and acknowledge that person and to depend upon his love for us, even if it is hard for us to let go of our plans.

It is much the same with acknowledging God by receiving the person of his Spirit. If during a financial crisis I suddenly receive an anonymous hundred-dollar check in the mail, I am grateful to God for his love. If, however, I suddenly get very ill during a financial crisis, it is hard to be grateful to God and to praise him. Only if I choose God's plan for my life over my own plan can I acknowledge God and be formed by him. This sensitivity to the Spirit of God working in every circumstance rests on receiving the person of the Spirit in the experience of sonship. As sons, we choose to trust (have faith) that our lives are better off being formed by God's loving plan than they are if we are in control.

In summary, we can consider Romans 8:14, "All who are led by the Spirit of God are sons of God." Yielding to the Spirit means yielding to the experience of our Father's love which forms a transformed mind. A struggle is inherent in being faithful to this spiritual way of thinking that sees God's plan unfolding in every detail of our lives. It is a struggle to let go of our plans, our false identity which we can control. The thoughts and temptations that come to us during the day are the areas of struggle where we must choose to be led by the Spirit of God.

It is not a matter of willpower, but of yielding to God's love, to his Spirit. Our alternative is to be led by the world, the flesh, and the devil.

## *Actively Praising*

What practical helps are there to yield to God's love and his Spirit in this way? Two things that can root us more deeply in our scriptural identity as sons and daughters of God are actively praising and apocalyptic thinking. Not only can they reinforce and deepen our security in God's love, but they can also help discern where we are resisting it.

Actively praising the Lord for an "interference" in our lives can be a practical help in acknowledging God's loving presence and plan and receiving a transformed mind. There is, however, no magic process to achieve the transformed mind which brings about a shift in our posture. Though done under the power of the Spirit, we need active vigilance in putting off the old and yielding to the new. The practical help of actively praising the

Lord for seeming interferences in our lives is merely a way of maintaining that vigilance.

St. Paul, in his great pastoral concern for those he fathered in Christ, is concerned that renewed thought patterns replace the old. When we become a new creation everything is totally new. Our environment does not radically change but everything else does—our response to it, the way we perceive it, our thought patterns about it. It is not a matter of being in a different world, but being under a different Lord and so seeing the world differently. The worldly way of thinking in the old creation sees weakness, trial, and distress as occasions for fear, bitterness, and depression. The spiritual way of thinking in the new creation acknowledges God working through trials and sees them as occasions for grace to abound even more. This acknowledgment of God's working can change the way we feel and behave.

Our way of thinking, of course, is not so black or white. A spiritual way of thinking is precarious. Unless we constantly strive to receive it fully, we will suddenly discover how far we have slid down the mountain. Some areas of our lives fall easily under Jesus' Lordship. Others, however, steeped in a worldly way of thinking, require a struggle on our part to bring under Jesus' Lordship. This process is complex and unique to each individual, yet Paul's words of "Rejoice in the Lord always! I say it again—Rejoice!" (Phil 4:4) are meant for everyone and apparently for all circumstances.

Consider the following scripture passages as descriptions of how a Christian should respond to weakness, trial, and distress. In seeing the thought patterns of the transformed mind, we can begin to get a glimpse of scripture's vision for dealing with difficulties in personal relationships. The first step in dealing with such problems is to change our own mental thought patterns about them.

> Count it all joy, my brethren, when you meet various trials, for you know that the testing of your faith produces steadfastness. And let steadfastness have its full effect, that you may be perfect and complete, lacking in nothing. (Jas 1:2-4 RSV)

> More than that, we rejoice in our sufferings, knowing that suffering produces endurance, and endurance produces

character, and character produces hope, and hope does not disappoint us, because God's love has been poured into our hearts through the Holy Spirit which has been given to us. (Rom 5:3-5 RSV)

Beloved, do not be surprised at the fiery ordeal which comes upon you to prove you, as though something strange were happening to you. But rejoice in so far as you share Christ's sufferings, that you may also rejoice and be glad when his glory is revealed. (1 Pt 4:12-13 RSV)

These passages are from different contexts, but note how they direct a Christian's response to weakness, trial, and distress. We are to rejoice, to be filled with hope, realizing trials are for the good. We should praise the Lord instead of grumbling and complaining. Even in seemingly disastrous situations one is never to fall into the trap of the worldly way of thinking "It is horrible that ....," "It is terrible that....," "It is catastrophic that...." Rather, one is to praise God for it, rejoicing in hope, even if it goes against the grain. When we encounter real evil, we cannot praise God for the evil, but we can praise him for the good we know he can draw from the evil. Actively praising is not meant to be unauthentic, but it brings our resistance to the light, activates in us the spiritual way of thinking, and keeps us rooted in the truth even when we do not feel the truth.

As Merlin Carothers puts it in his best-seller *Prison to Praise*:

Jesus didn't promise to change circumstances around us, but he did promise great peace and pure joy to those who would learn to believe that God actually controls *all things*. The very act of praise releases the power of God into a set of circumstances and enables God to change them if this is his design. Very often it is our attitudes that hinder the solution of a problem. God is sovereign and could certainly cut across our wrong thought patterns and attitudes. But his perfect plan is to bring each of us into fellowship and communion with him, and so he allows circumstances and incidents which will bring our wrong attitudes to our attention.[10]

In the new creation, difficulties take on a new meaning because of the new vision with which we perceive reality. No longer is the dominant thought one of "this difficulty is an obstacle to what I want. This is terrible!" because what I want has been superseded. What the difficulty prevents is no longer what I want, for more than anything else I want to "enter through the narrow gate" (Mt 7:13). This detachment, even from the good things I see and want, is not a matter of a negative attitude toward them, but of a spiritual perspective that puts our Father's plan first.

"But how narrow is the gate that leads to life, how rough the road, and how few there are who find it!" (Mt 7:14). The very difficulty is the means by which what we want can happen. The transformed mind can perceive what God is doing through the difficulty as a good thing (whereas the old mind can only perceive the difficulty as a horribly catastrophic thing) because it is bringing about the purity of heart which keeps us on the narrow path and leads us into the kingdom. Our immediate desire and plan, which the difficulty interferes with, is willingly sold in order to buy the pearl of great price—God's kingdom, his plan. By persevering through the difficulty, we will gain the maturity and tested virtue which will keep us on the narrow path into the kingdom. Just like Peter, as we grow older in the Spirit, circumstances will lead us where, at first, we would rather not go (Jn 21:18).

Actively praising God for our problems might at first glance seem superficial: "Praise the Lord and all your problems will go away." If praise is indeed superficial, it remains an external band-aid put over the festering wounds of our real thoughts. But praise is meant to be a basic orientation of our thought patterns which creates the inner environment to clean out the festering wounds of our thoughts and to "bring every thought into captivity to make it obedient to Christ" (2 Cor 10:5).

Vocally praising God for difficulties can be a good way to "get a handle" on how our inner thoughts should be focused. Being rooted in God's personal love leads to trusting him in faith. Sin, however, abounds. Frequently, we are not rooted in God's love and an insecurity follows which clutches or despairs or resents.

We need help in reminding ourselves of God's tender concern for us and that the situations we are in are working for the good only if we respond to God. Praising God for the difficulties we are in is just such a help. Such is Job's claim, "The Lord gave and the Lord has taken away, blessed be the name of the Lord" (Jb 1:21).[11]

Actively praising evokes in the conscious and unconscious levels of our thoughts the basic truths of the transformed mind—God's personal love *for me*; the presence of his Spirit with us; our union with him even in afflictions; how things are working for the good, so that we might be purified and prepared for loving. Hence we can say "yes," and accept our circumstances and praise God for his plan. Sometimes the dynamics of such praise are not conscious, yet at times they are and it is often a help. The power, though, is in the Spirit's indwelling, flooding our hearts with God's love. Being conscious of praising and verbalizing is simply actively placing faith in the Spirit's power within us. We are tapping the source of power, for where sin abounds, grace abounds even more.

When we actively seek to cultivate thought patterns of praise, we become sensitive to other thought patterns within us that "argue" with us about it. When I am in the midst of a difficulty and praise God for it, something inside often says "no." Other thoughts begin to be exposed and they need to be confronted and dealt with so that our praise can be pure and not half-hearted. This is a good tool through which the Lord can purify us and point out the very areas where he wants his Lordship to be more extensive.

In *Praise: a Way of Life*, Fr. Paul Hinnebusch makes this point strongly in a description of how active praise can help root us more deeply in our scriptural identity as sons and daughters of God.

> . . . I have to say Yes to every situation in which I find myself, no matter how miserable it may be, whether this misery stems from my own sinfulness, or from the sinfulness of those about me, or from the sinfulness of those who went before me. I have to accept myself as I am and where I am. I have to accept my

situation as it is, praising the Lord who is Lord of all of this, Lord of every detail of my life, working in all things for my good through my yes to him . . . In life's troubles, all of us have a tendency to bewail our fate and to waste our vitality and energies on resentment, on feeling sorry for ourselves, and on blaming others for our difficult situations . . . But in doing all of this, we sink only more deeply into the swamp of our own misery. Resenting others and blaming them, even if their sins are responsible for our difficulties, is not the solution to our problems. The decisive factor in every difficult situation in our life is our own right response to it, our Yes to God's loving providence which works for good with those who love him.[12]

## *Apocalyptic Thinking*

The second practical help to securing us in our sonship is apocalyptic thinking. This is the scriptural view of ourselves and the world. It is a matter of spiritual vision and discernment, not historical predictions about the end of the world.[13] Apocalyptic thinking is a practical help in appropriating our scriptural identity as sons and daughters of God.

An apocalyptic urgency about coming to God more deeply and intensely living the gospel is at the heart of being led by the Spirit as sons of God. Thought patterns that compromise and water down the gospel must be spit out of our mouths instead of affirmed by our words and actions. Examples of compromising words are, "We have to be prudent, so we should go ahead and devise our own plans." "I'm depressed/angry/resentful, but that's the kind of person I am." "It's not possible to do everything you ought to do, so . . ." etc.

The word "apocalyptic" is not limited to a historical end-time, but more broadly applies to the vision that sees to the spiritual heart of the matter. Apocalyptic means revelation, in the way a stage is revealed when the curtains open. Our apocalyptic vision perceives the battle on the stage of life between God and the evil one which underlies our struggles and for which we are the battleground. It creates an urgency that can't stand a lukewarm gospel that compromises with the world.

As Pope Paul VI said in his January 26, 1977 general audience:

> We must open our eyes. We live in difficult times. That Jesus who instills courage in us and wishes us to trust in his assistance and his divine art of turning to our spiritual and superior advantage all things, even those which we perceive as contrary to us and painful, when, through the voice of the Apostle Paul, we know "That in everything God works for good with those who love him" (Rom 8:28), is the same Jesus the Master who warns us repeatedly to be vigilant; who wishes us to be attentive to the signs of the times; who announces to us in advance the unhappiness that is, so to speak, innate in the Christian profession; and who again by means of The Apostle himself, exhorts us to live defended by the armour of God in order to be able to resist evil. The Christian life is a struggle. The condition of those who have chosen Christ as their model, their guide, their redeemer, cannot be fearful, or uncomfortable or uncertain.[14]

The apocalyptic thinking of scripture sees the struggles we experience not merely as psychological, historical, and emotional but as a battle between God and Satan for us, who have the free will to choose. This apocalyptic thinking gives us an urgency about how we respond to our thoughts. It makes the day of the Lord present to us.

When we are intensely living the gospel, the day of the Lord is at hand for us and we know the urgency of it. It is akin to Einstein's general theory of relativity which tells us that in the presence of an intense gravitational mass, space-time bends. In the presence of someone intensely living the gospel, space-time bends and the day of the Lord is already at hand along with its urgency. It is a matter of vision, not prediction. Apocalyptic thinking which sees God and Satan battling, with us as the battleground, orients us to take our thoughts seriously and to "bring every thought into captivity to make it obedient to Christ" (2 Cor 10:5).

When we are intensely living the gospel with the apocalyptic thinking that goes along with it, we experience the distress in our life, the *thlipsis* or labor pains of childbirth that are ushering in a new age. "I tell you all this that in me you may find peace. You will suffer (*thlipsis*) in the world. But take courage! I have overcome the world" (Jn 16:33).

When Jesus speaks of finding peace in him, he is speaking of the peace and joy of being one with him, knowing him, receiving eternal life in the midst of suffering and distress. The peace he speaks of has nothing whatsoever to do with the absence of warfare, an end to psychological tension, or a sentimental feeling of well-being.[15] The Greek word used here for suffering and distress is *thlipsis* with its meaning of the pressures of childbirth. In labor we are sad, for the apocalyptic time is at hand. We feel the urgency of it. Yet we can look to the birth of the full kingdom coming soon, assured by the first fruits of the Spirit present now. Then we will no longer remember our *thlipsis* in our joy of being born into the kingdom and bringing others with us.

Apocalyptic thinking sees that difficulties are overcome with perseverance, knowing that our struggles are not wasted. More than that we can rejoice, for Jesus has struggled and conquered, and our perseverence in struggling joins us to him and leads us to him. With apocalyptic thinking, we expectantly suffer the labor pains for the joy of the birth about to come. As Michel Bouttier expresses it, "Joy, a signal from the world to come, breaks out even in the midst of the *thlipsis* (distress), since every tribulation brings with it the pains of childbirth and the time of release."[16]

The apocalyptic struggle we experience is the struggle, portrayed in chapters seven and eight of Romans, of choosing the inner man as led by the Spirit over and above the flesh. The struggle does not end when the Spirit comes; rather, that is when the struggle really begins. In concluding this section, let us reflect on Dunn's summary of the apocalyptic thinking portrayed in Romans 7:14-8:25:

> In these verses the believer's experience is clearly depicted as an experience of warfare between flesh and Spirit. It is not a warfare from which the believer can distance himself and take sides as though he were a neutral observer or umpire. On the contrary, he finds himself on *both* sides; as believer he lives on both levels, flesh and Spirit, *at the same time;* the division runs right through the believing "I." It is because he lives on two levels at once that he constantly has to choose between

the two levels—flesh or Spirit. "I" in my "inner man," as renewed mind, as man of Spirit, have to choose against "I" as flesh. By the power of the Spirit it can be done. But the choice has to be made, and made repeatedly if life and not death is to triumph at the last.[17]

## *A Posture Shift*

At a given moment a thought of any kind might come to our minds. We can choose to be led by the Spirit as sons of God or to yield to the flesh in a worldly way of thinking. Over a longer period of time, consistent choices form a thought pattern that becomes a habit. Though not fixed and final, the habit becomes the likely way of responding to thoughts. If we choose to be led by the Spirit of God as sons of God, then this spiritual way of thinking brings about a posture shift within us. A child-like posture of vulnerability and compassion develops which changes the way we feel and behave.

As we are present to the Spirit and become a new creation, our transformed mind can become rooted in the conviction of God's personal love for us. "Yet in all this we are more than conquerors because of him who has loved us" (Rom 8:37), "knowing that he who raised up the Lord Jesus will raise us up along with Jesus" (2 Cor 4:14). We begin to live a new life of being in love with God and trusting in what he is doing with us. "The life I live now is not my own; Christ is living in me. I still live my human life, but it is a life of faith in the Son of God, who loved me and gave himself for me" (Gal 2:20).

The miracle of the new creation is grounded by faith in God's personal love for me and effects an entirely new thought pattern saturated with hope. The basis for our new response of hope is confidence in God's love for me, being in touch with him, and convinced that "God makes all things work together for the good" (Rom 8:28). Because of this we are able to relax in trust and begin to experience a posture shift from fear to faith, from uptightness to vulnerability, from isolation to compassion. It gradually changes the way we feel and behave, freeing us to be more deeply in touch with our identity as sons and daughters of God and with the presence of the Spirit.

As we experience this posture shift, we begin to see God working more and more in our daily lives. The new level of God's speaking to us and directing us becomes alive as we acknowledge God and are present to his Spirit. I would like to illustrate this point with an experience from my own life while I was writing this book.

One day I left my home in Rutherford to go to a library in New York City and work on this manuscript. I had planned on coming home late so I could put in a full day's work and finish this very chapter. Four hours before the scheduled work time was over, I began to feel tired and slightly ill. The thought then came into my mind that I should go home early, even right away. I rejected this thought immediately. I wanted to finish this chapter by that night. Going home early would interfere with my plans. Besides, I did not feel tired or ill enough to warrant leaving early; it was hardly anything. The thought of leaving early annoyed me.

Suddenly, it struck me that God was speaking to me through this; he wanted me to leave early and go home. I tried to put this idea out of my mind but it kept coming back more and more strongly. Eventually, I realized my plan to finish this chapter was blocking God's plan. I had no idea of what God's plan was, but it clearly involved leaving right away. As I decided to focus on God's plan, I felt excited about what might be up.

I left the library at once. As I went home I felt a heightened expectancy about what God's plan might be. I looked around at the people on the subway and bus and wondered if the Lord wanted me to be praying and interceding for someone in a special way. I remember never having enjoyed riding the New York subways so much. I wanted to be led by God and to discover what his plan was.

When I finally got home to Rutherford, there was a message for me from some people in the community. I called them. They said some crisis had happened and they needed to talk to me that night. They had called our house in the afternoon and were told I would not be in till late. Their need to talk to me was so urgent that they prayed and asked God to do something to allow it to be possible! We had a good and fruitful talk that night. But I was even more excited at being in touch with how directly God wants to be working in every detail of our lives.

This was a posture shift experience for me. When I first felt tired and slightly ill, I was afraid that my plan for finishing the chapter would be curtailed. I felt annoyed: how horrible it was that *my* plans were being interfered with! I could have stayed there in a posture of "how horrible that things aren't the way I want them." If I had been locked into my plan strongly enough, I am sure I never would have sensed that God was trying to speak to me. Needless to say, I would have been in a lousy mood all night. Yet I came to see that God was speaking to me and I decided to follow him.

In making this decision for God, I became more deeply aware of how God speaks to me and how his Spirit directs my life. My decision for God was nothing more than acknowledging him, his love, his plan, and being present to his Spirit. In choosing to lean forward, to enter into what God was doing, it became so easy to have a hopeful perspective, to become excited, to receive a posture shift. I felt faith in God's love instead of fear that my plans would be messed up. I felt vulnerable to what the Spirit wanted to do with me instead of an uptightness that would block out the Spirit. I felt compassion for those I was with that evening instead of being isolated and withdrawn. That "trivial" decision for God freed me to be more deeply in touch with my identity as a son of God with the presence of the Spirit. It even eventually brought about a better chapter, which you are now reading!

This posture shift comes from choosing to be led by the Spirit of God as a son of God. Consistently chosen, it forms a habitual spiritual way of thinking. This sonship thought pattern effects a posture shift that transforms our emotions, expectations and judgments. It transforms our relationships.

In this chapter, we have explored our thought patterns and the basis for the right posture for expectations and judgments. We saw our scriptural identity as sons and daughters of God, and the spiritual way of thinking that comes from it. The practical aids of actively praising and apocalyptic thinking can help root us more deeply in our sonship identity which brings about a posture shift.

CHAPTER THREE

# SCRIPTURAL EXPECTATIONS: COMPLETING OR COMPETING?

In this book, we have asked some difficult questions. What does it mean to be pure of heart as we call one another to holiness? How should I approach my brother or sister when there is a fault to be pointed out? What should my posture be? How can I authentically support instead of condemn or discourage? Our initial answer can be summed up in the words "vulnerability based on a transformed mind which acknowledges God's plan." To be vulnerable is to resist being in control in a way that chokes ourselves or others. It is to risk being open enough so that other people and the things they say can enter in and affect us. The transformed mind is one which acknowledges God's plans and resists clinging to our own plan, even if it has been formulated "for the glory of God." This brings about a posture shift whose test and reinforcement is actively praising and apocalyptic thinking.

So far, we have been examining the transformed mind required for a Christian approach to judgments and expectations in relationships. In the next chapter we will consider fraternal correction in scripture. Now we turn to scripture on expectations, especially those scriptural expectations that ought to complete, yet frequently compete.

In our community life, we often see how people's expectations reveal their worldly or spiritual way of thinking. Examples include expecting the laws to be rigidly adhered to for their own sake, expecting to solidify our identity by being better than others, expecting to copy another's vision or impose our vision on others. A spiritual way of thinking leads to different expectations: expecting to love and be faithful to the law as a support to loving, expecting to be deeply rooted in our identity as sons and daughters of God with the unique gifts he has given us, expecting to be impelled by our vision without imposing it on others. The worldly way of thinking tends to compete with others. A transformed mind expects to complete others.

A worldly way of thinking leads to expectations that tolerate the bad side of a good gift as a necessary evil, whereas a transformed mind trusts that God's power wants to deal with the bad side while reinforcing the good gift. A worldly way of thinking gives us expectations that are narrowly limited to the horizons of our plans. A spiritual way of thinking expects God's plan to be broader than the plan we have come to see and so expects others to be doing what we individually are not called to. What does scripture tell us about how to approach differing expectations and to discern the thought patterns behind them? This is the chapter's question. We will answer it in a dialectic way that contrasts differing expectations in a sharp relief so that we can perceive the subterfuge of our thought patterns.

What do we mean by "expectations?" "Expectations" means something that we look for and anticipate coming. Often our expectations become conscious only when they are not fulfilled. If we expect the law to be rigidly adhered to for its own sake, we realize this when others don't follow the law. Our expectations in relationships are what we consider reasonable, just, proper, due, or necessary. While some expectations can be made explicit among people by agreements or covenants, most are implicit.[18] Such unspoken expectations are satisfactory when a common understanding brings about similar expectations, but at times we need to make expectations explicit. Our relationships can flounder at either extreme. Unspoken expectations can cause friction, breakdowns, and cross purposes when expectations are different. On the other hand, rigidity, immaturity, and lifelessness can come from legally spelling out every minute expectation.

Like material possessions, expectations can have their proper place in our lives or they can become the center and focus which we cling to tightly. When we cling to them and they are not fulfilled we can feel greatly upset, angry, devastated, and depressed. When expectations have their proper place and Jesus is at the center of our lives, unfulfilled expectations bring milder feelings of disappointment, irritation, or the sadness which says that something is unfortunate yet not all that crucial. This contrast between clinging to our expectations and plans rather than holding them loosely in light of God's expectations and plan is exemplified in James, "Here is the answer for those of you who talk like this: 'Today or tomorrow, we are off to this or that town; we are going to spend a year there, trading, and make some money.' You never know what will happen tomorrow: you are no more than a mist that is here for a little while and then disappears. The most you should ever say is: 'If it is the Lord's will, we shall still be alive to do this or that.' But how proud and sure of yourselves you are now! Pride of this kind is always wicked" (4:13-16).

The expectations we have are the basis for the judgments we make. If I expect the law to be rigidly adhered to, I will tend to judge law-breakers harshly regardless of their deeper purpose and motivation. Expectations are a necessity; one cannot avoid them. The dream world of never having expectations, thereby never being hurt or disappointed, is totally unrealistic and undesirable. The real solution is to bring differing expectations into the light and let Jesus reveal his Lordship there in the process. Thus, the cure for wrong expectations is not to ignore them, but to seek correct ones. We ought to expect the law to be generally followed, but only as a means to love.

For insight about right expectations, specifically in the area of relating to one another, we now turn to scripture, focusing on key areas of differing expectations. These are: the Old Testament method of regulating expectations in relationships, the Law, and how it was changed when Jesus came; the apostles' expectations of position and status and how Jesus dealt with it; and the early communities' expectations of how to live together in the tension of law and Spirit, truth and love, and pluralism.

## *New Wine in Old Covenant Wineskins*

The Old Testament Jewish nation gradually evolved over a long period before Jesus came. We will review the evolution briefly and contrast the Old Covenant wineskin with Jesus' new wine.

The prime examples here are John the Baptist's expectations of Jesus, and Jesus' expectations of the Old Covenant. There is a mysterious tension that arises from the contrast, for the New Covenant which competes with the Old also completes it.

Israel was a covenant community, and the Old Testament method of regulating expectations in relationships was the Law. The fundamental idea of the covenant is expressed in Exodus 19, where the Lord says to Moses:

> Tell the Israelites: you have seen for yourselves how I treated the Egyptians and how I bore you up on eagle wings and brought you here to myself. Therefore, if you harken to my voice and keep my covenant, you shall be my special possession, dearer to me than all other people, though all the earth is mine. You shall be to me a kingdom of priests, a holy nation. (v. 4-6)

To the Jews the action of a personal God in a historically evolving relationship was clear. God punishes Egypt with plagues, helps the Hebrew slaves in the dramatic escape through the Red Sea, provides for them in the desert, and finally brings them to Sinai. God has acted powerfully in their lives; he has chosen them. On this basis God initiates the covenant agreement that involves their obedience. The people respond by saying, "everything the Lord has said, we will do" (v. 8).

The covenant forms Israel and establishes the people as a community. They were "a covenant community" as the title of Daniel Rhodes' study of Exodus indicates.[19] The expectations in relationships within the community were regulated by the law of the covenant, minutely spelled out in Exodus, Leviticus, and Deuteronomy. In a study of the consequences of the covenant, George Buchanan notes three carefully worked out practices of covenant communities in history that were key for their life—initiation procedures, the requirement of community love, and exclusion procedures.[20] Their life was regulated by these laws—the wineskins—which protected their relationships and common life together.

The covenant and Law evolved in Israel over time. As in any set of explicit expectations between persons, the covenant between God and Israel was hard to articulate. The heart of the matter is to be something for and with one another, to be committed together in a specific relationship. Since this relationship is hard to label, it is often described in a set of laws that specify the expectations of the relationships. For Israel, the heart of their expectations was to be a people following God; it was described as expecting to adhere to the Law. The hard-to-label reality of the relationship is a matter of the heart. The easier-to-articulate description of the relationship involves external behavior.

Originally, this set of laws with their sanctions was purely religious for Israel. There was no civil machinery to enforce the Law. With the coming of the monarchy, the legal traditions of the covenanted community were taken over and even displaced by the king and his court. The monarchy had a civil structure with agencies to enforce its law, which at times was in conflict with the Law of the covenant. Yet during the monarchy, the prophets kept alive the true idea of the covenant and condemned the failure to live up to it. Finally, the Deuteronomic reform returned to the ancient Mosaic concept of the covenant people.[21]

This tension between the covenant as a matter of the heart and as a matter of required behavior is reflected in contrasting passages of scripture from different times. One can compare, for example, the early "At the time I have appointed, you shall be careful to present to me the food offerings . . . " (Nm 28:2) with "I will place my law within them, and write it on their hearts" (Jer 31:33).

The New Covenant in Jesus, which continues the Mosaic religion by fulfilling it, is a radical transformation of the old way to regulate expectations in relationships. Instead of the Law, there is the Spirit. D. Hillers has said that "to call what Jesus brought a covenant is like calling conversion circumcision, or like saying that one keeps the Passover with the unleavened bread of sincerity and truth."[22] The mysterious tension begins to emerge here. What Jesus does completes the Old Covenant and so it is the New Covenant. Yet it also is so beyond the Old that it seemingly competes with it and can be called a New Covenant only by stretching and symbolizing the meaning of "covenant."

Mendenhall's classic study concludes that "the stipulations of the covenant (of Jesus) are not a system of laws to define in detail every obligation in every conceivable circumstance, but the law of love."[23] While this might be the prophet's Old Covenant ideal, it was never successfully translated into the life of Israel. St. Paul wrote that "our sole credit is from God, who has made us qualified ministers of a new covenant, a covenant not of written law but of spirit. The written law kills, but the Spirit gives life" (2 Cor 3:5b-6; cf Rom 7:6; Gal 3:3). The new wine of Jesus is the expectation of the Spirit.

When Jesus came, he met hardly anyone's expectations. The conservatives expected someone to reinforce the Mosaic institution. The liberals expected someone to overthrow the Roman institution, and the man in the middle expected "peace" and was scared to death of the demands of the gospel. Even John the Baptist was confused by Jesus. Let us consider John's expectations of Jesus. In Matthew 11:2f we read, "Now John in prison heard about the works Christ was performing, and sent a message by his disciples to ask him, 'Are you he who is to come or do we look for another?' "

John the Baptist had a certain expectation of "he who is to come," the one who would baptize in the Holy Spirit and fire (Mt 3:11) and for whom he was preparing the way by baptizing with water for the sake of reform. John's expectation of "he who is to come" was that "he will clear the threshing floor and gather his grain into the barn, but the chaff he will burn in the unquenchable fire" (Mt 3:12). Even though John made the judgment at the Jordan that Jesus was "he who is to come" (Mt 3:13-17), later in prison, after he hears of what Jesus is doing, he realizes that Jesus does not match his expectations. And so he questions his earlier judgment and asks Jesus the rather embarrassing question "Are you he who is to come or do we look for another?"

John was apparently expecting the reign of God in terms of fiery judgment and the Law—the separation of grain and chaff. Jesus, however, postpones the separating till his coming in glory (Mt 25:31f), and so John is left confused. God who works in the Spirit rarely meets our expectations of the law. John expected "he who is to come" to reveal the definitive truth in such a way that the grain is gathered into the barn and the chaff into the fire. Instead, "the blind recover their sight, cripples walk, lepers are cured, the deaf hear, dead men are raised to life and the poor have the good news preached to them" (Mt 11:5). Certainly good things, yet what about throwing those who don't believe into the fire?

While it might be easy for us at a distance to see how Jesus was completing the ministry of John the Baptist, the Baptist's expectations made it extremely difficult for him to identify the wonder-working Jesus who preached the kingdom as "he who is to come." Kraeling even goes so far as to question whether John ever really fully accepted Jesus.

> There is for John no possible meeting ground between the wonder-working preacher of the kingdom and the transcendent "man-like one" who destroys the wicked in unquenchable fire, save on the assumption of a break with his fundamental convictions, for which there is no adequate justification.[24]

John's preaching was looking forward to the end-time, the chief mark of which for him was the fiery judgment. Jesus proclaims that the kingdom is at hand, but says the fiery judgment will come later. The Baptist's wineskin does not know how to hold this new wine of Jesus. As Dunn points out, "As soon as the note of imminence characteristic of John's preaching was supplanted or at least supplemented by the note of fulfillment characteristic of Jesus' preaching"[25] the Baptist and his followers had to ask their embarrassing question: where is the judgment proclaimed by the Baptist as the chief mark of the end-time?

John was interested in telling people about what was right in the light of the impending judgment. He told people to reform their lives (Mt 3:2) and condemned the Pharisees and Sadducees, pointing out the wrath and fire soon to come. His comment to Herod, "It is not right for you to live with her" (Mt 14:4) cost him his life. The Old Covenant, centered on the truth and witnessing to the condemnation of those not living in truth, could never quite adjust to its fulfillment in Jesus' message of love and healing which postpones the time of judgment.

If Jesus was a source of confusion even to his forerunner John, we can imagine what a source of confusion he was for most people. Almost everyone was tainted with the worldly way of thinking that was locked into the Law, a way of thinking which limited their vision for God's plan. Perhaps that is why, when Jesus answers John's embarrassing question, he concludes by saying "Blest is the man who finds no stumbling block in me" (Mt 11:6).

One could point to other passages which highlight the same tension, as when Jesus' disciples pick corn on the sabbath (Mt 12:1-8; Mk 2:23-28; Lk 6:1-5) or when he heals on the sabbath (Mt 12:9-13; Mk 3:1-5; Lk 6:6-10). Jesus apparently disobeys the Law. What were Jesus' expectations of the Old Covenant?

As mentioned above, the heart of a covenant relationship is to be something for and with another. It is hard to articulate this deeper commitment of the heart, and so it is often expressed by describing what the relationship might look like in practice. Jesus was always in touch with the deeper heart level, whereas others frequently were stuck in descriptions of external behavior. To the Pharisees, upset when his disciples ate corn on the sabbath, he said, "If you understood the meaning of the text 'It is mercy I desire and not sacrifice,' you would not have condemned these innocent men" (Mt 12:7). In healing on the sabbath he says, "clearly, good deeds may be performed on the sabbath" (Mt 12:12). Jesus describes the Scribes and Pharisees who are so out of touch with the heart of the covenant relationship as people who "strain out the gnat and swallow the camel!" (Mt 23:24).

An insight into Jesus' expectation of the Old Covenant can be gleaned from Jesus' discussion with the Pharisees about divorce. "(Jesus) said, 'What command did Moses give you?' They answered, 'Moses permitted divorce and the writing of a decree of divorce.' But Jesus told them: 'He wrote that commandment for you because of your stubbornness' " (Mk 10:3-5). Jesus expected the Old Covenant to be reinterpreted in light of what he knew for certain in his heart through his relationship with his Father. As Dunn puts it, it was "a certainty which compelled him to set aside even the authority of Moses when the two were not compatible."[26]

The expectations of the Old Covenant wineskin clung to the external behavior which was merely an attempt to flesh out the heart of the covenant relationship to God. Because it clung to the Law with its condemnatory posture toward others, it made no sense to put the new wine into it. "People do not pour new wine into old wineskins. If they do, the skins burst, the wine spills out, and the skins are ruined. No, they pour new wine into new wineskins, and in that way both are preserved" (Mt 9:17). In a sense, the New and Old Covenants do compete. The New Covenant fleshes out the heart of the covenant relationship to God in Jesus and the Spirit instead of the Law. It brings with it a posture of being vulnerable and compassionate. New wineskins are needed; one cannot just complete the old wineskins.

Yet that is only half the picture. We must also consider these words of Jesus, "Do not think that I have come to abolish the law and the prophets. I have come, not to abolish them, but to fulfill them" (Mt 5:17). The mysterious tension that arises from this contrast is an essential part of the gospel that affects our expectations. Should we expect the New Covenant to compete with the Old or complete it? Either expectation is insufficient. It must be both, even though each seems to exclude the other. One can take an analogy from modern physics and compare this to the wave-particle duality of light. Is light a wave or a particle? It cannot be both. But the answer depends on when you ask the question and what the circumstances are. Our expectations need to be broadened to adapt to the mysterious tension of the gospel. A worldly way of thinking can't expand and adjust like this; only a transformed mind can.

## *An Identity Without Comparing*

John the Baptist was at the end of the Old Covenant with its expectations. Jesus said that "history has not known a man born of woman greater than John the Baptizer. Yet the least born into the kingdom of God is greater than he" (Mt 11:11). The apostles, by contrast, are at the beginning of the New Covenant. The struggles they had with their status expectations—wanting an identity by comparing themselves with others—are enlightening for us. We will look at key passages that show how the apostles had expectations of a position better than the others, and then see how Jesus dealt with their views. Out of these reflections on how to stop approaching others in a worldly way will come the implications of kingdom expectations for our own lives.

Consider the extent to which the apostles compared themselves to one another: "An argument started between them about which of them was the greatest" (Lk 9:46 JB). "A dispute arose also between them about which should be reckoned the greatest" (Lk 22:24 JB). "They came to Capernaum, and when he was in the house he asked them, 'What were you arguing about on the road?' They said nothing because they had been arguing which of them was the greatest" (Mk 9:33, 34 JB). "At this time the disciples came to Jesus and said, 'Who is the greatest in the kingdom of heaven?' " (Mt 18:1 JB). " 'Promise that these two sons of mine may sit one at your right hand and the other at your left in your kingdom.' ... When the other ten heard this they were indignant with the two brothers" (Mt 20:21, 24 JB).

These status expectations of the apostles revealed their thought patterns: "I haven't made it unless I'm on top." They had compromised their identities, making who they are equivalent to their ranking on a comparison test. Seeing themselves with such a competitive attitude soon led to competitive evaluations and judgments. "A dispute arose."

What a contrast to their first calls, when their identities were established as men purely and simply dependent on following Jesus, without comparing themselves: "They left everything and followed him" (Lk 5:11 JB). "Leaving everything behind, Levi stood up and became his follower" (Lk 5:28 JB). "And at once they left their nets and followed him" (Mk 1:18; Mt 4:20 JB). "He called them, and immediately they abandoned boat and father to follow him" (Mt 4:22 JB).

What began as pure surrender to the kingdom and self-forgetful generosity seems to have degenerated into a selfish vying for first place. Perhaps the glory the apostles saw in the miracles and at the Transfiguration went to their heads and they wanted to control it, to be able to call it forth on command. Perhaps they misunderstood the kingdom to come and were caught up in solidifying their positions. Perhaps they wanted to know if they were of greater importance than the Jews who did not believe. Whatever the reasons, how did Jesus deal with these status expectations?

> Jesus knew what thoughts were going through their minds, and he took a little child and set him by his side and then said

to them, " . . . For the least among you all, that is the one who is great." (Lk 9:47, 48 JB)

And he said to them, "The kings of the Gentiles exercise lordship over them; and those in authority over them are called benefactors. But not so with you; rather let the greatest among you become as the youngest, and the leader as one who serves . . . But I am among you as one who serves." (Lk 22:25-27 RSV)

So he sat down, called the Twelve to him and said, "If anyone wants to be first, he must make himself last of all and servant of all." (Mk 9:35 JB)

So he called a little child to him and set the child in front of them. Then he said, "I tell you solemnly, unless you change and become like little children you will never enter the kingdom of heaven. And so, the one who makes himself as little as this little child is the greatest in the kingdom of heaven." (Mt 18:2-4 JB).

Jesus then called them together and said: "You know how those who exercise authority over the Gentiles lord it over them; their great ones make their importance felt. It cannot be like that with you. Anyone among you who aspires to greatness must serve the rest, and whoever wants to rank first among you must serve the needs of all." (Mt 20:25, 26)

Jesus dealt with the status expectations of his apostles by correcting them ("it cannot be that way with you"), channeling them ("if anyone wishes to rank first . . . "), and transposing their expectations into the new values of the kingdom (" . . . he must remain the last . . . "). Jesus does not attempt to destroy their desires and expectations for greatness. Rather, he teaches them how to translate their desires and expectations into the kingdom, and arrive at the exact opposite conclusion than they had. We ought to expect . . . to be a child, a servant, to be last. Jesus uses the imagery of a child and a servant to help them root their identity in values of his kingdom, using images which come from his own experience of his Father in prayer and the Spirit in mission.[27] It is much easier to leave one's nets than it is to receive the transformed mind and thought patterns that see last as first, service as greatness, and being a child as status. Nevertheless it is these values that give us our true identity.

There is a beautiful post-resurrection scene that shows Peter's struggle with tenacious competitive status expectations which confuse his identity:

> Peter turned around at that, and noticed that the disciple who Jesus loved was following. Seeing him, Peter was prompted to ask Jesus, "But Lord, what about him?" "Suppose I want him to stay until I come," Jesus replied, "How does that concern you? Your business is to follow me" (Jn 21:20-22).

Peter, as many of us do, compares himself to another person, and wants to know "what about him?" Jesus knows that such comparisons and status expectations would mean a cracked foundation in Peter's life. The problem is approaching our gifts, call, or identity like an exam that everyone takes: either I've passed or failed, made it or not made it, and so either I'm better or worse than you. Suddenly I am interested in "what about him?" It leads to thinking "It is terrible that I can't do this or don't have that job. I must not be worthwhile to others. Others are selfish. Or, they are better than I am, etc." This is the worldly way of thinking with all its worldly expectations.

Jesus knows that these judgmental attitudes will undermine the transformed mind and so he tells Peter, "how does that concern you? Your business is to follow me." Jesus knew that constantly comparing oneself to others always boomerangs and leads to slavery. It does not allow the diversity of gifts in the Body of Christ to flower. It prevents us from exploring the meaning of the "follow me" that Jesus addresses personally to us. If we are to be free, our identity must come from our relationship with the Lord, from our response to the unique "follow me" addressed personally to us.

The apostles, who are at the beginning of the New Covenant, strived for an identity by comparing themselves with others. In their desire for a position of status and power, they climb over one another and become divided, losing both their singleness of heart and the unity among themselves. Jesus corrects and channels their status expectations by transposing them into the new values of the kingdom. The implications of the kingdom expectations of being a child and servant is a conversion that clarifies and frees our identity, as well as our relationships.

## *Impelled Without Imposing*

We have been focusing on key areas of differing expectations. We considered how the Old Testament method of regulating relationships—the Law—was radically transformed when Jesus came. Our expectations must be broadened in order to adapt to the mysterious tension of the new and the old both competing and completing. The apostles struggled to root their identity, not in the worldly pattern of competing, but in the kingdom expectations of being a child and servant. Now we turn to some of the early Christian communities described in scripture and discuss their experiences and expectations of how to live together.

Expectations are based on what is valued. If we were perfect, then what we value would always have the right balance. Yet we are sinners loved by God and so we emphasize some values to the risk of others. Communities do that too, including the New Testament communities. This is not all bad, nor entirely due to sin, since different individuals or communities have different visions, missions, and vocations, different parts to play in God's overall plan.

Christians must observe certain limits in their emphasis. An extreme emphasis on the Law or the Spirit to the exclusion of the other is wrong. There is also a common ground that should be valued highly. For example, Christians should be both filled with the Spirit and willing to have explicit expectations of what that implies. Yet, different emphases and expectations within the broader Christian vision are appropriate for different people or communities according to their vision, mission, and vocation. By considering the differing expectations of some New Testament communities, and the difficulties these communities ran into, we can provide background for expectations in our own relationships. The worldly thought pattern that causes difficulty here thinks that the vision that impells us must be imposed on others. It thinks God's plan is limited to the part of it that we see.

Paul's letter to the Galatians shows the tension between the expectations of the Judaizers' Law and the freedom of the Spirit. After a lengthy defense of his authority and doctrine (1:11-2:21), Paul finally gets to the heart of the matter, "You senseless Galatians! . . . how did you receive the Spirit? Was it through observance of the law or through faith in what you heard? How could you be so stupid? After beginning in the Spirit, are you now to end in the flesh?" (3:1-3). Paul then attacks the Law and defends the freedom of Spirit-inspired faith.

The Galatians originally valued the freedom that came from the Spirit and faith. This is the message that Paul had preached to them, most likely on his first missionary journey.[28] Paul says that he had talked with James, Cephas, and John about the Gentile position that they were not required to follow any of the Mosaic Laws (2:9-10). After Paul left Galatia, however, Judeo-Christians from Jerusalem came urging the Galatians to adopt the practices of the Mosaic Law. This confused the Galatians and they began to be unfaithful to their call of Spirit, freedom, and faith. In Paul's mind it was clearly wrong for the Galatians to compromise their Christian faith by going to the extreme of the Law; it was a question of staying within Christian limits. It was also clearly wrong in Paul's mind for the Galatians to compromise their own unique charism, mission, and vision as a Gentile Church; this was a question of mission.

In contrast, the Jerusalem Church at first considered it necessary for those who belonged to it to obey at least some Mosaic laws (Acts 15:28-29). The Epistle of James, addressed to the twelve tribes of the dispersion, is sensitive to false faith unproven by good works (2:14-26)—a significant contrast to Paul's concern in Galatians. James values the Law enough to warn people not to speak ill of others because it is "speaking against the law" (4:11). Yet Paul strongly opposes these emphases for the Galatians. In warning them against being misled by the flesh, he emphasizes the Spirit (Gal 5:16) not outlining the limits of the Law (Gal 5:18). His norm for discernment is the fruit of the Spirit (Gal 5:22).

We may partially understand why Paul and the Jerusalem Church do not agree on this question by understanding the historical perspective and context in which the different letters were written. The fuller understanding, however, can only come by seeing the vocation of the Gentile Church at Galatia. The broader Christian call embraces the more specified calls of the Galatians, the Jerusalem Church, and the twelve tribes of the dispersion. The Jerusalem Church thought its way of living with the Law was *the* Christian call. The Twelve probably found it difficult to distinguish between the essence of Christianity which they had a spiritual gift to preserve and their particular style of Christianity.

In God's plan, the Gentile Churches would vastly outnumber the Judeo-Christian Churches, much to the initial surprise of the Twelve. And so the vocation of the initial Gentile Churches was to be totally free of the Mosaic Law even though this Law was acceptable in other Christian Churches. The balance for the Galatian Church is different from the balance of the Jerusalem Church, yet both are embraced by the broader Christian call.

The tension between the Law and the Spirit in Galatians exemplifies the different community visions of the Jewish-Christian and Gentile Churches. It would be easy to imagine that the expectations of the Church at Jerusalem were so rigid that it would have confused its own call to observe the Mosaic Law with the Christian call to all men—Gentiles as well as Jews. Yet God had a larger plan. God had to send the Spirit-filled Peter a vision (Acts 10:9f) before he would be open to the Gentiles and stop viewing the Jewish dietary laws as necessities. Perhaps it is precisely the difficulty of broadening one of the Twelve's vision that led to the calling of Paul as an apostle to the Gentiles unformed by the Jerusalem community or its vision (Gal 1:17).

The lesson we learn about our own expectations is this: while we ought to be impelled by the vision God has given us, we need to be cautious about trying to impose it on others. Do we ever expect our brothers and sisters to do what we do and to do it the way we do? If so, we need to be cautious. Maybe that is the right thing. But it might be something right for us. We need to discern if we are affected by a worldly way of thinking that is so centered on ourselves that we can't imagine God doing something else. Different visions are meant to complement one another in God's plan, not compete.

## *The Bad Side of a Good Gift*

There is a completing/competing tension in expectations. We have seen it in the tension of new wine in Old Covenant wineskins, in the apostles' struggling to free their identities from comparisons to others, in communities' differing visions. Another way of approaching this tension of expectations is realizing that every good gift has a bad side. When a charism is being authentically cultivated and intensely lived out, the main problem to be dealt with is frequently simply the bad side of the good gift.

The cure for the bad effects of the gift is not to eliminate the gift or to de-emphasize it, but to receive the support needed to minimize its bad side. A good example is the gift of "truth" with its bad side of "a lack of love." A person or community who has a gift to see the truth, focus on it, be faithful to it, and so forth, often has the bad effect of not loving others in the process of sharing the truth. Clearly, truth and love are meant to complement one another. Paul wrote to the Ephesians, "Speak the truth in love" (Eph 4:15 RSV). Yet every good gift has a bad side, and if the Ephesians have a gift to "stand therefore, having girded your loins with truth" (Eph 6:14), let us see what the bad side is and how the Lord deals with it.

The book of Revelation shows the tension of valuing truth more than love in its letter to Ephesus in 2:1-6:

> To the angel of the church in Ephesus write: "The words of him who holds the seven stars in his right hand, who walks among the seven golden lampstands. I know your works, your toil and your patient endurance, and how you cannot bear evil men but have tested those who call themselves apostles but are not, and found them to be false; I know you are enduring patiently and bearing up for my name's sake, and you have not grown weary. But I have this against you, that you have abandoned the love you had at first. Remember then from what you have fallen, repent and do the works you did at first. If not, I

> will come to you and remove your lampstand from its place, unless you repent. Yet this you have, you hate the works of the Nicolaitans, which I also hate. (RSV)

The elders at Ephesus had once received a prophetic warning from Paul, "take heed . . . fierce wolves will come in among you, not sparing the flock; and from among your own selves will arise men speaking perverse things, to draw away the disciples after them. Therefore be alert . . . " (Acts 20:28-31 RSV). The elders would undoubtedly have taken this warning seriously, perhaps militantly preparing to safeguard the truth and resist such men, especially from within their own ranks.

Timothy is called the first bishop of Ephesus and is encouraged to safeguard the truth, "remain at Ephesus that you may charge certain persons not to teach any different doctrine" (1 Tm 1:3 RSV). The warnings are repeated often and understandably so—Ephesus was the greatest harbor of Asia, a politically active city, the center for the worship of Artemis with hundreds of sacred prostitutes attached to the temple, a haven for criminals seeking asylum. Magic was rampant. The Ephesians' patient endurance in watching over the truth in response to Paul's warning proves fruitful—they became so that they could not tolerate wicked men, such as the Nicolaitans who compromised the truth of the gospel with paganism.

However, in the process they so over-emphasized and so valued the "truth" that they sacrificed their early love for one another. One can imagine a community that has become anxious about being "pure" when it comes to the "truth' and, in the process, it inadvertantly falls from love into fear, gossiping, rigidity, suspicion, coldness.

William Barclay comments on Revelation's "But I have this against you, that you have abandoned the love you had at first" in a section he entitles, "when orthodoxy costs too much."

> But much more likely what this means is that the first fine rapture of Christian fellowship and love for the brotherhood is gone. In the first days the members of the church at Ephesus had really loved each other; they had been a band of brothers; dissention had never reared its head; the heart was ready to kindle and the hand was ready to help. But something had

gone wrong. It may well be that heresy-hunting had killed love; it may well be that the eagerness to root out all mistaken men had ended in a sour and rigid othodoxy. It may well be that orthodoxy had been achieved, but at the price of fellowship. When that happens, orthodoxy has cost too much. It is so often true that when a minister is first settled in his parish and in his charge there is a warmth of fellowship and a wealth of good will; and then something goes wrong; and the fellowship is exchanged for bickering; and the comradeship becomes suspicion; and the first love is gone. All the orthodoxy in the world will never take the place of love.[29]

Such is the problem in Ephesus, yet Revelations 2:1-6 quoted above puts it in the context of being the bad side of a good gift. The Risen Christ who is in their midst praises the Ephesians' deeds, labors, and patient endurance. He is glad that they cannot tolerate wicked men and does not in any way suggest they should slack off in order to achieve balance. He knows they are doing this for him and they are not becoming discouraged. He is reinforcing the good gift: the diligent protection of the truth.

Yet he has one thing against them: they have turned aside from their early love. Something has gone wrong and the Risen Christ points out the three steps to dealing with the bad side of their gift: (1) Remember—"remember then from what you have fallen," (2) Repent—neither give up nor blame the circumstances, (3) Return—"do the works you did at first." He tells them to repent of the bad side of their gift which overemphasizes the truth at the expense of love.

We can see the same dynamics working in us, in the bad sides of good gifts. In our expectations of others or ourselves we often see only the bad thing and so are annoyed and discouraged. Or we might tolerate the bad side as a necessary evil. When we see it as the bad side of a good gift we can put it in context, as the Risen Christ does in Revelation 2:1-6. We can reinforce the good gift and help minimize the bad side of it by remembering, repenting, and returning.

## *Pluralism: Paul and Barnabas*

In the last section of this chapter we will complete our discussion of the aspects of differing expectations by an example of New

Testament pluralism exemplified in Paul and Barnabas. Again we see what in God's larger vision is meant to complete, in our limited vision seems to compete.

In Acts we read of an interesting quarrel that reveals the tension between mission values and relationship values.

> On a later occasion Paul said to Barnabas, "Let us go back and visit all the towns where we preached the word of the Lord, so that we can see how the brothers are doing." Barnabas suggested taking John Mark, but Paul was not in favor of taking along the very man who had deserted them in Pamphylia and had refused to share in their work. After a violent quarrel they parted company, and Barnabas sailed off with Mark to Cyprus. Before Paul left, he chose Silas to accompany him . . . (Acts 15:36-40 JB).

Paul and Barnabas had an interesting relationship to start with. There was the Antioch incident where Paul clashed with Cephas "about the truth of the gospel" (Gal 2:14). Peter, wanting to maintain a good relationship with the Judaizers, stopped eating with the Gentiles. Paul "directly withstood" Cephas but in Paul's mind "Barnabas was swept away by their pretense" (Gal 2:13).

Barnabas was in the original Jerusalem community under the apostles (Acts 4:36) and Paul was not able to join the community until "Barnabas took him in charge and introduced him to the apostles" (Acts 9:27). Barnabas was sent from the Jerusalem community as an apostolic delegate to Antioch and, overloaded by the amount of instruction to be given, sent for Paul who helped him for a year (Acts 11:22-26). Barnabas was clearly in charge, signified by the order of names in Acts 12:25, "Barnabas and Saul returned to Jerusalem upon completing the relief mission, taking along with them John Mark." But Paul soon took the lead, for Acts 13:13 says "Paul and his companions (this includes Barnabas) put out to sea and sailed to Perga in Pamphylia. There John left them and returned to Jerusalem." Paul and Barnabas were close traveling companions and always seemed to be working together. Yet the Antioch episode, with the "truth of the gospel" highlighted against "peaceful relationships," must have flashed back in similar circumstances and been an underlying tension.

John Mark left Paul and Barnabas for Jerusalem about the same time Paul clearly began to be in charge (Acts 13:13). Although it has been conjectured that John Mark objected to Paul's ascendancy over his cousin Barnabas, it is more likely that the rugged country and alien culture had made Mark homesick for Jerusalem where a warm and close community gathered together to pray in his mother's house (Acts 12:12).[30] He was a disciple of Peter (1 Pt 5:13) who wrote down in his gospel what he heard from Peter.[31] In the quote above, Paul insists that Mark is not fit to be taken along on his second mission, yet in later years Mark and Paul are fellow prisoners (Col 4:10) and Paul writes to Timothy to "get Mark and bring him with you, for he can be of great service to me" (2 Tm 4:11).

At any rate, the point is that Paul and Barnabas' dispute has to do with their differing expectations. Paul values the mission and expects a successful one; Barnabas values the relationship with his cousin John Mark and expects a peaceful one. Paul, valuing his mission so highly, expects no "deserters" to be part of it since it might undermine the mission. Barnabas is likely taken aback by Paul's rigid, military reasoning and "sharply disagrees" citing, no doubt, the law of love, understanding, and forgiveness. The Greek here literally means "there occurred a provocation" implying a bitter quarrel.[32] The provocation likely involved a flashback to the Antioch incident—Paul reminding Barnabas of how he endangered the mission to the Gentiles by being "swept away" at Cephas' pretense, Barnabas reminding Paul of how he endangered the relationship with Cephas by poor diplomacy and how he showed no respect or love for Peter who held the keys. Barnabas finally chooses the relationship with Mark over the mission and sails to Cyprus with Mark. Paul chooses the mission over the relationship with Barnabas, and, left alone, chooses Silas to accompany him.

What an embarrassing incident for the early Christians to recall. Who was right? Who was wrong? I would like to suggest that they were both right about their conclusions because they were both being faithful to their different charisms. Both might be wrong since their dispute apparently showed a lack of love. Paul's charism emphasized the "truth of the gospel." His mission involved traveling and beginning communities; his vocation was the mission to the Gentiles. His background suited him well for it as he was not dependent on what others thought about him. Grace, as we know, builds on nature.

Barnabas' charism emphasized loyalty and love for his cousin Mark and for fellow Christians such as those in the Jerusalem community who shared their goods with "everyone according to his need." Barnabas' mission involved the ongoing formation and strengthening relationships that sustain a community which is one's home more than one's mission. His vocation was to be an apostolic delegate sent out from the Jerusalem community, always conscious of connecting new Christians to home base. For Barnabas too, we see grace building on nature; his very name means "son of encouragement" (Acts 4:36).

The charisms, missions, and vocations of both men are within the broader Christian call, though too much emphasis in either direction would be dangerous. Each needs to complete the other in God's larger plan. Yet the differences are real and the clash, given the circumstances that highlight the differing expectations, was perhaps inevitable. In the smaller scope of our limited vision, we can only see how they competed. We do not see God's way of indicating who he wants where. Some gifts complete each other best by not being in the same part of the Church. Scripture might want to assure us that diversity and pluralism, within their proper limits, are perfectly acceptable even if they make loving more difficult, which in turn incites arguments. Not that arguments are acceptable, but at times they might be hard to avoid. We should be careful not to reject another's charism, mission, or vocation simply because it clashes with ours.

The scriptural expectation for tensions in God's larger plan is to complete. It is in our narrow perspective that we perceive it as competing. The study of new wine in Old Covenant wineskins points out the need for our expectations to be broadened in order to adapt to the mysterious tension of the gospel which confused even John the Baptist. The apostles wanted an indentity by comparing themselves with others and so became divided. Jesus corrected their status expectations by translating them into the kingdom credentials of being a child and servant. The difference of vision between the Jewish and Gentile Christian communities highlights the importance of being impelled by our vision instead of trying to have it imposed on others. The way the Risen Christ approaches the truth/love problem in Ephesus is to treat it as the bad side of a good gift, and we should do likewise with the faults of our brothers and sisters. Finally, the Paul and Barnabas controversy helps us to see that clashes, if they come from authentic pluralism, could be God's way of indicating who he wants where in order to complete his larger plan. These scriptural insights help us to know how to approach differing expectations and, through a spiritual way of thinking, discern when they should complete one another and when one is right and the other is wrong.

CHAPTER FOUR

# FRATERNAL CORRECTION IN SCRIPTURE

In Chapter Two we have seen our scriptural identity as sons and daughters of God issue forth in a transformed and renewed mind that acknowledges God's plan and brings about a posture shift. The transformed mind is deeply conscious that our Father, who both tenderly loves us and requires absolute obedience, is in control. We can let go of our plans and the false identities we create. The practical aids of actively praising and apocalyptic thinking ground us in our identity as sons and daughters of God and help us discern where we still resist our scriptural identity.

In Chapter Three we reflected on the scriptural expectations that ought to complete, yet frequently compete. We saw how our relationships need to be led by the Spirit, not minutely regulated by the law. Jesus corrects the apostles' status expectations with the kingdom values of being a child and servant. If the apostles compete with one another, they will judge one another on that pass/fail basis, and Jesus does not allow it.

The tension between law and Spirit in Galatians points out the different community visions of the Gentile and Jewish-Christian Churches. While we need to be impelled by the vision God has given us, we also need to be cautious about imposing it on others. The completing/competing tension in expectations is often simply the question of how to deal with the bad side of a good gift. As we saw in the Church of Ephesus, the good gift needs to be reinforced, while correcting the bad side of it by remembering, repenting, and returning. In the dispute between Paul and Barnabas, we see again apparent competition which in God's plan is a matter of completion. People with different charisms harshly judge one another when there is merely a clash of charisms unless they realize what authentic pluralism is and realize they are only a part of what God is doing.

Let us return to the questions. What does it mean to be pure of heart as we call one another to holiness? How should I approach my brother and sister when there is a fault to be pointed out? What should my posture be? How can I authentically support instead of condemn or discourage? From Chapters One and Two, the answers could be summed up in the words "vulnerability that acknowledges God's plan and is secure in our identity as a son or daughter of God."

From Chapter Three we could add the following: we must be so securely rooted in our identity as a son or daughter of God, that we (1) are freed from judging according to the law; (2) are freed from searching for our identities by competing with others, thus allowing each of us to focus on what it means *for me* to follow Jesus; (3) are aware God has a larger plan than we can see and so while we need to be impelled by the vision given to us, we ought to be cautious about imposing it on others; (4) can fully exercise the good gift he has given to us while seeing that the bad side of it stays within Christian limits; (5) can confront a clash of charisms with another person without condemning or attacking the other, but realizing the importance of his charism in God's overall plan.

In this chapter we will review fraternal correction in scripture. We will examine Old Testament wisdom on correcting others, the New Testament balance on judging others, and fraternal correction in Matthew 18. We expect to gain further insight into our basic questions and again expect the Holy Spirit to be speaking to us about our own posture and relationships in the process.

First, though, what is fraternal correction? How can we define it? The *New Catholic Encyclopedia* has this to say:

> Fraternal correction is an admonition given to another to protect him from sin or to induce him to give up sin. It is called "fraternal" to distinguish it from paternal correction, which is administered by a superior in his capacity of father, and from

> judicial correction which is given to a person after he has been proved guilty by a formal process of law. Fraternal correction is an act of charity and is numbered among the seven spiritual works of mercy, which are the effects of charity. Fraternal correction can sometimes be obligatory. For just as one can at times be obliged to aid another in his bodily needs, as when he is seriously ill or wounded, so one can sometimes be bound to assist a fellow man in his spiritual needs, particularly when his soul is wounded or likely to be wounded by grave sin.[33]

I would like to extend this basic understanding of fraternal correction in two ways for the purposes of this book.[34]

First, much of what is said about fraternal correction extends to paternal correction. The difference lies in our relationship with the other person: are we in authority or under authority? The major difference is that if we are under authority to the person correcting us, and if his judgment falls within the scope of his authority's competence, then we need to obey what he says rather than merely consider it seriously. For example if a co-worker suggests some improvements in our work, we ought to consider seriously what he is saying. If our boss suggests some improvements in our work, we ought to obey him. It is not enough to just consider his words. This difference between fraternal and paternal correction will be explored more fully in Chapter Six.

Second, while fraternal correction is, strictly speaking, limited to matters of right and wrong, much of what we say about it can be extended to matters that do not involve righteousness. If someone is about to gossip, fornicate, or do something else clearly wrong (e.g. see 1 Cor 6:9-10 and Gal 5:19-21), then fraternal correction is indicated and the person involved in wrongdoing ought to ask forgiveness if appropriate. However, if someone is mispronouncing a word, making a poor business deal which is not morally wrong, relating in a non-constructive way, or some other behavior that does not involve wrongdoing, we can still use some principles of fraternal correction. We should appreciate and utilize such "extended" fraternal correction. When we do, the person has nothing to apologize for but simply resolves to do better. At the same time, when we are giving such "extended" fraternal correction, we ought not to put the same seriousness on the need for the other person to respond as when it involves wrongdoing.

## *Wisdom in Correcting Others*

The motivation for fraternal correction is a desire to maintain unity and love. How do we go about it? Wisdom dictates that we offer correction to people in different ways depending on their circumstances, openness, and our relationship with them.

As we approach our brothers and sisters, vulnerability and compassion must be permeated with wisdom. The Old Testament wisdom books have a clear approach to fraternal correction which is based on avoiding hatred for one's brother ("You shall not bear hatred for your brother in your heart. Though you may have to reprove your fellow man, do not incur sin because of him." Lv 19:17) and avoiding a break between people ("Admonish your neighbor before you break with him; thus you will fulfill the law of the Most High." Sir 19:26). Fraternal correction is encouraged as a way of active love ("Better is an open rebuke than a love that remains hidden." Prv 27:5) and as the approach which bears fruit in the long run ("He who rebukes a man gets more thanks in the end than one with a flattering tongue." Prv 28:23). Unity and love motivate fraternal correction.

With this as a background, the wisdom books distinguish between the way to correct a wise man and to correct a fool. Consider the following passages from the Book of Proverbs:

> If you correct a conceited man, you will only be insulted. If you reprimand an evil man, you will only get hurt. Never correct a conceited man; he will hate you for it. But if you correct a wise man, he will respect you (9:7-8 TEV).

> Anyone who loves knowledge wants to be told when he is wrong. It is stupid to hate being corrected (12:1 TEV).

> Poverty and shame befall the man who disregards correction, but he who heeds reproof is honored (13:18).

> Conceited people do not like to be corrected; they never ask for advice from those who are wiser (15:12 TEV).
>
> He who rejects admonition despises his own soul, but he who heeds reproof gains understanding (15:32).
>
> An intelligent person learns more from one rebuke than a fool learns from being beaten a hundred times (17:10 TEV).
>
> If you beat an arrogant man, the simple learn a lesson: if you rebuke an intelligent man, he gains knowledge (19:25).
>
> If you get more stubborn every time you are corrected, one day you will be crushed and never recover (29:1 TEV).

These proverbs have a dual purpose. They are meant to encourage us to be open to correction, but they also indicate a need for wisdom in the way we correct different kinds of people. What works with a person who is open and appreciative (a wise man) does not always work well with a person who is closed and resistant (a fool, an arrogant man, stupid, senseless, stiff-necked). We need wisdom.

Part of the wisdom we need involves timing and patience. It would be a mistake if, upon learning what fraternal correction is, we immediately told a friend about everything that needs to change in his life. Major personality problems need time and work. Similarly, we shouldn't correct every instance of brusqueness, irritation, or annoying traits right on the spot. On the other hand, some things have to be reconciled soon, perhaps immediately. It depends on the relationship, the degree of trust, the leading of the Spirit. We ought to be careful about plunging into fraternal correction imprudently.

Another person's faults are usually blind spots, for the fault is often the bad side of his or her good gift. What is obvious to us is usually not at all obvious to the other person. Often the fault is obvious to us because we have a gift to see it. Sometimes, for example, it is hard for me to know if I am really present to others. Some brothers and sisters can tell me instantly when I am withdrawing—they have a gift to see it, and it is obvious to them and they can point it out. With the support of such feedback, the bad effects of a person's gift can be minimized as the gift continues to function and be reinforced. In the process, we and the person draw closer together in our support for one another. It is crucial to have a posture of vulnerability, from which we open ourselves, and compassion, with which we suffer with another.

A posture of vulnerability and compassion makes it easy for those who are securely rooted in their identity as sons and daughters of God to be open and appreciative when we bring things into the light. Yet even with a posture of vulnerability and compassion, people are closed at times and resistant to this kind of feedback and support. Additional wisdom is needed to determine how much feedback people can receive and to understand how best to support them.

In our community experience we have come to distinguish three levels of openness. Each has different implications for how we approach a person with fraternal correction. The ideal level is when a person is open and appreciative. He is not only open to having things brought into the light, but is also truly appreciative when they are brought out. He knows his need for support, he desires to draw closer to others through this need, and is secure enough not to be threatened by it. Bringing things into the light is a normal part of his brother/sister relationships, through which he is able to continually grow.

On the next level is the person who is open yet resistant. He is open to correction and wants things to be brought into the light, but it is hard for him. He feels resistant, uptight, threatened, defensive, annoyed, or upset when another mentions his weaknesses. While wanting honest feedback, he also resists it. This person needs to work through his feelings and come to a deeper security and understanding.

Finally, there is the person who is closed and resistant. He not only resists correction emotionally, but he also resists it in principle. He is closed to correction because it is too threatening to his false self-image. He prefers to stay in the dark. Attempting to help such a person work through his feelings is a frustrating experience because he has not fundamentally opted to be open. Such a person needs clear, honest feedback—the truth spoken to him in love—which confronts him with the consequences of his choice. Helping him to realize the death-implications of his closedness can support him in making a fundamental decision to be open.

Wisdom requires that people who are at different levels of openness be corrected differently, though always in the posture of vulnerability and compassion. Only when someone is open and appreciative can he see clearly the "topic" which is brought into the light. Only then can he receive direct support. For the person who is open and resistant, the "topic" will create an array of difficult feelings. In such cases the "topic" will have to wait while the person resolves the feelings that it brings up. When someone is closed and resistant, neither the "topic" of correction nor the difficult feelings created will be fruitfully handled. Both will have to be put aside temporarily while lovingly confronting the person with the truth about his fundamental option. In other words, unwise love that corrects everyone the same way will be fruitful only some of the time, and will often be frustrating and confusing.

Nevertheless, we should never limit people, for in fact each of us probably shows all three attitudes toward correction at various times. In one area of our lives we might be open and appreciative of correction. In another we might be open and resistant; in yet another, closed and resistant. Comparisons with other people are hazardous. We may think we are more open and appreciative than others, but often our sore spot has not been touched. Each of us has his or her good gifts with their concomitant bad sides or weaknesses that need support.

Wisdom in correcting others points to the importance of our unity. Unity is easily shattered in the absence of fraternal correction. For individuals, different approaches are appropriate depending on whether the person is open and appreciative, open yet resistant, or closed and resistant. The purpose and context of correction is always unity and returning to the first love.

## *The New Testament Balance on Judging*

Let us consider what the New Testament has to say on judgments of others. At first glance scripture seems to contradict itself about calling people to holiness, fraternal correction, and the proper judging of others this involves. Numerous passages forbid judging others while many others recommend it, even insist on it.

Consider Matthew writing "If you want to avoid judgment, stop passing judgment. Your verdict on others will be the verdict passed on you. The measure with which you measure will be used to measure you" (7:1-2). Paul writes to the Romans " . . . every one of you who judges another is inexcusable" (2:1). To the Corinthians he writes " . . . so stop passing judgment before the time of his return" (1 Cor 4:5). James says that "the one who speaks ill of his brother or judges his brother is speaking against the law . . . who then are you to judge your neighbor?" (4:11-12). Apparently, Christians are not to judge others.

But then we read Matthew's advice about fraternal correction, "If your brother should commit some wrong against you, go and point out his fault . . . " (18:15). We hear Paul's advice to those who resisted making a judgment about the incestuous man, "Is it not those inside the community you must judge? God will judge the others" (1 Cor 5:14) and to "correct him as you would a brother" (2 Thes 3:15). Paul tells the Colossians to "admonish one another" (3:16) and tells Timothy that the servant of the Lord should be "gently correcting those who contradict him . . . ." (2 Tm 2:25). In writing to the Galatians, Paul says "My brothers, if someone is detected in sin, you who live by the Spirit should gently set him right . . . " (6:1). James ends his letter by recalling that "The case may arise among you of someone straying from the truth, and of another bringing him back" (5:19). Apparently, Christians *are* to judge others.

The apparent contradiction in interpreting scripture comes from the ambiguous meaning of the Greek word translated as "judging." One of the meanings of judging others is the sense of forming an opinion about what is happening. Another meaning is to condemn or judge harshly.[35]

If we are to support and love one another, then we need to "judge" what is going on in the first sense—to form a right opinion about events and actions. For example, if the other shepherds in our community are to support me by helping me not to be in control the wrong way, then they have to make a judgment when that begins to happen. When they first started telling me this a few years ago, I would argue with them about it, claiming that it wasn't true and that they shouldn't judge anyway. Then I began to tolerate their comments and gradually came to accept and appreciate them. My initial resistance had to do with a misunderstanding about what judging others meant. My co-workers shouldn't judge me in the sense of harshly condemning me, but there was nothing at all wrong with their "judging" me in the sense of seeing what is happening, forming a conclusion about it, and acting on it by sharing with me so that I could correct it. They may not be right every single time, but usually they are.

What is unconditionally demanded by scripture is that such evaluations or judgments of one another are done with a posture of love, vulnerability, and compassion. We know that God will judge us. Thus our judging of others excludes superiority, hardness, and blindness to our own faults, and also safeguards a readiness to forgive and to intercede.[36] The "do not judge" passages of scripture are telling us two things: (1) make sure our posture is loving, not harsh, (2) do not condemn others by saying that they are no good. If we do that to others, then we are told that God will do the same to us.

Scripture's approach to judging others is that compassion must undergird our thoughts and words about others. Instead of condemning others, we realize we all have the same human frailties, though their effects might be very different in our lives. This realization should not lead to a pessimistic resignation, however, because we are empowered by faith and believe that God mysteriously uses even our failures in his plan. We experience God being with us through Jesus being passionately with us, which is to say that God has compassion for us precisely in our weakness. Because we experience God's love for us in our weakness, we are able to be passionately with (compassion) others in our lack of perfection. While being able to honestly face difficulties in others' behavior, we experience the grace whereby "mercy triumphs over judgment" (Jas 2:13).

Yet it would be a mistake to think our judgments are to be mild, meek, and soft. In commenting on fraternal correction, Xavier Leon-Dufour stresses Paul's forcefulness. The believer should practice fraternal correction according to Jesus' precept (Mt 18:15; cf. 1 Thes 5:14; 2 Thes 3:15; Col 3:16; 2 Tm 2:25). Paul does this with vigor, not hesitating to use the rod (1 Cor 4:21), nor to hurt feelings if there is a cause (2 Cor 7:3-11). He incessantly instructs and warns his children (1 Cor 4:14; Acts 20:31).[37]

This is a gospel paradox which the modern mind finds hard to understand. How can you love someone so much that you are forceful to the point of using the rod? Judging others in the proper way does at times mean being forceful. The goal is not for the other person to feel good, but for the other person to be supported. A few years ago, for example, when someone would point out to me that I was trying to be in control in the wrong way, I didn't feel good about it at all. Yet I do in retrospect, realizing it was a tremendous support.

We probably need to remind ourselves that Paul's forcefulness comes from the intensity of his love. He regards his people tenderly and affectionately as his children because he is their father in Christ. When he warned the Ephesian leaders strongly, it was to the point of tears, of loving concern, not raging anger (Acts 20:31). Paul's relationship with them was one of openness, vulnerability, tenderness, and trust. It is in this context that Paul corrects them with forcefulness.[38]

## *Fraternal Correction in Matthew 18*

Now that we have a general orientation to scripture's approach to judging, let us study in more depth Matthew 18, the most crucial passage about fraternal correction. At first it might seem that only verses 15-20 deal directly with fraternal correction, but modern scholarship has shown how the entire chapter conveys one message: the ground rules needed if God's peace is to permeate our personal relationships.[39] First of all let us recall the structure of the chapter, and then read through the text.

1. The Transformed Mind—THE GOSPEL PARADOX (verses 1-4). True greatness in the kingdom of God is to be like a child.
2. Practical #1—ENCOURAGE (verses 5-9). The evil of scandal and radically avoiding it.
3. Practical #2—CARE FOR (verses 10-14). The care of sheep going astray.

4. Practical #3—DESIRE UNITY (verses 15-20). Fraternal correction and the fruit of reconciliation.
5. Practical #4—FORGIVE (verses 21-35). The reason for limitless forgiveness in the kingdom of God.

*The Transformed Mind—THE GOSPEL PARADOX* (verses 1-4)

At this time the disciples came to Jesus and said, "Who is the greatest in the kingdom of heaven?" So he called a little child to him and set the child in front of them. Then he said, "I tell you solemnly, unless you change and become like little children you will never enter the kingdom of heaven. And so, the one who makes himself as little as this little child is the greatest in the kingdom of heaven (1-4 JB).

*Practical #1—ENCOURAGE* (verses 5-9)

Anyone who welcomes a little child like this in my name welcomes me. But anyone who is an obstacle to bring down one of these little ones who have faith in me would be better drowned in the depths of the sea with a great millstone round his neck. Alas for the world that there should be such obstacles! Obstacles indeed there must be, but alas for the man who provides them! If your hand or your foot should cause you to sin, cut it off and throw it away: it is better for you to enter into life crippled or lame, than to have two hands or two feet and be thrown into eternal fire. And if your eye should cause you to sin, tear it out and throw it away: it is better for you to enter into life with one eye, than to have two eyes and be thrown into the hell of fire. (5-9 JB).

*Practical #2—CARE FOR* (verses 10-14)

See that you never despise any of these little ones, for I tell you that their angels in heaven are continually in the presence of my Father in heaven. Tell me. Suppose a man has a hundred sheep and one of them strays; will he not leave the ninety-nine on the hillside and go in search of the stray? I tell you solemnly, if he finds it, it gives him more joy than do the ninety-nine that did not stray at all. Similarly, it is never the will of your Father in heaven that one of these little ones should be lost (10-14 JB).

*Practical #3—DESIRE UNITY* (verses 15-20)

If your brother does something wrong, go and have it out with him alone, between your two selves. If he listens to you, you have won back your brother. If he does not listen, take one or two others along with you: the evidence of two or three witnesses is required to sustain any charge. But if he refuses to listen to these, report it to the community; and if he refuses to listen to the community, treat him like a pagan or a tax collector. I tell you solemnly, whatever you bind on earth shall be considered bound in heaven; whatever you loose on earth shall be considered loosed in heaven. I tell you solemnly once again, if two of you on earth agree to ask anything at all, it will be granted to you by my Father in heaven. For where two or three meet in my name, I shall be there with them (15-20 JB).

*Practical #4—FORGIVE* (verses 21-35)

Then Peter went up to him and said, "Lord, how often must I forgive my brother if he wrongs me? As often as seven times?" Jesus answered, "Not seven, I tell you, but seventy-seven times. And so the kingdom of heaven may be compared to a king who decided to settle his accounts with his servants. When the reckoning began, they brought him a man who owed ten thousand talents; but he had no means of paying, so his master gave orders that he should be sold, together with his wife and children and all his possessions, to meet the debt. At this, the servant threw himself down at his master's feet. 'Give me time' he said 'and I will pay the whole sum.' And the servant's master felt so sorry for him that he let him go and cancelled the debt. Now as this servant went out, he happened to meet a fellow servant who owed him one hundred denarii; and he seized him by the throat and began to throttle him. 'Pay what you owe me' he said. His fellow servant fell at his feet and implored him, saying, 'Give me time and I will pay you.' But the other would not agree; on the contrary, he had him thrown into prison till he should pay the debt. His fellow servants were deeply distressed when they saw what had happened, and they went to their master and reported the whole affair to him. Then the master sent for him. 'You wicked servant,' he said 'I cancelled all that debt of yours when you appealed to me. Were you not bound, then, to have pity on your fellow servant just as I had pity on you?' And in his anger the master handed him over to the torturers till he should pay all his debt. And that is how my heavenly Father will deal with you unless each forgive your brother from your heart" (21-35 JB).

Scripture scholars generally agree that in Chapter 18 of Matthew, not only are earlier traditions (for example, Mark 9:35-50) presented again, but they also are woven together in a different way and re-interpreted into a new final form, which speaks directly to the evangelist's community. The evangelist was intelligent as well as inspired. "He understood the material he inherited. He selected what was relevant to the Christian community."[40] In a recent study which looks at the final form of Matthew's Gospel, especially Chapter 18, in order to recover Matthew's viewpoint and where his community "was at," William Thompson concludes:

> Matthew presents Jesus as a Teacher of Wisdom who predicts his own future, and in the light of that prediction instructs his disciples about life in Christian community. These instructions indicate that scandal and sin were dividing the community. Matthew interpreted this tension as a foretaste of the widespread internal corruption of the last days (24:10-13), and it led him to a deeper understanding of the traditional sayings of Jesus. He arranged and composed this section of his gospel to help the members of his community confront the problem of internal dissension.[41]

As we go through Matthew 18, we may gain wisdom on what our expectations and judgments should be if we are living in the kingdom already present *with special reference to* relationships that are tense, unpeaceful, and, in the larger context of a community, torn by internal dissension. Matthew is not speaking theoretically about ideals or laws. He is giving very practical advice on how to bring peace to relationships individually and communally.

We need to take Matthew 18 seriously for our own situation. It is as relevant to us today as it was to Matthew's community. It shows us how to deal with tense, unpeaceful relationships. Thus, we need to study the passage with an eye toward determining what the Lord is saying to us about our relationships—now.

## The Gospel Paradox (18:1-4)

The first part of Matthew 18 is about how true greatness in the kingdom of God is to be like a child. It reveals the foundational gospel paradox. The transformed and renewed mind knows our identity as a son or daughter of God, not as someone more important than others.

Jesus' directive is addressed to all the disciples, not merely to the Twelve. He tells us to make ourselves little, humble—*tapeinoun* in Greek. That Greek verb does not occur often in the New Testament. We see it in the paradox of the gospel law, "anyone who *humbles* himself will be exalted" (Mt 23:12 JB). We see it when Paul explains the paradox of his preaching, "I preached the gospel of God to you free of charge, *humbling* myself with a view to exalting you" (2 Cor 11:7). We see it again in the Philippian hymn that tells us to take on Christ's attitude, "It was thus that he *humbled* himself, obediently accepting even death, death on a cross! Because of this, God highly exalted him" (2:8-9). James writes of the same paradoxical law, "Be *humbled* in the sight of the Lord and he will raise you on high" (4:10).

A spiritual way of thinking is being revealed here. The preparation for dealing with lack of peace in a relationship is to be like a child, to actively enter into the paradoxical gospel law by becoming lowly, humbled, emptied, vulnerable. Yet all the while we trust that in doing so God will then exalt us, and bring us into his glory. This being as a child, this humbling of ourselves which trusts in God's exaltation, undergirds all the rest of the advice in Matthew 18 which tells us how to offer fraternal correction in a Christian community on earth.

The humility Jesus requires of us has nothing whatsoever to do with a low self-image or feeling bad about ourselves. To the contrary, these things are problems in a Christian's life and find their source in focusing on ourselves. If we misunderstand humility and "making ourselves lowly" as having a low opinion of ourselves, then we might think that we should never correct others because we can't trust our perceptions, understandings, and judgments.

The humility that Jesus speaks of has to do with our posture of trust in God. Humbling ourselves, making ourselves lowly, means that we so trust in God's care that we can simply speak the truth without pressuring, manipulating, or forcing. It is a paradox: we yield to death and God empowers a resurrection.

When we want something very much, it is easy to subtly pressure, manipulate, or force others into providing it. However, a child-like posture of humility leads us to make our needs known, to speak the truth but never to apply pressure to have it our way. It values the unity and love in the relationship too much to "use" the relationship to get what we want.

For example, consider a situation where we are part of a group trying to come to a common decision. A worldly way of thinking would have us argue, apply pressure, belittle people who disagree, gossip, form factions, and do whatever is necessary to get our way. A spiritual way of thinking would have us be humble, like a child, stating clearly what we think ought to happen and why, and trusting in God to take care of things. Unity in the process is more important than a good idea in the conclusion. The gospel paradox is that when we let go and trust in God, what we want happens better anyway.

## Encouragement (18:5-9)

The second section of Matthew 18 is about the evil of scandal and radically avoiding it. Its practical advice is to encourage others.

The child, the little one, means any Christian who has humbled himself, emptied himself, and made himself vulnerable to his brothers and sisters. It means someone who has let go of manipulating and trusts in God. Jesus tells the disciples that in accepting and receiving any such Christian, they are accepting and receiving him. Jesus is giving us a letter of introduction to other Christians, including those we have a problem with. He is saying, "these are my friends. Treat them as you would me, for we are one." He pleads with us to accept them, assuring us that in receiving them, we receive him.

We need to take radical steps to avoid leading astray a little one, a Christian who has given up worldly ways of relating in order to trust in God. The word "lead astray" means to cause another to stumble, to hinder, weaken, or completely destroy his faith in Jesus. A Christian who has emptied himself has faith that God will exalt him. If we are in a relationship with another Christian which is so discouraging for him that it undermines his faith that God will exalt him, then Jesus tells us we are in trouble. We must radically avoid all conduct, expectations, and judgments which might cause a fellow disciple to grow weak in his faith. Not only are we to be like a child, but we are to go to any extreme to avoid discouraging others from being like a child. If our stubbornness with a fellow disciple causes him to lose his childlikeness, then we are in trouble with the Lord.

In practice, this means being careful to see that our posture is a loving one. For example, we must always share in a way that builds up the other person; we should never simply dump our feelings onto another. When there is any problem with another, we need to deal with it right away: "the sun must not go down on your wrath" (Eph 4:26). Otherwise a reservoir of negative feelings can build up to the point where, when we do share, the person feels attacked. This can create a scandal where we weaken the other's faith that God will exalt him.

This rigorous concern for the faith of a little one who trusts in God does not mean that we should avoid the intense and forceful fraternal correction that Paul displayed at times. But it does mean that the more intense and forceful fraternal correction is, the deeper must be the love relationship within which the fraternal correction happens. Our experience is that even when a person is in an especially fragile emotional condition, bringing up difficulties does no harm to their faith if it is done in the midst of an intense love. The person might find it hard, but it doesn't undermine his or her faith.

## Care for Others (18:10-14)

The third section of Matthew 18 is about the care of sheep going astray. Its practical advice is to care for others very actively and to respect them.

Jesus has told us that the basis for our kingdom life is being like a child, being emptied, vulnerable, and thus entering into the faith posture where God himself can exalt us and bring us into his glory. Then he warns us severely not to be stumbling blocks to our brother's childlike faith. Furthermore, we are not even to "despise" one of these little ones. The rare Greek verb used here "expresses the opposite of love and devotion—look down on, despise, scorn, treat with contempt."[42] Jesus has moved into the realm of our thoughts and attitudes. He is giving us a clear directive about how not to think of brothers and sisters who have exposed their hearts to us. We must always deeply respect them, no matter what wrongs have been committed.

Even though others may have begun to stray from the rest of the community, we are never to despise them, because they have a privileged relationship with their heavenly Father. The mysterious phrase, "their angels in heaven constantly behold my heavenly Father's face" means that the paradoxical gospel law has been mystically fulfilled; they have been exalted and brought into the glory of God. "Through their angels in heaven these little ones constantly enjoy a special relationship to the Father."[43]

Matthew has an interesting distinction from the parallel passage in Luke 15:4-7 which simply speaks of trying to find lost sheep and fully expects to find them. Matthew has an "if." The first part of verse 13 is best translated as "if it comes about that he finds it" or "if he actually finds it." As one scripture scholar says, "The probable condition indicates that the successful outcome of the search is not assured. The shepherd may not always find the one sheep going astray."[44]

Matthew had enough experience of confused and insecure members of the community to distinguish between "going astray" and "being lost."[45] The straying sheep is likely to be a disciple who has begun to stray from the community. The rest of the community is warned against despising him, for he is related to the Father and the Father does not want him lost. Instead of despising him they should focus on caring for him and drawing him back. Yet Matthew, fully in touch with the reality of his community life, refuses to pretend that no sheep will ever be lost. The disciple who begins to go astray can be saved by the pastoral concern of others, and the Father's will is for us to reach out in care and concern.

Very often it seems that one sheep strays at the very moment our hands are full with the ninety-nine. We could be easily tempted to ignore the one going astray and concentrate our efforts on those who are faithful. Jesus is telling us that this is a temptation to be resisted. We should never ignore "problem relationships" with those who are weak, using the excuse that we have no time because we are with the ninety-nine who are strong.

What happens when a large part of a community goes astray? How do you deal with the tensions that develop beneath the surface among the hundred sheep as the spirit of the community goes astray?

A common problem in communities is subterfuge, where the spirit of a community gets bogged down, an uneasiness and distance develops, and love grows cold. The usual source of this problem is the one identified by passages quoted earlier (Lv 19:17; Sir 19:26): neglect of fraternal correction will lead to disunity.

The scenario might unfold like this. One person in the community is annoyed at something another did or did not do. Instead of sharing it with the other person and resolving it, the individual keeps it inside where bitterness and resentment can develop. If this behavior becomes common, the tone of the community life begins to change subtly. People avoid one another. They feel unable to share freely together and conversations become superficial. People begin to trust their self-protections instead of God. If many people keep things in the dark, the atmosphere of the entire community is poisoned. What is to be done? How do we actively care for the brothers and sisters in these circumstances?

In our own experience, we have developed a three-step process that helps to clear the air and return to our first love. First, the leaders of the community need to take responsibility when such a situation develops. They address the entire community about the seriousness of the situation and the need for everyone to take an active responsibility for it. Second, the entire community needs to come together for a time of prayer and penance where the Holy Spirit can move each of our hearts. The focus of such prayer is: "how do I need to take responsibility, repent and ask forgiveness?" The question is not "how should everyone else do this?" Three, after sufficient time, the community should come together to share what people have heard in prayer and how it has affected them. Time should also be available after the meeting when individuals are encouraged to be reconciled.

Special attention and support should be given to those who find the process difficult. Of course, it would be far better to correct things at the beginning before it becomes a community-wide problem. Experiences such as these make us grateful for the gift of fraternal correction which, when regularly responded to, can help the community to stay on track.

## Desire Unity (18:15-20)

The fourth part of Matthew 18 is about fraternal correction and the fruit of reconciliation. Its practical advice is to desire unity with one's whole being.

To enter into Jesus' mind as we read these words, we must adopt the childlikeness which undergirds this whole chapter. We should have the humility of a child which brings even awkward things right out into the light. We should not beat around the bush in giving correction, but say it clearly and briefly. As in the previous section Matthew "stressed the shepherd's concern for his flock rather than the successful outcome of his search,"[46] so here he wants to emphasize our desire for unity with the one who does wrong rather than the successful outcome of the procedure outlined.

Jesus directs a threefold procedure to individual disciples. All of the second person pronouns are singular in verses 15-17. Each individual wronged must take the initiative to reach out to the wrongdoer, never despising him, in the hopes of reconciliation. We need to put the complaint into words, so we do not brood and poison ourselves and wind up despising our brother or sister.[47] First there is a private meeting, then a meeting with witnesses, then with the Church. Always the goal is to win the brother back, not to get back at the brother. "It is a question of persuasion rather than rebuke or condemnation."[48]

As with straying sheep, the brother may ignore all three attempts at winning him back. In that case, then treat him as you (singular, referring to the brother who had a wrong committed against him) would a tax collector or Gentile. The nuance of the Greek means "it is a matter of personal attitude and conduct rather than official ecclesiological condemnation."[49] While some would interpret this as meaning the brother should avoid further contact with him (Matthew's realism comes out clearly), others suggest "it is a challenge to win him with the love which can touch even the hardest heart."[50] Recall that Jesus loved tax-collectors, Matthew among them. Yet their behavior is clearly not to be imitated (Mt 5:46-47, 6:7). Matthew's intention is to stress the need to be so desirous of unity that we bend over backwards in the threefold attempt to be reconciled. He never intended to set up self-righteous rules for condemning people.

In the verse about binding or loosing (the second person pronouns become plural), Matthew applies the bind/loose image to the brother ignoring/being won back at any part of the threefold process. Matthew might be recalling this saying of Jesus to stress the fact that the wrong can be loosed, both on earth and in heaven, that a successful attempt at reconciliation has God's own power to wipe out the wrong that was done. When unity is re-established, God's power allows things to be better than if the wrong and reconciliation had never occurred. Matthew, being a realist, does not pass over the opposite possibility.

What the Jerusalem Bible translates as "if two of you on earth agree" actually means "be in agreement, be in harmony, be of one mind."[51] The process of reconciliation should always bring people to one mind. Hopefully, it brings the brother and the wrongdoer to one mind as the wrongdoer is won back, and the fruit of such unity is a powerful prayer that is granted anything—even a total loosing from all the bad effects of the disunity. Unfortunately, at times it brings the Church to one mind over and against the wrongdoer who ignores it and refuses to be won back. In either case, though, the precious unity which is granted any request in prayer is the fruit of concern, love, an outpouring of time and energy, and a respect for one another. This is costly unity indeed, yet unbelievably powerful. At all costs, we must desire unity. In commenting on Matthew 18:15-20, Barclay writes, "Basically this passage means that we must never tolerate any situation in which there is a breach of personal relationships between us and another member of the Christian community."[52] We must desire unity with our whole being.

There are different levels of unity appropriate to different relationships—a marriage, a group of leaders, a community, a prayer group, a group of people living together, any brother or sister in the Lord. The quality and depth of unity depends on the kind of relationship, whether people are formally committed to one another or spontaneously gathering, the maturity of the people, and other factors.

We cannot apply the Matthew 18 approach in the same external way to our spouse and at our parish council meeting. Yet the principles are the same. If our brother has done some wrong against us and it is dividing our heart against him, we need to go and talk with him about it. We shouldn't repress it, gossip about him, or complain to others. We ought to share directly with him. The depth of our sharing is determined by the level of unity appropriate to the relationship. This can usually be discerned by discussing the matter until we experience peace in our hearts about what has happened.

If the other person does not listen, we ought to ask for the support of a third party and, after that, the support of our pastor. The focus must always be unity and love.

## Forgiveness (18:21-35)

The last part of Matthew 18 explains the reason for limitless forgiveness in the kingdom of God. Its practical advice is to forgive others.

As soon as Jesus has finished speaking about the energy that must be expended in winning a brother back, Peter asks the typical question, "Lord, I can tolerate going through the whole business of reconciliation if you tell me to, but if it keeps happening it is only reasonable to give up on the person. Right?" "Wrong," says Jesus. One never, never gives up on a brother or sister. Forgiveness must be extended limitlessly. Most likely,

Peter's question reflects the actual state of relationships in the Matthean community, a situation where members may have had Lamech's attitude: "If Cain is avenged sevenfold, then Lamech seventy-sevenfold" (Gn 4:24).[53]

The reason for limitless forgiveness in the kingdom of God is clarified in the contrast between the master's merciful conduct (moved with pity, the master wrote off the debt) and the servant's heartlessness and harsh punishment of any who owed him the smallest debt. The contrast is extreme. The huge amount the master is owed is ten thousand talents. Ten thousand is the highest possible number in Greek, and a talent is the highest unit in currency.[54] The small fraction owed the servant is a hundred denarii. It is a contrast between $10,000,000 and $20, a mere fraction indeed.

God, our Father, has cancelled our huge debt with great tenderness and compassion, being so passionately with us that his Son Jesus became flesh. As St. John put it, "if God has loved us so, we must have the same love for one another" (1 Jn 4:11). If we do not, there is again the stern warning of what will happen to us. Matthew wanted to stress unlimited forgiveness to counteract the scandal which was running rampant in his community. In Matthew's Gospel, after the Our Father there is an additional warning to help the members of his community with this. "If you forgive the faults of others, your heavenly Father will forgive you yours. If you do not forgive others, neither will your Father forgive you" (Mt 6:14-15).

The master's forgiveness goes even further than the appeal for patience, perhaps because the master knows the only two options are condemnation and unlimited forgiveness. It is not possible for the servant to ever repay his master such a huge amount, even if he worked the rest of his life. As the master is moved with pity and released the servant, ripping up the I.O.U., so we must do likewise with our brothers. What they "owe" us is nothing compared to what God has released us from, even if it is our "legal right" to exact it. When we forgive our brothers from our hearts, letting go of the debt or grudge, then we ourselves are freed. A single act of non-forgiveness has a disastrous effect on the one not forgiving. When we are holding onto a resentment, a grudge, or bitterness, it has a hold on us, and chokes us. Matthew is sternly warning us that when we do that to others, God will do it to us. "Blest are those who show mercy, mercy shall be theirs" (Mt 5:7). His practical advice is to forgive others.

## *Conclusions*

As we conclude our examination of scripture, let us recall the starting point; we are rooted in our scriptural identity as sons and daughters of God. It is out of this transformed mind that we can acknowledge God's plan and let go of our false identities and private plans. The result is a posture shift that affects the way we feel and behave. The practical aids of actively praising and apocalyptic thinking both support this spiritual way of thinking and are a means of discernment to see where worldly ways of thinking still prevail.

We then saw the completing/competing tensions in scripture where we learned the lessons of being centered on loving and obeying God as our Father; not getting trapped in a rigid, literal interpretation of the law; being centered on following Jesus the way I am called, not competing with others to be the greatest; being impelled by the vision God gives us but not imposing it on others; reinforcing the good gifts people have in the process of dealing with the bad side of them; valuing others' charisms even when they clash with ours.

What does Chapter Four have to say to the questions: What does it mean to be pure of heart as we call one another to holiness? How should I approach my brother or sister when there is a fault to be pointed out? What should my posture be? How can I authentically support instead of condemn or discourage?

Adding to the answers above we could say the following. We need to approach brothers and sisters differently when there is a fault to be pointed out depending on their openness and attitudes. If they are open and appreciative, we can approach them expecting to directly help them with the fault being pointed out. If they are open yet resistant, we will need to approach them expecting to only indirectly help them with the fault being pointed out. The direct help will be aimed at the feelings that are stirred up by it. If they are closed and resistant, we will need to approach them expecting the fault to be pointed out only as a means to the end of helping them be open to relationships at all. Here it is mostly a decision on their part, but one which they may not realize is crucial for their lives.

From our study of the New Testament balance on judgments, we saw that the notion that a Christian should never judge in any way is a misunderstanding. The truth is that one should never condemn, and our posture should always be loving.

Matthew's advice to a divided community to bring about peace in their relationships is:

1. Be grounded in the gospel paradox of the transformed and renewed mind where we humble ourselves and take on a vulnerable posture like children, trusting in God.
2. Encourage our brethren, taking a responsibility to see that we never undermine their childlike faith by our relationship being a stumbling block.
3. Actively care for those who have begun to stray, focusing our energies on drawing them back, not despising them.
4. Desire unity with our whole heart. Do not let poison breed within us, but go to the person and "make every effort to preserve the unity which has the Spirit as its origin and peace as its binding force" (Eph 4:3).
5. Limitlessly forgive. Fully release our brother or sister and cancel the debt. Let go of anything which is holding them, keeping in mind a healthy fear of the Lord.

# *Part Two*

# *Christian Tradition*

CHAPTER FIVE

# PURITY OF HEART: THE DESERT FATHERS

The theme of this book is the posture of vulnerability and compassion that underlies a Christian's relationships, becoming most apparent in the area of expectations and judgments. Fraternal correction and our expectations of others, then, becomes an ideal laboratory in which to consider our posture in relationships in a way that opens us to the Holy Spirit's transformation. Our approach is to reflect on wisdom about this from scripture, Christian tradition, and contemporary sources in light of our community's experiences in relationships. It is neither a systematic study of all available wisdom on our theme nor a journal account of our experiences. Its goal is the sharing of wisdom from selected sources in light of our experience so that we can receive practical help in how to love in relationships, especially in the delicate areas of judgments, expectations, and fraternal correction.

In Chapter One we considered our relationships with others and the vulnerable posture necesary to come into deeper unity. The process of our transformation by the power of the Holy Spirit is one of struggling with our posture—giving up worldly protections to receive graced vulnerability, letting go of harsh condemnations to take on compassionate judgments.

Part One of the book focused on scripture's wisdom in a variety of areas. In Chapter Two we explored the prerequisite of a transformed mind that sees God's Spirit working in our daily lives. We saw the importance of our scriptural identity as sons and daughters of God which allows us to be secure in his personal love for us. The transformed mind acknowledges God's plan instead of clinging to our own, and brings with it a posture shift, a transformation of our whole attitude. The practical aids of actively praising and apocalyptic thinking help us to enter into the transformed mind more deeply and point out areas where we are still resistant to God's way of viewing things.

Chapter Three explored the dialectic expectations of completing and competing, juxtaposing apparently contradictory expectations with a view toward resolving their conflict by seeing them in God's larger plan. Insight into God's resolution of conflicting expectations is crucial if we are to have the right posture in our judgments. The compassionate new wine of Jesus completes the old wineskin, yet apparently also competes with the old wineskin—the expectation of fiery judgment now so that others may be condemned immediately. It completes the right expectation of God coming to save; it competes with the wrong expectation of harshly condemning those not living according to the letter of the law.

The apostles' wrong expectations that they would gain their identity from the status of being first competes with Jesus' view of things. Thus he leads them into the right expectations—they are to be as a child, a servant whose identity is formed in God alone. The tension between the different community visions of the Jewish-Christian and Gentile Churches highlights the right expectation of being impelled by our vision and the wrong one of imposing it on others. In considering the bad side of the Ephesians' good gift of truth, we saw how crucial it is to reinforce the good gift of truth while rejecting the wrong expectation that its bad side—a rigidity lacking in love—will unavoidably permeate the situation. Finally, in the Paul-Barnabas dispute, we see the clashing charisms of a mission and relationship orientation. Both persons wrongly expect one to be right and the other to be wrong. The right expectation is that in God's larger plan their diversity and pluralism is meant to complete one another by serving in different parts of the Church. Knowing how to interpret the dialectic of contrasting expectations helps one to enter the right posture for judging others.

In Chapter Four, the wisdom, love, and unity which are the motivating purpose and posture for fraternal correction clearly emerges. Wisdom makes clear how we need to be flexible in correcting others, depending on their openness and attitudes. If they are open and appreciative, then we can support them directly by pointing out the problem. However, if pointing out the problem brings up many feelings they find hard to cope with, then they will need support primarily with working their feelings through. If they are closed to any correction at all, they will need support in realizing the implications of their decision to be closed. If the motivating purpose of pointing out another's problem is to love and support the other person, then we will be flexible in approaching them. If our primary desire is to express our feelings, we will frequently find ourselves dumping our feelings on others, with destructive consequences.

Matthew's advice to his divided community was also found relevant in bringing peace to our own relationships: be grounded in the gospel paradox where we humble ourselves and become vulnerable like children while we trust that God will exalt us; encourage those we are correcting; actively care for them; urgently desire unity with them; and limitlessly forgive.

Part Two of this book examines Christian tradition in order to tap certain key resources selected in light of our experience of entering into deeper relationships in the Lord. This chapter is about the purity of heart involved in our thought patterns and judging our brothers and sisters as seen by the Desert Fathers. The next chapter deals with St. Thomas Aquinas' views on the questions of how to judge others. Chapter Seven looks at some key Church documents which help us to see the practical applications of a posture that respects others.

Scripture's exhortation about our identity, expectations, and judgments in relationships is a narrow path to follow, a hard saying to accept. Yet we today are not the first ones who have tried to follow that narrow path. Our Christian tradition is filled with believers who have tried and succeeded. They are certainly a consolation and an inspiration for us.

The Desert Fathers who were the early fourth century initiators of the monastic movement are a case in point. They left everything in their world in order to live either alone, or more commonly in groups, in the deserts of Northern Africa. Their immediate goal was purity of heart, their way to reach the ultimate end of the kingdom of heaven.[55] Abbot Moses, called the chief of the saints in the desert of Scete, explained that they were so caught up with attaining purity of heart that:

> We undergo all sorts of toils not merely without weariness but actually with delight; on account of which the want of food in fasting is no trial to us, the weariness of our vigils becomes a delight; reading and constant meditation on the scriptures does not pall upon us; and further incessant toil, and self-denial, and the privation of all things, and the horrors also of this vast desert have no terrors for us.[56]

The reason these monks were so urgently caught up in seeking purity of heart might be a startling discovery for us. They realized that the very "world" they had fled for the sake of the kingdom of God, was still very much in their own hearts. Instead of finding immediate perfection, they found spirits of gluttony, fornication, avarice, anger, dejection, listlessness, vainglory, and pride.[57] These had to be fought to attain that purity of heart which alone could lead them into the kingdom of God.[58]

With this in mind, we can now consider their wisdom on judging others, on guarding our thoughts, and on the apocalyptic vision which supports Christians in their urgency to intensely live the gospel without compromise.

## *Judging Our Brother*

The Desert Fathers' urgency in their search for purity of heart had striking effects on their posture in judging others. We can see in some of their stories or sayings how the typical worldly responses of revenge and harsh condemnation color their judgments of others. Yet their sayings stress how the oldest monks, who had learned purity of heart, helped the younger ones be freed of their worldly responses. Let us look at these sayings which are lessons in the right posture for fraternal correction.

> One of the brethern had been insulted by another and he wanted to take revenge. He came to Abbot Sisois and told him what had taken place, saying: I am going to get even, Father. But the elder besought him to leave the affair in the hands of God. No, said the brother, I will not give up until I have made that fellow pay for what he said. Then the elder stood up and began to pray in these terms: O God, you are no longer necessary to us, and we no longer need you to take care of us since, as this brother says, we both can and will avenge ourselves. At this the brother promised to give up his idea of revenge.[59]

This story can be easily transferred to our own lives to exemplify the kind of judgment we make on others when they insult us. Our first, worldly, reponse is to take revenge, to get even. A spiritual way of thinking tells us to leave the matter of punishing the individual up to God. But the worldly way of thinking, wanting to make "that fellow pay for what he said," is frequently stronger and wins out. When we do that, we are denying God, refusing to acknowledge his plan, and undermining the spiritual way of thinking. When the Holy Spirit shows us the implications of what we are doing, we need to repent and give up the idea of revenge. Let us look below the surface into the realm of our hearts by considering the monk's heart response in this story.

Notice the progression of events and what changes the monk's heart.[60] First, the monk has a wrong done against him; in this case it was the statement of another against him. Let us call this point A: it is the *A*ctivating event. Point B, our *B*elief system and thoughts, is unspoken. It must be inferred. The monk's emotional response is to be upset, angry, and tempted to get back at the other. Let us call this point C; it is the *C*onsequent emotions. Then comes D, a *D*ecision for revenge. Notice that in this story, as well as in our own lives, a belief system, point B, is activated by A and causes C. Our belief system can be either a worldly way of thinking or a spiritual way of thinking. In either case, A does not cause C; the unspoken B causes C.

The monk's initial response to the activating event of being insulted must be read between the lines. Perhaps the monk's worldly belief system might be something like, "Oh, how horrible being insulted is. How could he ever say anything like that? What will other people think? This ruins my plans to be well respected, etc." This thinking at point B is a thought pattern in the realm of expectations and judgments. What follows is the consequent emotional response at C—upset and anger. Then comes D: the resulting *D*ecision for revenge based on these emotions. This is a typical worldly way of thinking with its consequent fruit.

When he comes to the older and wiser monk for advice, he experiences a transformation to a spiritual way of thinking. What changes? The activating event of being insulted cannot change since that is simply a historical fact. But the older monk explains by parable the implications of the decision for revenge based on his consequent emotions of anger and upset: if I must take revenge, then there is no need for God. This point is addressed to B; it is a new thought pattern. Through this the younger monk realizes the irrationality and perhaps sinfulness of his expectations and judgment at point B—his worldly belief system or thought pattern. Again, reading between the lines, the younger monk may say to himself something like "the insult happened, but it is not all that horrible. Everybody has their faults, we're all in the same boat together. It would have been nice if he didn't insult me, but it is not a disaster that he did. God will provide what is needed and I trust he is working through this for the good." What follows from this new spiritual way of thinking at B is a new emotional response at C. Perhaps the monk even feels somewhat hurt or angry, but not with the intensity that overwhelms him and leads to a decision to take revenge.

It is certainly possible, given our free will, to resist even the intensely negative emotions that come from the worldly way of thinking and to make a decision to not take revenge anyway. But a will power approach is not the best solution on two counts. First, it makes the right decision harder to make; we are likely to fail from time to time and do the right thing less frequently. Second, even if we make the right decision to not take revenge, we are trapped by our feelings. We are not free to relate to the person in a loving way and our negative thoughts and feelings will often be non-verbally expressed in spite of ourselves. The right decision and actions are good, but not good enough. The Lord's solution is to give us purity of heart—a spiritual way of thinking that frees the way we feel and makes it easier to more consistently make the right decisions.

Such a spiritual way of thinking that leaves revenge in the hands of God does not mean we ignore what people do to us. The monk, for example, might seek out his brother to be reconciled with him. Wrongdoing should usually be pointed out to others, but with the attitude of wanting to be one with them and lovingly support them—not to attack them or take revenge. We find fraternal correction becoming fraternal conflict when purity of heart is replaced by a worldly way of thinking. At times we might realize that we have merely been overly sensitive, reading into what a person has said or done when there is no real wrongdoing. Here we do not necessarily need to seek out our brother, but simply to resist the temptation and repent of entering into a worldly thought pattern.

Let us consider another saying of the Desert Fathers which sheds light on their discipline of custody of the heart or guarding one's thoughts:

> A brother in Scete happened to commit a fault, and the elders assembled, and sent for Abbot Moses to join them. He, however, did not want to come. The priest sent him a message, saying: Come, the community of the brethren is waiting for you. So he arose and started off. And taking with him a very old basket full of holes, he filled it with sand, and carried it behind him. The elders came out to meet him, and said: What is this, Father? The elder replied: My sins are running out behind me, and I do not see them, and today I come to judge the sins of another! They, hearing this, said nothing to the brother but pardoned him.[61]

This story, too, can be easily transferred to our lives. People commit a fault and we call everyone together to embarrass them instead of pointing it out to them privately in a way that encourages them, actively cares for them, intensely desires unity, and limitlessly forgives. The elders of Scete are violating every principle of fraternal correction as we do ourselves at times. As the

Holy Spirit reveals to us what we are really doing, we need to repent and pardon instead of punish. Perhaps the support the brother needed was an elder privately pointing out his fault and helping him to do better.

Notice again in this story the progression of the *A*ctivating event, the *B*elief System activated by it, the *C*onsequent emotions, the resulting *D*ecision and what changes the elders' hearts. First, a brother committed a fault; it is the activating event A. Perhaps the elders' emotional response (C) is to be incensed, so much so that they decide (D) to call an assembly to judge the brother, even inviting Abbot Moses to it. Again, A does not cause C; B causes C. B is the elders' belief system or thought response to A, which must be inferred. It might be something like, "How horrible that he committed this fault. If he can't be like we are, we ought to punish him for his own good. He is messing up our plans to have a holy community, etc." This thinking at B is a thought in the realm of expectations and judgments. What follows from it is the emotional response at C of being incensed and then the wrong decision to punish him.

Now when Abbot Moses presents the parable of the sand running out of the basket full of holes, what changes? Fact A does not change, nor is it disputed, since it is simply a historical fact. But as Abbot Moses unfolds his parable, the elders realize the irrationality and perhaps sinfulness of their expectation and judgment at point B—the impurity of their hearts, their worldly way of thinking. We can infer that the elders, after they have entered into a spiritual way of thinking, now say to themselves something like, "He committed the fault but it is not all that horrible. Everybody has their faults, we're all in the same boat together. It would have been nice if it didn't happen, but it is not a disaster that it did. We shouldn't shirk our responsibility to point out the brother's fault, yet God will provide what is needed. We should forgive, and trust that all is working for the good in God's plan." What follows from this new thinking at B is a new emotional response at C. This is a posture that is free to forgive. It provides a basis for more easily making the right decision.

It is important to note here that the Desert Fathers did not say we should pretend the brother never committed the fault. They did not try to ignore it, nor did they shirk their responsibility to provide proper fraternal correction. They did, however, avoid condemnatory judgments based on a blind self-justification which refuses to forgive until proper punishment is meted out. They lived a love that was passionately *with* their brothers.

The Desert Fathers' attitude in judging others was based on purity of heart. It involved being purified from a worldly way of thinking that causes an upset and anger and easily leads to the wrong decisions to seek revenge, punishment, and fraternal conflict. Purity of heart freed them to lovingly support others through fraternal correction which all experienced as a life-giving process.

## *Guarding Our Thoughts*

As the stories above indicate, the Desert Fathers frequently had to deal with the problem of impurity of heart, a worldly way of thinking. This problem had its most striking effect, perhaps, in the posture for judging others, yet it affected all their relationships and all aspects of their lives. The importance that purity of heart had for them led them to develop an understanding of how to guard their hearts and their thoughts.

Their method of "custody of the heart" or "guarding of one's thoughts" meant being careful of the very first thoughts (point B) we have about a person or situation. They tried to determine if these thoughts reflected a spiritual or a worldly way of thinking. This method is meant to be a practical help for our whole life, including expectations and judgments in relationships.

Abbot Moses, in speaking of the origins of our thoughts and how to discern them, says:

> Above all we ought at least to know that there are three origins of our thoughts, i.e., from God, from the devil, and from ourselves ... We ought then carefully to notice this threefold order, and with a wise discretion analyze the thoughts which arise in our hearts, tracking out their origin and cause and author in the first instance ... lest haply some beast, if I may say so, relating to the understanding, either lion or dragon, passing through has furtively left the dangerous marks of his

> track, which will show to others the way of access into the secret recesses of the heart, owing to a carelessness about our thoughts.[62]

The way a monk sought purity of heart was by guarding his thoughts, the doorway to his heart. When thoughts of revenge or condemnation entered his mind, he needed to be watchful enough to prevent such evil thoughts from entering his heart where they could be the controlling influence on his desires, speech, and action. In exposing such thought patterns to the light, he protected himself from similar thoughts being carried in through the thought patterns already established.

To illustrate this, let us reconsider the story I related earlier about my distress in the library. I had wanted to do a full day's work but began to sense that God wanted me to leave, to go home early. That was the activating event. The response in my own thoughts, emotions, and decisions was predictable when a worldly way of thinking is the controlling influence. I became centered on protecting my plans and eliminating all interference. A spiritual way of thinking would have centered me on being vulnerable to God's plan, opening myself to the surprises of the Holy Spirit.

When I did sense God trying to say something to me, I resisted it. As I first sensed God might have a plan different from mine, I was uninterested. I tried to put it out of my mind. I knew what I wanted to do and I feared that God's plans were going to interfere with my life. It would have been easy to externally "follow the Spirit," to leave the library thinking "If I have to, I have to; but I'm not going to like it." But this would have bothered me inside. I might feel bitter, angry, sarcastic, withdrawn, or abandoned, and I would tend to blame it on others and complain. If the subway or bus were late, I would get angry. When I got home and heard someone had called, I would be annoyed, "Why can't they ever leave me alone?" My posture would negatively affect all the people I would have come in contact with and, in a vicious circle, cause me to complain and withdraw from them even more. This worldly thought pattern certainly does not have God as its author.

While I did resist the sense that God was speaking to me, I began to realize that God wanted to work through what looked like an interference. I saw how focused I was on my own plan. This was hard for me because I thought I *was* following the Lord's plan. I believed he wanted me to be writing this book. And he did, but I was clinging to my detailed plans to do it instead of relaxing in the Lord's timing. I was clinging so tightly that when God said he had something more important for me that particular night, I did not want to hear him. When I did, I felt he was interfering with my life.

Not only did I have to realize that my plan was different from the Lord's, but I had to actively *choose* to follow his plan. If I had realized our plans were different but never chose to follow his, I would have externally "followed the Spirit" but with the negative posture described above. As I decided to focus on God's agenda, to choose *him* in the present moment over *my* work for him, I began to feel excited. I experienced a posture shift as I chose to follow God's plan and become conscious of his Spirit working very directly in my daily life. This thought pattern has its origin in God.

The discipline of guarding our thoughts means reflecting on them to see if our first thoughts about a situation come from God or elsewhere. This is a means of immediately checking to see whether we are entering into a spiritual thought pattern or a worldly one. At the beginning it is easy to re-orient our thoughts, guarding against a worldly pattern. Once we have entered into a worldly pattern, though, it is harder to be freed from it.

A question that naturally arises here is whether it is actually possible to eliminate evil thoughts altogether. The answer of the Desert Fathers is "no" on one level, but "yes" on another. It is not possible to prevent evil thoughts from presenting themselves to us, but we can refuse to yield to them in the way that allows them entrance to the inner chambers of our hearts. When Abbot Serenus was asked about this very question he said:

> No one who has experienced the conflicts of the inner man, can doubt that our foes are continually lying in wait for us. But we mean that they oppose our progress in such a way that we can think of them as only *inciting* to evil things and not *forcing* . . . as there is in them ample power of inciting, so in us there is a supply of power of rejection, and of liberty of acquiescing . . . It is therefore clear that each man goes wrong from this; viz.,

> that when evil thoughts assault him he does not immediately meet them with refusal and contradiction, for it says: "resist him, and he will flee from you" (Jas 4:7).[63]

Evil thoughts will present themselves. How horrible he is for doing that. How different he is from me. Who would ever do anything like that. He deserves to be punished. My plans are being interfered with. But they can merely incite, not force us to evil things. In other words, we don't have to dwell on such a thought, turn it over in our minds, taste it, ponder it, follow through on its line of thinking. The thought is like an initial burst of energy, but unless we actively perpetuate it with the motor of our mind, it will soon die. Purity of heart does not mean the elimination of such intitial evil thoughts, but rather the rejection of those thoughts as a basis for our thought life. For if we do assimilate them, it will be just a short while until they become the basis of our speech, and then the basis of our actions. The reason they can become a controlling influence on our thoughts, speech, and actions is not their inherent power, but the power we give them by maintaing them, perpetuating them, and increasing them a hundred fold.

And so the Desert Fathers developed a method for custody of the heart, or guarding of one's thoughts, a way to put into practice what Paul wrote to the Romans, "... be transformed by the renewal of your mind, so that you may judge what is God's will, what is good, pleasing and perfect" (12:2). It is a process whereby our consistent vigilance over initial thoughts cooperates with the Spirit's transformation of our minds in a way that brings forth the fruits of the Spirit. Consider the words of Abbot Abraham, a monk noted for simplicity of life, in a chapter on how a monk ought to keep guard over his thoughts:

> A monk's whole attention should thus be fixed on one point, and the rise and circle of all his thoughts be vigorously restricted to it; viz., to the recollection of God: our mind, unless by working round the love of the Lord alone as an immovably fixed centre, through all the circumstances of our works and contrivances, it either fits or rejects the character of all our

> thoughts by the excellent compasses of love, will never by excellent skill build up the structure of that spiritual edifice ... but will without foresight raise in his heart a house that ... will be miserably destroyed by the fall of his building.[64]

"Working around the love of the Lord alone" is the discerning criterion for the guarding of one's thoughts. Is this expectation or judgment of mine in keeping with the compassion of Jesus? The monks who constantly prayed the Psalms would remember Psalm 118:5, "yes, our God is merciful" and Psalm 79:8, "may your compassion quickly come to us" and would apply these words to expectations and judgments of one another. Whether a thought resonates with God's own love tells us whether we should let the thought penetrate more deeply into our hearts.

A practical help the Desert Fathers developed to aid in maintaining purity of heart was this guarding of our thoughts. It involves seeing whether the first thoughts we have come from God or another source. Since evil thoughts can never force us to evil but only incite us, we don't have to yield to them and can resist them. Love is the criterion of discernment for guarding our thoughts, and on that basis we can know whether we ought to let a thought more deeply into our minds and hearts.

## *Apocalyptic Vision*

The apocalyptic vision of the Desert Fathers sees through the surface struggles to penetrate the spiritual heart of the matter where the struggle between God and the evil one exists. This "X-ray" vision allows them to experience with joy the labor pains of the birth of the kingdom. Caught up in the urgency of attaining purity of heart, they turn to prayer as an environment where they absorb a spiritual way of thinking and attain purity of heart.

Abbot Moses, as quoted earlier, counted as nothing all his trials, fasting, weariness, toil, and privation. He did so because he was so urgently caught up in seeking the purity of heart which would lead him to the kingdom of God. Let us quote him at length to see his apocalyptic vision that frees him to experience distress as the labor pains of being born into the kingdom of God. He is speaking of the desire to cling to God continually and says:

> For everything depends on the inward frame of mind, and when the devil has been expelled from this, and sins no longer reign in it, it follows that the kingdom of God is founded in us, as the Evangelist says "... the kingdom of God is within you" (Lk 17:21). But nothing can be within you but knowledge or ignorance of the truth, and delight either in vice or virtue, through which we prepare a kingdom for the devil or for Christ in our heart; and of this kingdom the Apostle describes the character, when he says "the kingdom of God is not a matter of eating or drinking, but of justice, peace and the joy that is given by the Holy Spirit" (Rom 14:17) .... where the kingdom of God is, there most certainly eternal life is enjoyed, and where the kingdom of the devil is, there without doubt is death and the grave.[65]

If one abides in justice, peace, and joy, then one is most certainly in the kingdom of God. If one abides in injustice, discord, and the sorrow that leads to death, then one is in the kingdom of the devil. This is the apocalyptic vision that gives perspective to the trials and distress of being born into the freedom of the kingdom, and gives us a sense of urgency about responding to the Lord step by step, moment by moment.

The Desert Fathers applied this urgency to our thoughts and prayer. They knew that the mind is an active thing, and it cannot be kept a semi-vacuum as we guard it from evil thoughts. As Abbot Nesteros said, "the mind of man cannot be emptied of all thoughts."[66] And Abbot Serenus said:

> (the mind) can never remain idle, but unless provision is made where it may exercise its motions and have what will constantly occupy it, it must by its own fickleness wander about and stray over all kinds of things until, accumstomed by long practice and daily use it tries and learns what food for the memory it ought to prepare, toward which it may bring its unwearied flight and acquire strength for remaining.[67]

Therefore, if we want to deprive our minds of evil thoughts, not only do we need to actively guard our thoughts so that the evil ones are denied deeper access, but we also need to actively dwell on the good so that it fills our minds.

And so the Fathers teach about continued recital of the Psalms, meditation on scripture and constant prayer: a whole variety of ways to fulfill Paul's injunction: "Your thoughts should be wholly directed to all that is true, all that deserves respect, all that is honest, pure, admirable, decent, virtuous, or worthy of praise" (Phil 4:8).

Paul is not giving theoretical advice on what would be nice, but very practical advice on what is necessary in order to create a mental environment that helps us cling to God. The Philippians were struggling to maintain their faith against opponents and were expecting to suffer for it (1:28, 29). So Paul sets forth the example of Christ emptying himself (2:5f), his own example of giving no thought to what lies behind but pushing on to what is ahead (3:13), and then gives them very practical advice on what to do (4:8) so that what their minds dwell on is a support in their struggle, not something that undermines them.

As we come to the Lord in prayer and dwell on the psalms, a scripture passage, the rosary, the Jesus prayer or whatever, we need to be urgently present to the Lord in prayer. Otherwise we bounce around from one good text to another and we vaguely wander through scripture, unable to absorb what God is doing in our hearts. We merely become a toucher or taster of spiritual meanings instead of an author and possessor of them.

As we remain urgently and faithfully present to God in prayer, we begin to experience his salvation more fully and fall more deeply in love with him. We no longer feel that we have to produce anything in prayer. We only want to cling to God, to enter the presence of God who is the same yesterday, today, and forever. We begin to know that just being present to him is all that is necessary, not getting words, or understanding a passage, or feeling close, or interceding, or even talking to him. Silence begins to be a channel to be more deeply present to the Lord in the course of ordinary existence.

The Lord begins to speak to us about the purity of heart that brings us into his deeper presence. As we gradually see the extent of our sinfulness and illusions in the light of God's love, our hearts begin to soften. I recall times when I would sit in prayer for hours, coming in touch with my sinfulness and illusions in the light of God's love. It was painfully purifying. I would recall St. Benedict's words, "it is not in saying a great deal that we shall be heard, but in purity of heart and in tears of compunction." I would learn to trust God as he cleansed and softened my heart, as difficult as it was. Such prayer was more a communication through silence and waiting than having any idea of what was happening. I would ponder over Lamentations 3:26, "it is good to wait in silence for the salvation of God." Over and over again I would pray Psalm 51, "Have mercy on me, O God, in your tenderness, in the greatness of your compassion wipe out my offense." God was cleansing me, purifying my heart, softening it to the point where I was vulnerable to him.

As we see with the apocalyptic vision that realizes we are coming closer either to God or the evil one, we become urgent about centering our minds on God and on those thoughts which will draw us to him. The pressures we experience in doing this are perceived as the labor pains of being born into the kingdom. We need to be urgently present to the Lord both in prayer and in the ordinary events of our daily lives. Our response to the present moment we live in, whether we are at prayer or daily activities, draws us closer to God or Satan. We need to be urgently responding, always seeing the incarnational presence of God in all that we do and giving ourselves to him as fully as possible. Centering our thoughts on God throughout the day flows from our time of prayer.

The foundation of prayer is to persevere in resisting the tendency to water down and compromise the good news of the kingdom of God in order to be comfortable or respectable. The heart of prayer is intensely living the gospel second-by-second with the apocalyptic urgency that catapults us into a deeper response to God. The "X-ray" vision of the Desert Fathers that perceives the spiritual realities behind the ordinary events is a practical help in being caught up in the urgency and labor pains that usher in the kingdom of God.

CHAPTER SIX

# HOW TO JUDGE OTHERS: AQUINAS

As we journey along the narrow path laid out by Jesus which leads to the Father, we need the help of the Spirit. In the scriptures, the Spirit gives an understanding of how to travel the narrow path in our relationships elicited in our judgments and expectations. The purity of heart demanded by the gospel is the Spirit's work and not our own. As we ponder over this material from Christian tradition, the Spirit will be teaching us how to cooperate with his work in our hearts. Let us be sensitive to his movement in our hearts as we read, so that our inner gyroscope for the journey along the narrow path will be increasingly fine-tuned.

The Desert Fathers teach us a great deal about the posture of judgments and expectations in our relationships. We have seen that judgments about our brothers and sisters are often distorted by a response to their actions based on a worldly thought pattern. Guarding our thoughts can protect us from the impurity of heart that creates disunity and biases judgments. Adopting an apocalyptic vision can give us the proper urgent perspective for responding to God in our relationships. All of this is good, yet at this point we are likely hungering to be more practical. In what circumstances is it right to make a judgment about another? How do we do it in practice? How do we deal with suspicions? Should we always give someone else the benefit of the doubt? Do we need authority to judge? To acquire some practical answers and wisdom about this, we turn to Aquinas.

St. Thomas Aquinas, who was about fifty when he died in the thirteenth century, was declared a Doctor of the Church in 1567 by St. Pius V. He came on the scene at a crucial time when the Church's tradition was being confronted with the rediscovery of Greek thought. His time of great cultural upheaval was not unlike our own. In the confusion produced by this confrontation, Aquinas played a pivotal role in designing a theological and philosophical system which remained Christian while it incorporated important elements from Aristotelian thought. He was a thinker of awesome stature, yet when asked if he were ever tempted to pride or vainglory, he replied "No," adding that if any such thoughts occurred to him, his common sense immediately dispelled them by showing him their utter unreasonableness![68]

As we turn to Thomas' wisdom on judgments and expectations in relationships, we will limit ourselves to a small part of his work in the *Summa Theologicae* entitled "on passing judgments."[69] In this section he answers some of the crucial practical questions that come up in our relationships. What is really meant by judging others? Does it mean observing what is going on and coming to a theoretical evaluation of the person or situation? Or does judging others mean going beyond observation to response, so that it becomes a matter of our external actions in relationship to them? Does judging others mean becoming responsible for them?

As Aquinas examines what judging others means, he turns to the critical questions of how to do it properly. How does one avoid unfair or rash judgments? Can judgments be based on suspicions? When is it wise or unwise to give people the benefit of the doubt? What is the role of agreements as an objective protection in judgments? What is the difference between someone in authority passing judgment and anyone else?

These are the areas of practical wisdom that we will study as we go through Aquinas' reflections on response or observation, rash judgments and suspicions, the benefit of the doubt, agreements and authority.

## *Response or Observation?*

What do we mean when we speak of judging others? We know different people can attach various meanings to the same word, thus causing needless confusion and disagreement. When we consider whether we should judge others, and if so, how to do it properly, what is the bedrock reality we are trying to understand? Is it a question of our external actions in relationship to a person—a matter of our exterior response? Or is it a question of our inner thoughts—a matter of correct observation and evaluation?

This question has important consequences. To illustrate it, consider the example of someone you work with who frequently sits and relaxes instead of actively doing his job. When you ask whether you should judge him and if so, how to do it properly, what is it that you are really asking? Are you merely asking whether it is proper to observe the situation and come to a conclusion in your mind about whether this person is lazy? It is a real question. After all, perhaps he is collecting his energies so as to be able to do his work even better, or perhaps he is troubled, or ill, or confused. Should we evaluate him in our minds like that? What would Christ do?

On the other hand, when you ask whether you should judge him, and if so, how to do it properly, do you mean something more? Do you mean not only making an evaluation, but also acting on the basis of it? You could act destructively by spreading gossip or slander; or you could act constructively, by taking steps to help the person work more responsibly. If you are his boss instead of his co-worker, you might ignore his behavior, talk to him about working harder, or fire him. Thus we can see how important it is to be clear about what we mean when we speak of judging others. Is it something that results in a practical response in our actions or an inner observation in our minds?[70] Whether we ought to judge, and if so, how, depends on what we mean by judging others.

Aquinas sees passing judgment as more of a response built upon observation than an observation alone. Therefore he says that good judgment requires two things: good observation and good disposition. The good observation is the "knowing power" which can get the facts straight and understand them correctly. This observation is a means to an end, a sound judgment with a view to doing something about that which is observed. The good disposition is the "loving power" which is bent on judging right, sets the goal for which our knowing power works, determines how to get there, and makes the sound moral judgment to follow through in action. These two requirements are the basis of passing judgment as a response to another.

"Knowing power" is a means to the end of "loving power." In Aquinas' terminology, "knowing power" is also referred to as our cognitive faculty or reason. "Loving power" is referred to as our right intentions or will. Our loving power sets our goal. The means to the goal is our knowing power which leads us to a judgment about what *ought* to happen. Our loving power then takes over and we make a decision, a moral judgment, as to whether we will *do* what we know ought to happen. In real life, loving power is scarcer than knowing power. Perfect examples are the people who are always giving good advice but can never follow it themselves! Commenting on this Aquinas writes:

> Judgment is correct when the cognitive faculty perceives a thing as it really is, and this comes from a healthily disposed power of perception; a well-made mirror reflects the images of bodies as they really are, whereas in one poorly-made they appear distorted and crooked. That a cognitive power is well-disposed to receive things as they really are at root is from nature, but its flowering is from practice or from the gift of grace. There are two sides to consider here. First and directly that of knowing power inasmuch as it is charged with true and correct concepts, not twisted ones. This is the task of sound judgment as a special virtue. Second and indirectly that of a well-disposed loving power, which enables a man to judge well in his wants; in this respect sound moral judgment is based on the habits of moral virtue, though this regards their ends, whereas the special virtue of sound judgment itself is rather about the means.[71]

In the example of our co-worker who is not doing his work, it would be our knowing power, if it is not distorted, that observes what is going on as it really is, evaluating it as laziness. While the ability to know correctly is a natural gift, it can be stifled by habitual non-use, misuse, or resistance to God's grace. It is also our knowing power that would come to a conclusion about what we ought to do, though our loving power sets up the goal toward which knowing power moves. If our loving power is misguided, then our knowing power brings us to gossip, slander, etc. If our loving power is well disposed, then our knowing power brings us to a conclusion to practically support our co-worker by helping him grow in responsibility and not be fired. Once our knowing power brings us to a conclusion, it is up to our loving power to put it into action and bring it about. Knowing power cannot be aborted and stopped short of action. It is a means to an end in this practical realm of our relationships with others. It ought to continue into loving power which issues forth into just action.

We make judgments all the time. Do I need to put gas in my car now or can I wait? How can I find out what kind of physical exercise I should be getting? These kinds of judgments may indirectly affect our personal relationships, but they are not the choices and questions we are specifically talking about here. What we are talking about is the kind of judgment that causes consequences in another person's life or directly affects our relationship with another.

For example, we might make the judgment in our mind that the chairman of a church committee we are on is ineffective in running meetings. As long as we keep this opinion to ourselves and do not let it affect our actions, it lies in the theoretical realm. It is a matter of affirming an understanding of the facts as correct—an observation.

Is it possible to make such a sharp distinction between what we think and what we do? Sometimes it is, and other times not. It depends on several factors: (1) how extreme is my opinion? (Is the chairman very ineffective or is he mildly so?); (2) how strongly held is my opinion? (Is he so obviously ineffective that no one could doubt it or does it seem that I am the only one with this opinion?); (3) how much do I believe this limitation affects others? (Does his ineffectiveness mess up everything or does it simply cause less clarity at meetings?) (4) how closely related am I to him? (Do we talk together almost every day or only every other month at the committee meetings?) The more we answer these questions in the first instance, the more our judgments can't help but spill over into our actions, speech, and attitudes. The more we answer in the second instance, the more we can separate thoughts and actions.

We need to carefully examine such a judgment if it leads to practical consequences: we stop coming to meetings; we complain about the committee chairman to others; we try to have the chairman replaced; or we try to do everything we can to help the chairman acquire the skills he needs. When a judgment is not purely theoretical but results in practical consequences, we first need to be sure that we have our facts straight and that we understand them correctly. For example, perhaps the committee is not working out well because it lacks a clear purpose or because the wrong people are on it. Or perhaps I am dissatisfied with the committee because my goals for it are different than the committee's goals. The first thing to examine is our knowing power.

Secondly, we have to examine our loving power. What is the goal to which our action is directed and what is its motivating force? Am I motivated by a spiritual way of thinking or a worldly way of thinking? Am I acting out of my negative feelings toward the chairman or a sincere concern and love? Am I concerned to love and support the person who is the chairman or do I just want the committee to function well? These are important questions to ponder if we are to judge and act rightly. For more significant matters, especially when our judgment will adversely affect another in a significant way, it may be necessary to discuss the matter with someone else.

As Aquinas puts it, if it is only a question about theoretical judgments or judgments about ourselves, then "there is no need for any judgment other than that of the virtuous man himself, who makes a judgment in the broad sense already referred to. In matters of justice (judgments with practical consequences that directly affect others), however, there is further required the judgment of a superior or umpire who might put his hand between us both (Jb 9:33)."[72]

When we pass judgments about others in the practical realm which issues forth in external actions, we ought to seek out an umpire's judgment also. When our judgment that our co-worker is lazy or our committee chairman is ineffective is not oriented to an action on our part, it is a simple observation. It is more serious to make the judgment that our co-worker is lazy or our committee chairman is ineffective when this judgment is oriented to an action on our part. In the latter case an "umpire" needs to be part of the judgment. We will return to this point shortly in dealing with authority.

Aquinas uses the terms "passing judgment" or "practical judgment" when referring to judging others as an action-oriented response that requires a good observation, not merely an observation that theoretically evaluates a person. The word "judgment" is commonly used in a broader sense, as either an action-oriented response or an inner theoretical observation. For clarity, he writes of "passing judgment" and "practical judgment." Yet he wants to be clear that we should understand judging others as an action-oriented response that involves both knowing power and loving power.

## *Rash Judgments and Suspicions*

When Aquinas speaks of judging others, he means an action-oriented response based on an observation. Yet even a good observation requires sound judgment. Given the clarity of what he means by judging others, he then tackles the question of whether we ought to pass practical judgments on others at all. He concludes that we can but there are conditions: "That it proceed from the bent of justice and . . . that it is pronounced according to the right reasonableness of prudence."[73] Otherwise the judgment is considered in turn an unfair judgment or a rash judgment as "when he judges doubtful or hidden things by unfounded guesses."[74]

To understand these conditions for judging others, we must first understand what Aquinas means by "justice" and "prudence." In his terminology, "justice" is the effect of good loving power, while "prudence" is good knowing power. It is because justice refers to our doing and prudence refers to our knowing that "we are not said to be just because we know something correctly . . . we are called just in that we do something rightly."[75] Aquinas says "justice is the habit according to which a person wills and does aright."[76] Prudence is prior to justice because you have to know what each person's due is before you can render to each his due and therefore be just. Aquinas says "prudence is knowing the things to be sought after and the things to avoid."[77] It is the practical knowledge of sound judgment about what to do in a situation we find ourselves in. It would be prudence on our part to know how to talk to our committee chairman about his ineffectiveness without condemning him. We would be just if we not only knew what to do, but also did it.

With an understanding of the meaning of justice and prudence, let us return to exploring what Aquinas is saying. A judgment must proceed from a motive of justice where we both want to do the right thing and in fact do it. Otherwise it is unfair. If, for example, our main concern in talking with a co-worker about his laziness is to dump our negative feelings on him, then the judgment is unfair. It can't be a fair judgment unless it proceeds from motives like wanting to love and support him in responsibility or from a concern for the work that needs to be done.

A judgement must be pronounced according to prudence where we know what the right thing is; otherwise it is a rash judgment. For example, from love and justice we may confront our committee chairman with his ineffectiveness without giving serious consideration to other explanations for the situation. This would be a rash judgment even though our motives are the best. The problem might lie in other factors like an ambiguous purpose or poor procedures for the committee. Or we might be upset because our goals are different than the committee's. In other words, to avoid rash judgments, we must know what the right conclusion is *and* how to put it into action.

A motive of justice preserves us from unfair judgments out of which come actions which do not respect others. This desire to do the right thing is the reason for outlawing destructive criticism from bitterness of spirit or anger. Constructive criticism based on love always respects others and is encouraging. Prudence preserves us from rash judgment when reasonable certainty is not present. This is merely the soundness of the knowing power upon which is based our loving power and actions.

A further question is, can we judge another if we are guilty of the same thing? Should we ignore it in this case? For example, if I am as lazy as my co-worker, does this make it impossible to love and support the other person by honest feedback? In other words, if we must deal with a problem in ourselves, do we therefore ignore it in another, even though this means they become more deeply rooted in a bad habit? Aquinas responds to this question:

> Augustine says, "If we find ourselves in the same sin as another, let us lament together and urge one another to strive together." It is not by acting thus that a man condemns himself so as to be condemned anew, but when by condemning another he shows that he also should be condemned for the same or similar crime.[78]

We do not, then, need to be perfect in an area where we are judging another. However, we do need to have compassion and invite the other into a mutual support in the problem area, not condemning the other for the fault. In the example above, it might mean saying something like this to our co-worker, "Listen, you and I have the same problem with the work here—we're lazy! It isn't right to let it go on like this. We're getting ourselves more deeply imbeded in a habit of irresponsibility which is bound to color the rest of our lives. It isn't fair to the work we're committed to doing. What do you say? Do you want to try and help one another in being more responsible?"

This kind of dialogue makes clear a presupposition—that the co-worker is a brother or sister in the Lord who has the same basic values that we do in Christ. As Paul writes, "what business is it of mine to judge outsiders? Is it not those inside the community you must judge?" (1 Cor 5:12). While all this wisdom on judging others has some relevance to any relationship, it is particularly intended for relationships that have a common bond in the Spirit and values of Christ.

Another question that arises after considering rash judgment is whether we can judge others when it is based on suspicion. Aquinas replies:

> The command, "Judge not," is explained by (Pseudo-) Chrysostom as follows, "By it the Lord does not forbid Christians reproving others because they seek their welfare, but that by vaunting their own righteousness Christians should despise Christians by hating and condemning others for the most part out of mere suspicion."[79]

He notes that a suspicion is an ill opinion founded on slight indications. The causes are (1) assuming the worst about others because we assume the worst about ourselves; (2) we already hate, despise, are angry with or envious of another, and so are prone by slight signs to think evil of him since everyone readily believes what he wants to believe; or (3) suspecting others because bitter experience has taught us to suspect everyone.

A suspicion is the vacuum of insufficient evidence improperly filled by one of the three things mentioned. We can judge the truth of Aquinas' analysis from our own experience. When we are aware of our own weakness and sins, don't we tend to project them on others? Often we tend to judge others harshly about things that are also our main problem. Perhaps we are lazy, and so the slightest sign of laziness in a co-worker causes us to judge him as lazy. When we're already upset with another person, don't we become blind to their good points and magnify the smallest bad ones? If we are angry with our committee chairman, any sign that he is not perfect might cause us to consider him inefficient. I suspect that all of us know someone we have difficulty judging properly because our feelings about him are so strong.

In commenting on the third way we can improperly fill the vacuum, Thomas recalls Aristotle's generalization, "old people are very suspicious, for they have often experienced the faults of others."[80] This Greek saying applied to "old people" could be accurately translated by the American proverb, "once bitten, twice shy." Who has not experienced being hurt by another's insensitivity and then, because of bitter experience, suspecting that others have the same fault?

Aquinas sums up by saying that suspiciousness implies a certain viciousness, and that it is found in three degrees of varying seriousness. They are (1) when on faint indications a man begins to have doubts about another's integrity. No one can avoid these thoughts, though they can be successfully resisted; (2) when on faint indications one holds for certain that another is wicked. Since this is not without contempt for one's neighbor, he notes that we must hold back from coming to fixed and final conclusions; (3) going so far as to condemn a man on suspicion.

The degrees of seriousness of suspicion increase as it grows from tainting our knowing power partially (doubts of another's integrity), to tainting our knowing power fully (holding for certain another's wickedness), to tainting our loving power (condemning another). They are of increasing seriousness because each includes the prior ones and so involves an ever-deeper turning from the light. Each step also implies external behavior ever-more harmful to the other.

In this section, Aquinas offers us a great deal of wisdom on how to judge others. Judging others, meaning an action-oriented response to them, is allowable but it requires justice and prudence; otherwise the judgment is unfair or rash. Even being guilty of the same sins as the one being "judged" should not hinder our judgment as long as we are compassionate and realize we are in the same boat together. Suspicion, which is an ill opinion founded on slight indications, is not a valid basis for passing judgment. We ought to guard ourselves against suspicion as the Desert Fathers did by the guarding of their thoughts. Suspiciousness grows increasingly serious as it goes from causing doubts about another's integrity, to holding for certain another is wicked, to condemning another—all on suspicion.

## *The Benefit of the Doubt*

After having determined that judging others means an action-oriented response in addition to observation, and that it is allowable given the conditions we have examined, Aquinas further considers the question of how to judge others and how not to. The fulcrum of his reflections is giving a person the benefit of the doubt.

Aquinas says that doubts should be interpreted in the more favorable sense. "Unless we have evident indications of another's wickedness, we ought to stick to a good opinion of him by giving him the benefit of the doubt."[81]

This is Thomas' positive remedy to the prior difficulty of basing judgments on suspicion:

> He who interprets doubts in the more favorable sense may happen to be mistaken more often than not. All the same to err frequently through thinking well of an unworthy man is better than to err less frequently through thinking ill of a worthy man, for in the second case an injury is inflicted, but not in the first.[82]

When we suspect someone has done something wrong, we ought to give the person the benefit of the doubt unless we have real evidence to the contrary. He qualifies this general answer by distinguishing between judging of things and of people. In judging of things we should not give the benefit of the doubt; rather we should judge as accurately as possible, judging them as they really are. "In judging about men, however, it is their good or evil which is the main point, inasmuch as they are held in honor or reproach in consequence. And so we ought to be inclined to judge them good rather than evil, unless there be manifest evidence to the contrary."[83]

We make practical judgments *so that* we can do something about it. It is not knowledge for the sake of knowledge, but knowledge for the sake of action. Our practical judgments occur in particular circumstances and they affect our behavior toward the things or people involved. For example, if I think the chair I am sitting on has very weak legs and may fall down, then I will act. I'll probably avoid the chair, repair it, or throw it out. It makes no sense to give the chair the benefit of the doubt, even though there is a possibility it is really sturdy. Making that kind of judgment about the chair is perfectly fine.

However, a practical judgment about another person is different. For example, if I think the person I am talking to about how I feel is a gossiper and can't be trusted to respect what I share with him, then that will affect my relationship to him. Much like the chair, I'll in some way avoid him, try to repair him, or throw him out. In any case, my behavior will affect him. My judgment that he is a gossiper has the consequence of holding him in reproach which affects my behavior towards him. It distances him from me and might encourage others to do likewise. Judging others is an action-oriented response. Given valid evidence, this might be the right judgment; but not if its basis is suspicions and doubts. That is why in practical judgments about others, we need to give them the benefit of the doubt.

So far that all seems to make good Christian sense. But what about a situation when you have the responsibility to make a decision where giving someone the benefit of the doubt can do harm to others? What if you are about to go skydiving and the person who wants to pack parachutes has shown some signs of irresponsibility? It might not be the wisest thing to give him the benefit of the doubt because of other factors involved! Or consider someone for whom you are pastorally responsible who has some signs of irresponsibility—a son or daughter, a member of your religious community of which you are a superior, a parishioner you frequently work with as a parish priest, a member of a committee of which you are chairman. Shouldn't you help them grow in responsibility? Even if you are just their brother and sister in the Lord, shouldn't you be helping them grow? If you are always giving someone the benefit of the doubt, then how do you fulfill other responsibilities such as loving in truth?

Aquinas says that furthering another's growth and preventing an unjust situation are more important than giving the benefit of the doubt. He explains how he approaches this question, introducing another qualifying distinction:

> One may interpret a doubtful point for better or for worse in two manners. First, by a working hypothesis, as when we have to apply a remedy for some evil, whether our own or another's; then to assume the worse is the safer course, since the cure for a greater ill is all the more effective with a lesser. Second, by deciding or determining how matters really stand. Then in judging of things we should make efforts to read them just as they really are; in judging persons, however, we should adopt the more favorable construction, as we have maintained.[84]

Thomas here is still considering practical judgments of others that involve action-oriented responses, but he divides them into two categories. The narrower category refers to situations where we ought to take some action to support another's growth or remedy an unjust situation; here we can use a "working hypothesis" and should not give the other the benefit of the doubt. However, for everything else apart from that, we should give the person the benefit of the doubt. Otherwise we begin to form fixed and unilateral conclusions about the other which cause him to be held in reproach. Others may notice it and gossip; we might complain about him to others; his reputation may get colored and his relationships are affected badly.

Consider, for example, someone who tells us that they will loan us their car so that we can go to an important meeting. Imagine that we know that this person often forgets such promises. How should we approach this? What does it mean to give the benefit of the doubt? We should not give him the benefit of the doubt in the sense of trusting his faulty memory. Rather we should use a "working hypothesis," assume the worst—that he has forgotten his promise. We might call him the week before the meeting to double check. However, we should give him the benefit of the doubt in the sense of trusting that he is well-intentioned, honest, and sincere.

It takes discernment and discipline to speak to people about their problem areas in a "working hypothesis" way without unilaterally deciding how "matters really stand" and getting locked into a negative way of relating to them. The discernment criterion is love. If it is more loving to give them the benefit of the doubt, do that. If it is more loving in a limited area not to, then don't. Instead, follow the "working hypothesis" so as to love them and others in the situation in the best possible way.

The working hypothesis is the practical judgment which is concerned with how I approach a situation and what practical steps would be wise. Deciding how matters really stand is the judgment which is concerned with the realm of how God sees the situation and whether the person is to be praised or condemned. Since we must responsibly and lovingly relate to the people in a given situation, we must have as accurate a working hypothesis as possible. Hence we should not interfere with the working hypothesis by giving the benefit of the doubt out of misguided love or justice. Since only God knows the graces given to an individual, only he, or in some cases the Church, can know how matters really stand. What the person intended, whether he could have done better given sin and the graces available are matters where we need to give the benefit of the doubt. They are not important for us anyway, since we are concerned only with how we should approach the situation, the common-sense realm.

Let us apply this to an example of a parish priest making a judgment whether a couple should be married. The parish priest needs a working hypothesis, not a decision on how matters really stand. He needs to take responsibility for accurately discerning whether it is wise for the couple to be married and, if not, for enforcing that decision within the context of the community. To give them the benefit of the doubt about their suitability for marriage would not be loving them since it might cause a disastrous situation. Yet in the judgment on how matters really stand—whether the couple is honest, sincere, responding to the graces they have—they should be given the benefit of the doubt. It is because of this distinction that a loving compassion can pervade a practical judgment that is difficult for a person to accept.

Aquinas favors giving people the benefit of the doubt even at the cost of accuracy and being correct. In judging of things we should never give the benefit of the doubt because accuracy is valued. However, with people, avoiding an injury to them or their good name is valued more highly than accuracy, and so we should give them the benefit of the doubt. For example, the parish priest ought to give the couple the benefit of the doubt about their honesty and sincerity. The one exception occurs when giving a person the benefit of the doubt might do them an even greater injury since some evil which has injurious long-term effects will not be dealt with. In that case we should take the route of a "working hypothesis" in the practical area that needs a judgment. For example, the parish priest should not give the benefit of the doubt about the couple's suitability for marriage. At the same time, he should refrain from extending that hypothesis to every area of a person's life. Love should rule and be the norm for discernment.

## *Agreements and Authority*

In developing his reflections on how to properly judge others, Aquinas considers agreements and authority. Should there be an objective criteria that is the basis of judging others? How do you interpret it and who does the definitive interpreting? What is the difference between someone in authority passing judgment and any knowledgeable person passing judgment?

Aquinas asks if judgment should always be passed according to the objective criteria of written laws. He notes that what is just (and to pass judgment is to determine what is just) arises either from natural right or from agreements among men. Written laws merely list natural rights but establish the agreements among men. And so while judgments should be passed according to written laws, if they conflict with natural rights then the written law is unjust and has no binding force. Laws should be interpreted according to their spirit, not their letter, whenever they might offend a natural right.

When groups of people gather together in communities, prayer groups, committees, or whatever, they frequently make agreements about how to relate together and about the extent of their responsibilities for one another. These agreements or expectations are the basis of many of the judgments we would make. For example, they are the basis for judgments that a person should be more committed, faithful, or should do something. Aquinas favors writing down such agreements and expectations to start with and basing judgments on what has been commonly and clearly agreed upon. Otherwise we might find ourselves judging others on the basis of what *we thought* we agreed to instead of what *in fact* we agreed to. It is easy to see how clear agreements can facilitate coming together with similar expectations.

Who has authority to interpret agreements? Aquinas concludes that since such judgments should be made according to written laws and since it is authority which wrote the law or oversees it, it must be authority which interprets it by applying it to a particular case.

This also holds for unwritten laws about relationships. There is a community context for practical judgments about others and our relationships. Some of this may be written down and some may not. In either case the community (of whatever kind) plays the definitive role in certain judgments that impose sanctions on another. Yet Aquinas does not say a judgment is wrong when it is rendered by someone lacking proper authority, since anyone can speak the truth. Here he distinguishes between passing a judgment which imposes sanctions and speaking the truth. It is one thing to talk to a co-worker about his laziness; it is another to arrange for him to be fired. In Aquinas' words:

> Declaring a truth does not induce any compulsion on the hearers to receive it; each is free to accept it or not as he wishes. Whereas passing judgment (in a way that imposes sanctions) carries with it a certain outward social pressure. Consequently it is unjust for a man to be judged (and have sanctions imposed) by one who has no public authority .... The habits of scientific knowledge and of justice are endowments of the individual person. A judgment is not termed usurped because they are lacking, but because of the want of public authority, which has the power of enforcement.[85]

Aquinas distinguishes between declaring a truth that involves no compulsion or sanctions and passing a judgment which involves sanctions—an action on the part of the "judge" that effects a social pressure. It might be fine to talk to our co-worker about his laziness. However, it is not our business to insure he gets fired if he chooses not to listen to us.

The first case involves declaring the truth in a way where the other is free to accept it or not as he wishes. This is the kind of judgment appropriate among brothers and sisters in the Lord. For example, we might tell a couple preparing for marriage that their proposed marriage is unwise due to their emotional development, present situation, or other reasons. We would share this judgment, what we know as the truth, in a way so that what we are saying is perfectly clear, but leaving the couple free to accept it or not as they wish. Their choosing to ignore what we are saying does not impose sanctions which affect their marriage plans.

The judgment which imposes a sanction induces a compulsion on the hearers to receive it. It is not merely an opinion but an authoritative opinion which is to be submitted to. It carries with it a certain outward social pressure. This is the kind of judgment appropriate to someone in authority over another. For example, consider someone who has authority in the Lord over a couple preparing for marriage (their parish priest perhaps) who is familiar with them and has come to the conclusion that they are not ready for marriage. This practical judgment induces a compulsion on the couple to receive it in a way another's similar judgment would not because he lacks authority. The couple might choose to ask the priest to reconsider his judgment; they may even appeal it to a higher authority. But they cannot take it or leave it. If they choose to ignore what he is saying, this will have consequences that affect their marriage plans and their relationship to the community they are in. Such a judgment, since it will impose sanctions on another, must be made by someone in authority. This is not because others could not make the correct practical judgment but because only authority can make an authoritative practical judgment, definitively enforcing it for those who remain in good standing in the community.

Any practical judgment, whether by a brother or sister in the Lord or by someone in authority, is the right determination on a practical matter that involves an action-oriented response. It is the case of knowing something *so that* we can do something about it. It is knowledge which is ordered to a useful practical judgment for the sake of action under the direction of love. However, the action we take is different, depending on whether we are in authority. For example, the parish priest who is in authority desires to know if a couple is prepared for marriage so that he can discern it and decide whether they ought to be married in the community at this time. If he says "no" to them, it *forces* them to reconsider the timing of their marriage plans and perhaps the plans themselves. A concerned brother in the Lord could speak the same truth, but the couple is *free* to take it or leave it. A concerned brother in the Lord might feel strongly enough about it and love them enough to not only share with them but also to give his input to the parish priest or personally refrain from going to the wedding. Yet it would be wrong if he organized opposition to the wedding in order to *force* them to reconsider it.

Aquinas affirms the value of agreements and the need to write them out so that judgments can be based on what we have *in fact* agreed upon. Authority ought to interpret the agreements and apply them to particular cases.

In conclusion, we can briefly review the practical wisdom St. Thomas Aquinas gives us on judging others. Judging others means going beyond observation to response, so that it becomes a matter of our external actions in relationship to others. Judging others means being responsible for them. Thus, passing judgments that impose sanctions ought to be done by those in authority who are responsible. Yet anyone can speak the truth and such judgments can have a personal effect on others. Unfair judgments are avoided by justice which is the fruit of loving power. Rash judgments are avoided by prudence which is knowing power. Judgments ought to be based on sufficient evidence, not on suspicions. People ought to be given the benefit of the doubt about the state of their hearts, but not in a bad situation that needs to be corrected. Here one must use a working hypothesis.

Aquinas' wisdom for our relationships builds upon the purity of heart focused on by the Desert Fathers and prepares us for the next chapter where, in the judgments of the Church, we can see the centrality of respecting freedom.

CHAPTER SEVEN

# RESPECTING FREEDOM: THE CHURCH

We have been considering some of the wisdom of tradition about our posture in relationships, especially the sensitive and complex areas of expectations, judgments, and fraternal correction. In the introductory chapter we saw that being vulnerable and compassionate were the fundamentals of a Christian's posture. In Part One we saw that the foundations of our relationships lies in our scriptural identity, the completing/competing tensions of scriptural expectations, and fraternal correction.

In Part Two we have discussed the Desert Fathers' wisdom about purity of heart and Aquinas' teaching about how to judge others. Purity of heart underlines the importance of basing judgments on a spiritual way of thinking that wants to support others, not the worldly pattern that clings to our plans and wants revenge and punishment. The Desert Fathers gave practical advice about ways to maintain purity of heart through guarding our thoughts and cultivating an apocalyptic vision. Aquinas helped us to see that judging others means being responsible for them: hence authority has a unique role. Aquinas also helped us see the right approach to rash judgments, suspicions, agreements, and giving the benefit of the doubt.

Now we turn to some recent decisions of the Roman Catholic Church to obtain an even deeper perspective on judgments, expectations, and fraternal correction in our relationships. This perspective is the need to respect other persons and their freedom in the process of judging.

Few things are more valuable for building love and unity in relationships or in a community than vulnerably sharing our hearts with others. Yet a person should never be pressured into sharing in this way; it always needs to be done freely. This has been the conclusion of the Church as set forth in decisions in the past century.

Respecting other persons and their rights is at the very heart of the gospel and Church teaching. Serious Christians do not push it to the side in order to get the task of "unity" or other "missions" accomplished. Vatican II clearly sees respecting persons as part of the gospel. The importance of never intimidating people and the practical guidelines to prevent this are discussed in the context of a recent American Bishops' statement on due process. Respect for persons is to permeate all of our expectations, judgments, and fraternal correction.

## *Vulnerably Sharing in Freedom*

The more deeply we can share our lives and hearts, the more deeply we can enter into relationships. In deeper relationships the questions of expectations, judgments, and fraternal correction quickly surface. Sharing our hearts, the process through which relationships deepen, brings awareness of our attractions and dislikes, our intentions, the special graces we receive, our weak spots, doubts and faults, our insecurities, the way we feel, our joys and our temptations.

We share our hearts to different degrees with different people depending on the relationship. With those we are close to, we might tend to share almost everything. With those we find hard to trust, we will be reluctant to share vulnerably with them, fearing they may not respect us, or use what we tell them to hurt us or laugh at us. The depth of sharing depends on our personality too. Some easily share their hearts with many people while others find it hard to share personally.

As expectations, judgments, and fraternal correction are worked out in a relationship, everything is made easier if people can share their hearts and respect one another. For example, consider two people, Tom and Larry, who are responsible for running a Life in the Spirit Seminar, which is a two-month weekly teaching series to help people enter into a renewed life in the Holy Spirit. Larry does not keep his agreement to carry out his share of the responsibility, and a problem occurs in his relationship with Tom. Tom might make the accurate judgment that Larry has not lived up to his responsibilities and that the occasion calls for fraternal correction.

If they keep everything on the level of external behavior, with neither man really sharing his thoughts and feelings, the process of fraternal correction might proceed somewhat formally and lifelessly:

**Tom:** "You didn't do what you said you would and the people taking the seminar aren't receiving what they ought to because of it. It also puts me in an awkward position."

**Larry:** "I realize that is true and it was wrong. Please forgive me."

**Tom:** "I do."

This is good, but is it good enough? Why didn't Larry fulfill his responsibilities? This process risks forcing Larry to live a will-power Christianity according to the law. If Larry were to share his heart, what is going on underneath the surface, he would receive more support and he could mature more readily. The relationship between Tom and Larry could grow stronger if Larry shared the problems that have interfered with his commitment. Tom might be able to point out to Larry a larger pattern of irresponsibility of which the current instance is just an example. Larry might be able to see his weak spot more clearly, and also receive support in overcoming it.

At the same time, such open sharing could damage Larry. If Larry shares his heart openly, Tom could respond by dumping all his negative feelings on him. He could use what Larry is saying to hurt him. Tom could do this without even realizing it. Indeed as the Desert Fathers' sayings make clear, he could even do it under the guise of offering spiritual help. If Tom is either unloving or unwise he could do more harm than good and cause Larry to withdraw.

Open, intimate sharing is a risky business. The more we can share our hearts, the more potential there is for unity, love, grace, and support in the relationship. Yet there is also more potential for hurt, pain, and withdrawal. What ought to happen? How do we know when we should share more deeply? Should we encourage others to share more deeply? Should such sharing be something we regularly expect? These are essential questions for our relationships.

Our own experience points to the value of encouraging people to share vulnerably, but using freedom as a criteria for discernment. People should always share their hearts in freedom, never because they have to, ought to, or are pressured to. They ought to be encouraged to share and be helped to see that their level of sharing will affect the kind of relationships they will have. Yet they should never force themselves to share or be pressured into it.

It is with this background that we want to look at the wisdom of the Church about the freedom we must have when sharing our hearts. The context of the Church's teaching is the community life of religious congregations down through the centuries. These are men and women gathered together to support one another in their committed life in the Lord and service. Yet the principles behind the Church decisions in this area have a broader application to all our relationships: family, church, prayer group, community, fellowship group, close advisor, etc.

What we have called sharing our hearts, Church tradition calls manifestation of conscience.[86] This refers to matters that would not normally be noticed by others unless we share them. Matters that others notice are no longer confined to the realm of our own conscience.[87] If someone who looks sad tells us he is depressed, he is not technically manifesting his conscience since his state is rather obvious. His condition has already entered the external forum and become public knowledge through his sad bearing.

The revelation of intimate and personal matters to others is referred to in the writings of St. Anthony of the Desert, St. Basil the Great, St. Jerome, John Cassian, and St. Benedict. For the first thousand years of Church history, the only purpose of such a sharing of one's heart was the spiritual advancement of the person who shares. For example, a person might make himself vulnerable to another by sharing struggles with sexual temptations in order to receive support in resisting and being freed from them. Whether this will, in fact, be a support depends on many things, such as one's ability to share one's feelings, others' levels of maturity, wisdom on how to deal with temptations, etc. But the purpose of such sharing is to advance spiritually.

In the middle ages—starting with Bonaventure and culminating in the Society of Jesus—religious communities with a superior expanded the purpose of vulnerably sharing one's heart. Superiors sought to know the internal dispositions of each of the community's members in order to support them in their spiritual growth, and also in order to make practical decisions about community assignments. It was a short step from seeing the manifestation of conscience as valuable to the social order in a community to making it a law that one had to manifest one's conscience to the superior at certain fixed intervals. For example, if a monk told his abbot that he had difficulty working well with a brother, then the abbot could use this information in several ways. He could separate the monks in their work in order to protect the ministry, or he could assign them to work together, so they could be healed.

With a gifted superior, this practice may very well be a blessing, and many have found it to be so. Yet the practice of using such personal information to make practical decisions about ministries makes it easier for things to go awry. Individuals are frequently out of touch with themselves, and are even less likely to know how to articulate those inner movements of the heart. There is a scarcity of highly gifted superiors and there is always the possibility that the superior would be someone lacking in either love or wisdom. Nevertheless, this practice might still be workable if the individual can use discretion. For example, if my superior is likely to misunderstand my discomfort with a brother as an intense dislike for him, then I would likely not feel free to share freely with my superior and would refrain from doing so. However, if my community has a law that requires me to share such matters, then I am in a serious dilemma. I have a choice between doing violence to myself by forcing myself to share or disobeying the law.

For the first eighteen centuries of its existence, the Church gave its approval to religious rules which prescribed the obligatory manifestation of conscience. Such sharing of hearts, however, was never the direct object of the Church's pronouncements, except for a brief statement by Clement VIII in 1603 prescribing that a daily opening of the interior movements of the heart and a manifestation of temptations be made by novices to their masters.

A change occurred in the Church's attitude around the middle of the nineteeth century. After 1800 years of approving obligatory manifestations of conscience, the Church de-emphasized and ultimately banned them. This returned the vulnerable sharing of one's heart to its original free and spontaneous character. The decisions that the Church made can be seen most clearly in Leo XIII's 1890 decree *Quemadmodum,* and in the 1918 Code of Canon Law for the Latin Church.

Leo XIII's decree recognized that vulnerably sharing one's heart with the head of one's community can be a help on the narrow road to the kingdom. It said that the purpose of such sharing is the spiritual advancement of community members as well as the maintenance and increase of peace in the community.

Yet the Pope noted that abuses had crept in and that some community heads had turned the practice into a searching examination of conscience where an improper power over others was exercised. The result was a danger to spiritual growth, anxiety of conscience, and disturbance of peace. Rome was regularly receiving appeals and complaints from members of various communities.

In light of this, the decree banned obligatory manifestations of the inward heart and conscience for all lay communities. It forbade heads of communities to in any way induce community members to vulnerably share their hearts with them. Yet the free and spontaneous sharing of one's heart was by no means discouraged.[88]

The proscription was extended to congregations of priests by the 1918 Code of Canon Law:

> All superiors are strictly forbidden to induce their subjects, in any way whatever, to make a manifestation of conscience to them. Subjects, on the other hand, are not forbidden to open their souls freely and spontaneously to their superiors; indeed, it is desirable that they go to their superiors with filial

confidence and, if the superiors be priests, expose their doubts and troubles of conscience likewise. (c. 530)[89]

The latter part of the quote makes clear that the Church did not intend to eliminate the manifestation of conscience. Canon Law condemns forcing a person to share his heart, but endorses free and spontaneous opening of one's heart as an aid to spiritual progress. The basic principles that apply to all of our relationships is clear: people should never be *expected* to share their hearts. This must always be done in freedom, without pressure or coercion.

A question that arises from the wording of the 1918 Code is whether *lay* superiors can receive others' doubts and troubles of conscience. A primary factor in this 1918 decree is the Church's belief that "such an intimate manifestation will be fruitful precisely because of the priest superior's scientific training in ascetico-moral theology. As a general rule, the same cannot be said of lay superiors."[90] Today, with education so widespread, this judgment would not apply so firmly. The basic point, however, is that the superior needs to have the appropriate wisdom and spiritual gifts, as well as basic maturity, to receive a manifestation of conscience.

Even at the time, though, the 1918 code included a mere non-encouragement to expose doubts and troubles of conscience to a lay superior, and a non-encouragement is different than a discouragement. Saints Benedict, Francis of Assisi, and Teresa of Avila were all lay superiors and were clearly good directors to whom it was desirable to expose one's doubts and troubles of conscience. Yet, at the time of the code, the average lay superior lacked extensive theological training, and the Church considered it best to encourage manifestation to priest superiors while not condemning it to lay superiors.

We have here the Church's clear decision to encourage sharing in freedom and to condemn any situation where it is forced or when a person is pressured into it. While the Church's decree legally pertains to religious life a century ago, its wisdom is still valuable for our relationships today. If a brother or sister is wise and loving, it is desirable to open our hearts to them. However, we should never do it unless we freely want to, though that does not mean we never experience the anxiety of risking such a confidence. Sharing our hearts in this way in the process of working through expectations, judgments, and fraternal correction allows for a deeper experience of unity, growth, support, and love than is possible when we limit ourselves to discussing external behavior.

One last clarification from Canon Law would be valuable. Canon 202 explains the difference between the external and internal forum, the word "forum" referring to a field or province of action rather than a place.[91]

The external forum pertains to external Church government—the executive, legislative, or judicial decisions that affect relationships. In the external forum, a religious superior can assign a ministry, a community council can legislate norms for style of life, a Church court can determine if a person is married to his first spouse or free to marry, etc. The decision made in the external forum carries with it the force of law or authority. Aquinas would say that the decision induces a compulsion on the hearers to receive it. They are not free to disregard it.

By contrast, the internal forum is within the province of personal conscience. Jurisdiction in the internal forum concerns actions pertaining to a person's guilt or innocence before God. The exercise of such jurisdiction is private, having no force of law and lacking the authority which belongs to the external forum. The sacrament of reconciliation, for example, belongs to the inner forum.

The practice of distinguishing between the superior (external forum—decisions about one's life) and the spiritual director (internal forum—counseling and absolution from guilt) arose in light of this distinction. This separation of spiritual powers was deemed wise because of the possibility of abuse. Canon 891, in this regard, condemns appointing a superior as one's confessor, though the condemnation only applies when the appointment is forced, not when a person chooses it and for a grave and urgent reason. Again, forcing a person to share his heart, especially to one who exercises authority over him, is forbidden. Sharing of one's heart always must be done freely or not at all.

We have seen that openly sharing our hearts with others in the process of working through expectations, judgments, and fraternal correction is a valuable means of growth, love, unity, and support. It brings us into deeper relationships. Yet sharing our hearts has its risks if the person we share with is not loving or wise. We can often sense this, and exercise discretion in what we share and to whom we share. We ought to respect this sense and never force ourselves to share against our will. Yet this does not mean we ought never to risk or overcome our inhibitions. Similarly, we should never force or pressure anyone into sharing their heart with us, even though it seems at times it would be very valuable. Yet this does not mean we ought never to encourage others to vulnerably share, as that has important implications for their relationships. Never, though, should we manipulate them into it.

## *Respecting Persons*

Never forcing anyone to openly share their hearts is a specific example of a larger principle in our relationships, that of respecting persons. Having a good feel for this fundamental gospel value goes a long way toward guiding us in our expectations, judgments, and fraternal correction. The need to respect persons is not peripheral to the gospel but is a part of its core. We see this clearly reflected in Vatican II, the most recent Church Council.

Vatican II gives insight into the Church's modern perspective on judgments and expectations in relationships. In Pope John XXIII's opening to the Council, he discussed "how to repress errors." He pointed out that errors are always the opinions *of people.* The errors are not the people themselves. Pope John's handling of this delicate question reveals a historical change on how the Church chooses to approach judging others. Pope John said:

> The Church has always opposed these errors. Frequently she has condemned them with the greatest severity. Nowadays, however, the Spouse of Christ prefers to make use of the medicine of mercy rather than of severity. She considers that she meets the needs of the present day by demonstrating the validity of her teaching rather than by condemnations.[92]

While Pope John is speaking in a particular context, the general principle comes through clearly—don't be severe, be merciful; don't condemn, demonstrate the validity of the positive. This principle has application in all of our relationships—whether with our spouses and children, our religious community, our friends, or others. Pope John is saying that unfortunately the tendency in the past was to be harsh; instead, be compassionate, be with others passionately as God in Christ was with us. Instead of condemning, witness by being authentic to the truth.

The Pastoral Constitution on the Church in the Modern World, a major document from Vatican II, sets forth a basic posture for properly judging others. One aspect of this posture is compassion, signified in the Constitution's opening sentence which speaks of the intimate bond between the Church and mankind: "The joys and the hopes, the griefs and the anxieties of the men of this age, especially those who are poor or in any way afflicted, these too are the joys and hopes, the griefs and anxieties of the followers of Christ."[93] How could one better express being passionately with others?

Another aspect of the basic posture for properly judging others is respecting them, revealed in the title of Chapter One of the Constitution, "The Dignity of the Human Person." In speaking of the dignity of the moral conscience, it states:

> In the depths of his conscience, man detects a law which he does not impose upon himself, but which holds him to obedience. Always summoning him to love good and avoid evil, the voice of conscience can when necessary speak to his heart more specifically: do this, shun that. For man has in his heart a law written by God. To obey it is the very dignity of man; according to it he will be judged. Conscience is the most secret core and sanctuary of a man. There he is alone with God, whose voice echoes in his depths.[94]

As we ponder the dignity of the person we are judging, how he is united with God in his most secret core, a respect grows for the person. This is a necessary posture if we are to properly judge him. The Council says that brotherly dialogue reaches "its perfection ... on the deeper level of interpersonal relationships" which demands "a mutual respect for the full spiritual dignity of the person." This is why we should never force a person to vulnerably share in a relationship. We must respect the other person's freedom.

The second chapter of the Pastoral Constitution discusses the community of mankind. It speaks of our vocation to community, our interdependence, the need to promote the common good and to foster reverence for the human person. This chapter includes a beautiful section about reverence and love for enemies (*adversarii*), which gives us insight into how we should approach difficult relationships.

> Respect and love ought to be extended also to those who think or act differently than we do in social, political, and religious matters, too. In fact, the more deeply we come to understand their ways of thinking through such courtesy and love, the more easily will we be able to enter into dialogue with them.[95]

The posture for properly judging is extending respect and love so that we come to understand the other's way of thinking. The principle is similar to the American Indian proverb—don't criticize another till you have walked a mile in his moccasins. The Constitution continues:

> This love and good will, to be sure, must in no way render us indifferent to truth and goodness. Indeed love itself impels the disciples of Christ to speak the saving truth to all men. But it is necessary to distinguish between error, which always merits repudiation, and the person in error, who never loses the dignity of being a person, even when he is flawed by false or inadequate religious notions. God alone is the judge and searcher of hearts; for that reason he forbids us to make judgments about the internal guilt of anyone.[96]

This echoes Aquinas' distinction between judging of things (the error) and the judging of people (the person in error). We can judge others in terms of the external forum, according to our judgments about the effects of their actions, moods, and motivations on others. However, only God can judge another in terms of the internal forum: the degree of their response to grace, their internal guilt, and the question of their salvation.

The Council makes clear that respecting persons is at the very heart of the gospel. In our relationships with others, especially in our expectations, judgments, and fraternal correction, we need to respect them. This respect for the full spiritual dignity of the person guides our practical approach to difficult interpersonal situations. It means that we use the medicine of mercy, not severity, with those who are in error; that we are compassionate because we share their joys and hopes, griefs and anxieties; that we lovingly try to understand their way of thinking rather than condemn them and disrespectfully shut them out. Respect for the person means we always need to distinguish between the error we are judging and the person in error. The person never loses his dignity, and must always be treated with respect.

## *Due Process*

The previous section clarifies the centrality of respecting persons. This principle must be applied to every area of our relationships, especially where expectations, judgments, or fraternal correction is involved. Let us apply this principle to one specific area where people are often intimidated or "rolled over." This area is the process of decision-making in organizations. The organization might be small and informal such as a committee or prayer group, or it can be large and structured such as a parish or a larger community. How do we respect persons in the process of working together in groups? The Catholic Church in the United States has inspected its own approach to this very question, and we turn now to its findings.

At the November 1969 meeting of the National Conference of Catholic Bishops, Father Robert Kennedy, chairman of a special due process study commission of the Canon Law Society, presented the results of his committee's studies. At that meeting the Bishops' Conference approved a resolution encouraging "more effective procedures by which human and ecclesial rights might be guaranteed at all times in the Church,"[97] and particularly encouraging the implementation of such due process procedures. Archbishop Bernardin noted that "the United States plan for due process was examined as a model for conciliation and arbitration for the rest of the Church."[98]

While due process is not yet a formal part of Church law, the U.S. Church's decisions have an important bearing on the posture one must have in judging others. Although due process is a formal procedure, the general principles embodied in it are relevant to our concern for expectations and judgments in our own relationships and social groupings.

The concept of due process has to do with the adequate protection of human rights and freedoms. These are protected in many ways: indirectly through education, the growth of moral consciousness, and development of character; directly by formal protection of law. Due process is the principle of justice according to which no one is deprived of any right without adequate justification and sufficient reason. It involves specific protections in administrative and judicial procedures, such as the right to be informed of proposed actions which might affect one's rights, and the right to be heard in defense of one's rights.

Due process is violated when the procedures by which a decision is reached are inadequate. For example, to make a decision that adversely affects someone without ever consulting him or making him aware of the discernment process is a violation of due process. Even though the decision may have been correct, the process of reaching it violates the person's rights. A person has a right not only to a just conclusion but also to a just process that respects him as a person. The principles of due process are also violated when the reasons for a given decision can be found to be insufficient to support the decision. This does not mean that the person concerned has had his rights violated whenever he disagrees with a decision or with the reasons for it. This is true only when the decision or the reasons given for it are determined to be unjust by objective criteria, usually as discerned by a qualified third party.

Due process protects the dignity, freedom, and basic rights of the human person. It is a means of assuring that people are respected, not rolled over. The Second Vatican Council has emphasized that these values are distinctively Christian and belong to the core of the gospel message.[99] Because of this the Church sees the origin of the due process issue in the ecclesiology of the Second Vatican Council and not in any particular problem that needs to be solved. It also sees the practice of due process that has evolved in Anglo-American jurisprudence as the fruit of the gospel, not as the importation of secular norms. As Father Kennedy puts it:

> For the Church to borrow some structures and procedures from Anglo-American experience would be nothing more than reclaiming Christian capital which we invested a long time ago. The dignity of the individual, his rights and freedoms and their recognition and protection have always been part of the Christian message and came to a particular flowering in Christian England several centuries ago. In post-Reformation times those values tended to get lost in the Church which, for historical reasons, found it necessary to emphasize the rights of authority rather than the rights of the individual person, but they continued to flourish in the civil society of England and were brought to this country. They stemmed from Christian England's understanding of the core of the Gospel message regarding the dignity of the individual. So in borrowing them from Anglo-American civil jurisprudence we do little more than reclaim for the governmental life of the Church the fruits of the Christianization of English society.[100]

Let us investigate what due process means in practice for a diocese and, by analogy, for our personal relationships and social groupings. We will limit ourselves to the aspect of due process that involves structuring administrative discretion. This aspect especially concerns individual members of a diocese who consider themselves aggrieved by administrative action on the part of persons in positions of authority in service to the Church. Such disputes may arise between individuals and a diocesan school board, a personnel board, a building commission, or a pastor.

Administrators and administrative bodies must exercise a large amount of discretion in their actions. No governmental system in history has ever left its administrators without significant discretionary power. None can, and the Church's governing authority is no exception. However, uncontrolled and unchecked discretionary power invites both abuses and suspicions of arbitrariness. To structure administrative discretion, due process makes four recommendations.

First, when an administrative authority is established in the diocese, the precise scope of the authority ought to be clearly delineated. The expectations for it need to be clear. Few things are more frustrating in the Church than not knowing who is responsible for a particular decision. Who is responsible for what needs to be spelled out clearly.

Second, an administrative authority ought to make policies and state them clearly. The expectations of how it will operate and how it will judge need to be clear. A school board should make known its standards for hiring and firing teachers. A personnel board should make known its criteria for recommending men for pastorates. A building commission should make known its standards for authorizing construction or demolition. A pastor should spell out his criteria for admitting students to the parish school in his parish. This clarification of policies, of operational procedures, and of criteria for judgments relieves tension and eliminates most people's complaints about arbitrary decisions. It assures consistency. It also provides a means to intelligently review a disputed decision: namely, to compare the particular decision to the preannounced standards.

Third, whenever discretionary power is exercised in such a way as to adversely affect the rights of persons in the Church, written findings of fact and reasoned opinions in support of the administrative decision should be issued. Such a procedure minimizes careless or hasty action, insures the consideration of important facts and ideas, and aids a person in knowing how to change his circumstances in order to obtain a favorable decision. Such reasoned opinions are, of course, built upon the first two principles—clear understanding of the scope of the authority and clear expectations of how it will judge.

Fourth, the administrative procedure which leads to decisions should not only be fair, but also should be seen to be fair. It is not enough that the process to arrive at a decision which affects someone's life be "objectively" fair. It is also necessary that the person affected be aware before the decision that a discernment process is going on so that he can be confident that the final decision is fair. Hence, it is a mandate of fundamental fairness that a person likely to be adversely affected by administrative action be informed of the proposed action, of the reasons underlying it, and be given adequate opportunity to respond. Likewise, it is a mandate of fundamental fairness that information concerning a person not be used as a basis for administrative action adversely affecting him without disclosing to him that this information is to be used. In addition, the person must have an opportunity to explain, rebut, or deny the "information" in question. Exceptions to preserve confidentiality and privacy are to be made only when it is in the interest of the community and not simply in the interest of an individual who does not wish to be embarrassed by the communication.[101]

Let us try to gain some insight into how these principles of due process apply to our own relationships—personally, in our families, communities, prayer groups, and committees.

First, we need to realize that even if we are not in a position of authority the decisions we make about others frequently affect them indirectly by affecting our relationships with them. If we notice that someone regularly comes late for meetings and conclude that he is irresponsible, this decision affects our relationship with him and we will be prone to act coolly toward him, or even to avoid him. That affects the other person. Since we can't avoid making decisions about others that will affect our relationships with them, we must be aware of their effects.

Second, we must clarify expectations with other people. As mentioned in Chapter Three, expectations can be formal or informal; written, verbal, or understood. If a relationship is going to be safeguarded from arbitrary decisions, then there must be a certain minimum level of clearly understood expectations. This minimum level varies according to the relationship. For example, do you expect a committee member to be present at a majority of meetings, or at every one?

Third, when we make decisions about others we need to carefully consider the facts and reason through the process of the decision. We must expend more energy in "fact-finding" and "reasoned opinion" to the degree that a decision will negatively affect our relationship with a person, or his rights. We may have to write out our decision process in order to clarify it. We do this not to quench our spontaneity, but to protect others.

Fourth, the decisions we make about others need to be fair not only in the sense of the above three steps, but also in the process of making them. We need to relate to the person during the decision-making process before coming to a fixed and final conclusion. If someone is always coming late to the meetings, we must talk to him about it before making a decision. Perhaps we will find that there is a good reason for his behavior and that, in fact, he is behaving responsibly. Perhaps the person will change because we talk to him. Even if the person is behaving irresponsibly and is unwilling to change, he won't be surprised by a "mysterious" change in our relationship to him or by a suggestion that he no longer be a member of the committee.

The recent Church decisions about due process, founded on the Second Vatican Council's sensitivity to the protection of human rights, have many applications to prayer groups and religious communities. They recall that a deep respect for persons must be the foundation for all our judgments which involve other people. Regardless of whether authority is formal or informal, administrative discretion is safeguarded when expectations are clearly spelled out ("this person is in charge of X, and here are the criteria by which he will discern what should happen in X."); when reasons for decisions are clearly spelled out ("in light of the preannounced criteria, this particular decision about X is justified because . . . "); and when people affected by the decision are informed that a discernment process is going on and are given a chance to give input before the decision is finalized ("I'm thinking about this situation involving X and would like to have your input about it before I come to a conclusion since it affects you."). These basic norms are used not merely to be polite or avoid trouble, but to respect persons in the process of decision-making in a group, insuring that no one is rolled over. The Second Vatican Council has made clear that this belongs to the very heart of the gospel, and in 1977 Pope Paul expressed that this sensitivity to an individual's rights ought to become a "new way of thinking."

> The new Code of Canon Law will give full priority to the protection of justice, in order that it may fully respond to the wishes of the (Second Vatican) Council ... The rights of the individual Christian are to be recognized and in consequence defended. Indeed, Canon Law should therefore proclaim the principle of juridical tutelage applied in equal measure to superiors and subjects, to dispose completely of any suspicion that ecclesiastical administration is arbitrary ... The protection of justice should be so highly regarded as to exalt the spiritual character of the life of the Church ... (These ideas should) form a new way of thinking.[102]

Respecting persons is at the heart of the gospel and should greatly affect all of our relationships, especially our expectations, judgments, and fraternal correction. Due process specifies the implications of this for organizations and relationships and points out that (1) who is responsible for what needs to be clear; (2) the criteria by which the person responsible will discern what ought to happen needs to be clear; (3) reasons for decisions that adversely affect a person's rights need to be clear; (4) people affected by a decision should be asked for their input during the process of decision-making and be aware of what is going on. Following these guidelines faithfully is a protection against the possibility that people will be rolled over in the process of our judgments.

## *Conclusions*

As we conclude Part Two, our discussion of Christian tradition, let us review what we have reflected on. The questions we have asked since the beginning of the book are: What does it mean to be pure of heart as we call one another to holiness? How should I approach my brother or sister when there is a fault to be pointed out? What should my posture be? How can I authentically support instead of condemn or discourage?

The answer from the first three chapters is that we must have a vulnerability that acknowledges God's plan and is secure in our identity as a son or daughter of God. We saw that we must be so securely rooted in our identity as a son or daughter of God that we (1) are freed from judging according to the law in a rigid, literal way that misses the heart of the law; (2) are freed from trying to find our identities by competing with others and instead are free to find what it means for me to follow Jesus; (3) are aware God has a larger plan so that we can be impelled by the vision God gives us without imposing our vision on others; (4) are fully using the good gift given to us while insuring that the bad side of it does not go beyond the scope of Christian limits; (5) can confront a clash of charisms with others without condemning or attacking them.

In Chapter Four we developed these answers by saying that we need to approach brothers and sisters differently about their faults depending on their openness. If they are open and appreciative, we can approach them expecting to directly help them with the fault being pointed out. If they are open yet resistant, our help needs to be directed toward helping them work through all the feelings stirred up when the fault is pointed out. If they are closed and resistant we ought to help them to see the implications this position has for their relationships.

Adding the answers from Matthew 18, we see that our posture needs to be grounded in the gospel paradox where we humble ourselves and become vulnerable like children. We are directed to encourage our brethern, taking a special care not to hurt them. We should actively care for those who have begun to stray, never writing them off. We ought to intensely desire unity with our whole heart and limitlessly forgive.

Let us reconsider the questions again, and continue to develop the answers in light of Part Two on Christian tradition. From the Desert Fathers we see that purity of heart needs to drain us of the worldly ways of thinking that are conducive to feelings of revenge, punishment, and attacking others. To be pure of heart means not to let worldly or evil thoughts penetrate the center of our hearts where they have a controlling influence. Rather, by guarding our thoughts and being caught up in the apocalyptic vision that sees the spiritual origins of the struggle, we can cling to God and be freed to love.

From St. Thomas Aquinas we gained important practical advice on how to judge. In order to authentically support instead of condemn or discourage we need to guide our knowing power by love. Coming to a judgment on the basis of doubtful knowledge, suspicions, or guesses is a rash judgment that does not authentically support a person. People ought to be given the benefit of the doubt unless they need to have our feedback so that they can deal with their problems. The guiding principle is love. While we are always free to judge in the sense of speaking the truth as we best judge it to be, it is unfair to induce a person to follow our judgment by definitively enforcing it unless we are in a position of authority.

In this chapter we have seen how much growth, support, love, and unity can deepen in the process of working through expectations, judgments, or fraternal correction if we vulnerably share our hearts with one another. Yet there is a risk since not everyone has the love or wisdom that enables them to support us. The guiding principle is freedom. We should never force ourselves or others to share deeply in any particular instance, though we should encourage such sharing in general. We saw that the foundational posture here is the principle of respecting persons, a principle which the Vatican Council puts at the heart of the gospel. The four due process guidelines give the practical application of this principle for our judgments that affect others.

# *Part Three*

# *Modern Sources*

CHAPTER EIGHT

# A TRANSFORMED MIND: PSYCHOLOGICAL INSIGHTS

Becoming vulnerable and compassionate in our judgments and expectations of others, and in fraternal correction, flows from a radical new way of thinking.

In light of our own community's experience of deeper, transforming relationships, we have reflected on some of the insights of scripture and Christian tradition. These reflections have yielded insights about our own relationships which God can use to transform our posture—the state of our heart. Fraternal correction, judgments, and expectations are particularly revealing topics that can help us become vulnerable and compassionate throughout our lives.

In Part One we saw scripture's wisdom on our identity as sons and daughters of God. This identity is the foundation for a transformed and a renewed mind that acknowledges God's plan in the unfolding of our daily lives. The practical helps of actively praising and apocalyptic thinking which flow from being children of God also secure us in our sonship more deeply and point out the areas where we still resist a spiritual way of thinking.

In the completing/competing dialectic of scriptural expectations we saw that a transformed mind broadens one's horizons to include the mysterious tensions of the gospel: it fulfills the law yet can live with wheat and weeds together. As we are rooted in our unique identities and follow Jesus, we are freed from competing with others or trying to "steal" their identities. We no longer feel a need to impose on others the vision we have received yet we are freed to be impelled by it. We see that many of our difficulties with others are manifestations of the bad side of their good gift, and our focus becomes to support them in using their good gift more purely. A transformed mind has effects in all these areas and even sees authentic pluralism in the larger vision of God where we can appreciate and value another's charism even when it clashes with our own.

With scripture's insight into a transformed mind as the foundation, we discussed fraternal correction in scripture. Being vulnerable and compassionate involves approaching brothers and sisters differently depending on their openness. We never condemn another, but the idea that we can never judge in any way is a mistaken understanding of scripture. Matthew's advice on the subject is to humble ourselves and take on a vulnerable posture like children, trusting in God. He then focuses on some practical helps: encourage people in the process of correction; don't give up on them but actively care for them by the process of correction; never let poison breed within us, but rather, desiring unity with our whole heart, enter into the process of correction by going to the person; and finally, be compassionate, limitlessly forgive in the process of correction.

Many Christians have lived according to scripture's insights on becoming vulnerable and compassionate. Part Two reviewed some of this wisdom from Christian tradition, highlighting the areas our community experience has found most valuable. From the Desert Fathers we see in the examples of judging one's brothers the need to be serious about maintaining a transformed mind. We should do this by guarding our thoughts and nurturing the urgency of the apocalyptic vision in prayer and praise. From Aquinas we gain helpful practical insights into the meaning of judging others and how to do it properly in particular situations. From the Church's own experience we glean crucial insights into the relationship context for judgments: vulnerably sharing with one another must be done in freedom and always with that respect for the other person which is constitutive of the gospel. In organized groups, the process of coming to decisions that affect others, or that involve judgments of others, ought to be governed by the four principles of due process. These principles, which find their source in the gospel, are: (1) a clear definition of the scope of authority; (2) clear criteria by which those in authority will judge matters within their scope; (3) the reasons for a judgment that adversely affects a person ought to be clearly spelled out to that person; (4) those affected by a judgment should be asked for their input in the process of coming to the judgment and they should be kept informed of how the process is progressing. These modern-day principles for respecting persons prevent abuses that violate the rights of people in the process of coming to judgments.

Here in Part Three we turn to contemporary sources for insights into our theme. Again, we select the sources we have found to be particularly valuable in our community experience. First, in this chapter, we will consider some psychological insights about a transformed and renewed mind: how our thought patterns affect the way we feel; how we can remove irrational ideas from our thought patterns; how we can use our feelings to discern our thought patterns; and how to experience a healing of our thought patterns.

Chapter Nine will consider some theological and epistemological insights on judging in our relationships. Chapter Ten will discuss some insights from our communal life and will apply the previous reflections to our relationships more extensively. The goal is to gain a deeper insight into the basis of vulnerability and compassion in our own relationships, highlighted in the topic of judgments, expectations, and fraternal correction. In order for this book to help us enrich our own relationships, it should be prayerfully read with an eye toward applying it to ourselves and our relationships, expecting the Holy Spirit to be speaking to us about it.

## *Emotional Responsibility*

A household of single men in our community had been living together for over a year. The heads of the community could see that their mutual support of one another had freed the men in many ways to serve well. Yet at times it was difficult for them to live together. Much of their difficulty was just the normal strain of a close life together. Sharing one's thoughts and feelings freely and in love is often difficult, especially if these feelings concern "silly" or "embarrassing" things. The men also had the usual difficulties knowing how to respond to another person with both compassion and integrity. However, their life together was a fruitful life of love and they were growing in the Lord.

Eventually, it seemed best that this particular group of men no longer live together but rather move into new households. The reasons for the change included the desires of some of the men for a different life-style, the larger community's need for a certain kind of household, and the need to form new households to accommodate newer people in the community who were being called into a household life. I was responsible for talking with the men about the change and working it out peacefully.

As I met with them, the men were all able to affirm that the change should be made. But the process seemed difficult, especially for one of the brothers. As we discussed it in the group it was clear that he felt uptight, nervous, and unable to relate well to the other people there. When I talked with him alone he said that every time he thought of the household changes he felt depressed and condemned. These paralyzing feelings would overwhelm him whenever he tried to share with one of the other brothers about the changes. He said he realized the household change was right, but it made him feel horrible. The feelings were getting increasingly worse and were causing him a great deal of suffering. He didn't know how to deal with his feelings, except by hoping they would settle down if he maintained the status quo and denied the need for any changes.

I asked the brother to verbalize the way he was thinking about the household changes. At first, he could only express the obvious facts we had talked about in the group: when all circumstances were considered, it was clearly best to change to the new living situations. I asked him if he was able to praise the Lord and acknowledge that God's plan for his life was unfolding through these changes. He said he hadn't tried to do that. I asked him to take a few minutes to think about praising the Lord for it; when he did, he got in touch with some surprising thought patterns.

He realized he was unable to praise the Lord for it. The reason was not that he felt the changes were objectively wrong, but because he thought the real reason for these changes was his own failure to relate well to the people he had lived with. Until that moment, he had not even realized he had such thoughts. He began to see that as soon as he thought he was a failure in relating to these people, powerful emotions would overwhelm him. He would think how terrible it was and what a horrible failure his whole life was. Suddenly he would find himself depressed, condemned and, when he was with the people he had lived with, tense and even paralyzed.

In this particular situation the brother had seen things incorrectly. It was simply not true that he was a failure in relating to the people. But because he had never been in touch with this thought pattern, it was never verbalized and shown to be false by others. He believed it was true and that it was terrible, and thus he was trapped in paralyzing emotions. As I helped him to see that he was not a failure, the depression and condemnation disappeared as if a faucet had been turned off. What the brother found even more freeing was a basic gospel truth: even if he was weak in some ways, his weakness is not a terrible thing at all but something God can use for our growth and healing. The brother can repent when necessary. There is nothing terrible about failing; everyone does it regularly in some area or another.

After the brother had been freed from his paralyzing feelings, he noticed that the thought, "I am a failure and this is terrible" still persisted and made him tense around the people he had lived with. He dealt with this by stopping and consciously getting in touch with the thought causing it. Once he did this, he could just recall the truth and the feelings would dissipate. Sometimes the truth was hard for him to believe and he needed someone else to remind him of it. This meant that he had to be able to tell some people about the thought patterns he was prone to and invite them to support him by speaking the truth. Not only was this a good example of a communal guarding of one's thoughts, but it was a very good way for others to be close to the man, to know him, and compassionately support him.

This story shows the importance of controlling thought patterns and guarding one's thoughts. This emphasis, which is present in scripture and in the teaching of the Desert Fathers, is also stressed in some modern schools of psychology. Albert Ellis, the founder of the rational-emotive school of psychology, explains that the initial judgments we make in our personal relationships and the unconscious expectations we have of others will determine much of our emotional life. His psychological insights about a transformed mind and our emotional responsibility will help us see more clearly what was going on in the example just given.

Often we tend to perceive various external events as the source of our negative feelings. We come to the "obvious" conclusion that we can relieve our negative feelings by changing something outside of ourselves—the event, the person, the circumstances. This mindset allows us to avoid personal responsibility for our emotional state and instead to blame people or things. At times we can and should blame external causes. If we are stabbed with a knife, the pain we feel has an external cause, and it is fair to blame our pain on whoever stuck the knife in us. However, in personal relationships, other people's ways of relating and the circumstances we find ourselves in are rarely the cause of our negative feelings. Our own thought patterns typically cause our negative emotions. Unless we understand this we will have a tendency to systematically misjudge situations and other people.

Dr. Ellis utilizes a three-step process to help us see the real source of many of our negative feelings. The first step is the event or situation that activates our thoughts. The last step is the emotions which follow from our thoughts. The true source of our emotions is the middle step—our thought patterns or belief system, activated by the event. To this three-step process we can add a fourth step—a decision about how to act in the situation.

An A-B-C-D schema might look like this:

A: Activating event or situation. This activates step B.
B: Belief system or thought pattern. Our thoughts about A.
C: Consequent emotions or feelings. These stem from step B, not step A.
D: Decision to act a certain way. Though it doesn't have to follow from the way we feel (C), it often does.

Our belief that an event A is terrible is a thought in the realm of judgments and expectations—Step B. Frequently our emotional response (Step C) to such a belief is intense, overwhelming, negative feelings. One doesn't need to have a special problem to feel this way; such feelings are part of a person's normal life. Often the decisions we make in our life flow along with these negative feelings.

It is possible to change our expectations and judgments at Step B to something more rational and realistic, something like: "I wish event A hadn't happened, but I can understand why it did, given reality, sin, human limitations, and circumstances. It is not terrible, or horrible, or catastrophic, but I would have preferred something else. Yet I trust that God will use this event to work for good in my life." When we change our expectations and judgments at Step B to something like this, our emotional response at Step C is also changed, sometimes surprisingly rapidly. Intensely negative emotions usually melt away, and what remains is a calmer response, even though one may still feel annoyed, irritated, or disappointed. This is not a process of repressing one's feelings (Step C) or of ignoring the facts and living in a make-believe land (Step A). Rather it is a process of authentically changing one's expectations and judgments about external events. These changes naturally have implications for our emotions. This process is very similar to the Desert Fathers' method of guarding thoughts. Using it frees us from blaming others or the situation for our bad feelings. It also frees us to enter into fraternal correction without "dumping" all of our negative feelings and blaming the person.

To apply this process effectively, we have to deal with the common but mistaken idea that "my feelings are my feelings and that's just the way they are. I need to express them. They are unrelated to my thoughts, beliefs, expectations, and judgments." This mistaken idea is frequently a reaction against tendencies to cope with negative feelings by repressing them. Repressing our feelings is unhealthy. Being in touch with our feelings allows us to share them in a way that both supports and draws us closer to others. Yet consistent, intensely overwhelming negative feelings are frequently only a symptom of wrong judgments based on a pattern of irrational expectations. While it is never healthy to repress the symptom of disease (in the realm of our emotions—Step C), the real solution is to get to the disease, the source of the emotions (in the realm of our thought patterns—Step B). The goal of this process is not to repress feelings, but rather to authentically change expectations and judgments along more rational, realistic, and compassionate lines. This in turn will have its inevitable effects on our feelings.

What is the connection between our thoughts (expectations, judgments) and our feelings? Drs. Ellis and Harper maintain that the close connection between human feelings and thought patterns is being increasingly proven by scientific studies:

> When we first began thinking and writing about rational-emotive therapy, in the latter half of the 1950's, we could cite little research material to back up the idea that humans do not *get* upset, but that they *upset themselves* by devoutly convincing themselves, at point B, of irrational beliefs about what happens to them at point A. The field of cognitive psychology, then in its formative stages, only included rare psychologists, such as Magda Arnold, who viewed emotions as linked with thinking. Since that time, hundreds of experiments have clearly demonstrated that if an experimenter induces, by fair means or foul, individuals to change their thoughts, they also profoundly change their emoting and behaving. Evidence that we feel the way we think keeps accumulating, steadily reaffirmed by the work of many experimenters.[103]

Ellis and Harper conclude that "*sustained* emotion normally requires repeated evaluative thought."[104] This means that feelings that last for a longer time than a passing mood and feelings which pop up regularly are normally caused by a thought pattern. We may not be aware of this pattern. This does not imply that all negative emotions can be controlled by one's thinking, nor does it imply that we should strive to become emotionless. Ellis and Harper are suggesting that inappropriate negative emotions—that is, emotions that are self-defeating, self-sabotaging, destructive, or hindering emotions—find their source in unreasonable beliefs. If so, then destructive emotions can be changed by a more rational pattern of thought.

Inappropriate emotions are basically those which interfere with or paralyze loving. These are not limited only to the more serious emotional problems that require special care, but apply to a whole variety of intense and less intense emotions which everyone experiences. Appropriate emotions, both positive and negative, are an essential part of human happiness. As Ellis and Harper note, "Certain negative emotions seem especially to aid survival. Thus if you did not feel displeased, sorry, regretful, annoyed, irritated, frustrated, or disappointed when you suffered hunger, injury, or defeat, would you feel motivated to keep out of harm's way and to continue your existence?"[105]

Appropriate emotions may include, at times, intensely experienced and even overwhelming emotions. Ellis does not recommend an emotionless life in order to achieve calmness. However, some intense emotions almost always interfere with loving, and these are the emotions he suggests we should change by changing our thought patterns. Our thought patterns are frequently so ingrained that we don't even realize they exist. In discussing how to differentiate inappropriate from appropriate emotions, and how to discover their source in our thought patterns, Ellis and Harper write:

> even your exceptional sorrow or displeasure may prove appropriate, assuming that you have some unusually strong wants or preferences and that these keep getting thwarted . . . Extreme sorrow and unhappiness, however, do *not* equal depression, despair, shame, or self-downing. And it still remains legitimate to discriminate between the former negative feelings, on the one hand, and the latter, on the other hand. Even 99 per cent unhappiness may not equal 1 per cent depression. The two feelings tend to rest in two different emotional continua . . . frustration, sorrow and sadness seem to arise when you strongly *prefer*, *desire* or *want* something and your preferences get blocked . . . Depression, despair, shame, and self-downing, however, arise from a *different* or *extra* set of beliefs; namely: "I absolutely *must* succeed . . ." And, when you don't succeed you then logically—because of the silly *must*—conclude: "I find it *awful* that I have failed! I *can't stand* my failure! I will *always* keep failing. I rate as a *rotten person* for failing so miserably!" With those highly irrational absolutistic beliefs, you make yourself depressed, despairing, ashamed, and self-downing.[106]

In light of the above psychological insights, let us reconsider the example of the man who changed households. We will do it in four steps according to the A-B-C-D schema.

Step A is the activating event: the change in households. The change is a fact which the brother learns about in a meeting. He can respond to it in a variety of ways.

Step B is the person's belief system or thought pattern which is activated by event A. Here the thought that comes to the person about the household change is: "This change means I've been a failure in relating to these people. This is horrible. This just confirms that I've always been a failure."

The first thing to note is that this thought is hidden. It is not a belief which the man has held consciously by seriously reflecting on it and affirming it. Rather, the thought arises in various circumstances and occasionally pops into consciousness, but is never grappled with reasonably. When the thought does pop up, the man "affirms it by default"; he allows it to slip back into the subconscious without rationally evaluating it. Most of the time the thought was below the level of consciousness. Only when the man tried to praise the Lord for the household changes did resistance to praise of his "failure" surface. Thus the hidden thought came into the light.

The second thing to note is that this thought is an irrational idea. The facts of the matter did not support it; the man was not a failure in his relationships with the people he lived with. Yet even if he were, the thought would still be an irrational idea since that kind of weakness is not horrible or catastrophic. Nor would such a weakness mean that the man is "a failure." This thought pattern simply is not rational and does not correspond to reality. This does not mean that the man had a special problem. He was surprised to realize that he was thinking like this. He was not consciously cultivating an irrational thought pattern, but was rather subject to a hidden irrational idea. We all fall victim to irrational thoughts at times.

The third thing to note about the thought is that the household change was evidently not the first event that had activated this thought. It had troubled the man numerous times in the past. It had developed into a hidden thought pattern or belief system which was activated by any event which could be misinterpreted along those lines. The hidden thought had been given free, though unconscious, reign because it had never been caught and evaluated.

Step C is the consequent emotions or feelings. The brother felt uptight and nervous as the group talked about their experience of living together. He felt depressed and condemned when he thought about the household changes. When he tried to talk to one of the brothers, he felt overwhelmed and almost paralyzed by these emotions. He presumed that these feelings which caused him so much suffering were caused by step A—the event of the household change. And so as the household changes progressed, the feelings grew worse. He felt powerless to do anything about them since he presumed they were caused by an event he could not control—the fact of the change in households. He felt better as long as he could avoid thinking about the household changes.

Things began to change when he came to the insight that these "horrible failure" thoughts at Step B caused the emotions he felt. He was able to distinguish between the fact of the household changes and the false idea that he was a horrible failure. He noticed that the first thought didn't bring any negative feelings whereas the second one brought them all. As he saw that the thought pattern was false, based on an irrational idea, the feelings disappeared. When the feelings returned, all he had to do was recall the false thought patterns causing them, realize they were irrational, and reaffirm the truth. The feelings would then go away. It was hard to do this alone at first and he needed someone else who could help objectify his thoughts and see their irrationality. He was freed!

Step D is the decision to act in a certain way. In our example, the person had first decided to avoid thinking about the household changes in order to avoid the negative feelings. This meant that he had to mentally maintain the status quo, which denied the need for any changes. He realized the changes were right so he didn't try to "block" them by trying to appeal the decisions or taking other external action. But he did "block" them internally by denying the real need for changes, thus making the process difficult for himself and making it hard for others to be in unity with him. Although he made the "right" decision in spite of his feelings (not to externally block the needed change), nevertheless his feelings would not allow him to enter into the process wholeheartedly. Another person might have decided to actively resist such a change, denying the obvious need for it, perhaps even spiritualizing their reasons: "Let's use some more discernment. If this change is really in the Lord, then we all ought to feel peaceful about it."

When the Step B thinking, "I'm a horrible failure," was corrected, then it was easy for the person to enter into the process with the right posture. His feelings were freed to support what he knew was right. The benefits would have been even greater for the person who might have made the wrong decision in light of his feelings. This person would not only have had his feelings freed but would have also received an intellectual insight, which had been blocked by his feelings, into what the right decision is.

This extended application of the A-B-C-D psychological insight into the dynamics of our thoughts points out the importance of our beliefs and thought patterns. It should help us achieve a transformed mind which is purified of its irrational ideas and mistaken beliefs, and which also knows how to uncover and discern them when they present themselves.

## *Irrational Ideas*

Ellis outlines several irrational expectations which inevitably lead to irrational ideas that cause and sustain emotional disturbance.[107] Among them are:

1. It is a dire necessity for an adult human being to be loved or approved of by virtually every significant other person in his community.

2. One should be thoroughly competent, adequate, and achieving in at least one important area if one is to consider oneself worthwhile.

3. It is awful and catastrophic when things are not the way one would very much like them to be; when one is seriously frustrated, treated unfairly, or rejected.

4. Human unhappiness is externally caused and people have little or no ability to control their sorrows and disturbances.

5. It is easier to avoid facing many of life's difficulties and to avoid taking responsibility than to undertake more rewarding forms of self-discipline.

6. One's past history is an all-important determiner of one's present behavior.

7. There is invariably a right, precise, and perfect solution to human problems and that it is catastrophic if this perfect solution is not found.

Here the contrast between the worldly way of thinking and a transformed mind is sharpened. The world represents many of these irrational ideas as truths; the gospel shows them to be illusions. For example, while it would be nice if everyone loved and approved us, it is certainly not something the gospel would have us expect. This list of irrational ideas is a good beginning for self-reflection about the root causes of much of our emotional upset.

Another group of psychologists, Farquhar and Lowe, have added to Ellis' list of irrational ideas.[108] They also present possible rational alternatives to the irrational ideas, truths to counter myths. They include:

1. *Myth*: each individual has a discoverable, internally consistent "self" and that one should strive to always behave in accord with "self." *Truth*: each individual is a complex composite of all emotions and that the true spice of living lies in accepting and experiencing one's emotional and intellectual shifts.

2. *Myth*: one's worth as a person is directly related to one's objectively discernible productivity. *Truth*: one's worth to himself rests in his aliveness and in his capacity to enjoy living.

3. *Myth*: anger is automatically bad, obscene, and destructive and that one should always curb his anger. *Truth*: anger is a normal human emotion which can be cleansing and nurturing. One should work at expressing anger as a communication of current feelings without attacking the personal worth and security of others.

4. *Myth*: people are very fragile and one should always keep one's thoughts to oneself in order to avoid hurting others. *Truth*: sharing one's perceptions can often be one of the most direct expressions of love a human can make.

5. *Myth*: happiness, pleasure, fulfillment, and growth can only occur in the presence of others and being alone is the worst possible human condition. *Truth*: happiness, pleasure, etc. can be experienced alone as well as with others and that being alone at times is a desirable human experience.

6. *Myth*: any sign of hostility, anger, aggression, or fear is a sign of broad, deep-seated problems. *Truth*: one should first consider that signs of negative emotions may be temporary or realistic expressions of inner emotions or feelings.

A question for reflection: what are some of the ways I approach situations that are based on an irrational idea (illusion) with its consequent emotional upset?

## *Discernment of Feelings*

A crucial question arises as we reflect on the insights of psychology. When I am not feeling at peace about a situation, how can I discern whether something is wrong with the situation or whether something is wrong with me and my thinking? This is a dual question: how do we discern our feelings (are they appropriate or inappropriate?) and then how do we use our feelings to see what is going on, where the problem lies, and what the solution is? To answer these questions we will consider first an example from scripture of discerning sorrow; secondly, the need to be familiar with our good gifts and their bad sides; thirdly, the approach of traditional spirituality that sees the need for deliverance, repentance, and compunction. As we examine the question of discerning our feelings from three somewhat different angles, we will begin to get a more complete feel for the answer.

First, then, the example from scripture of discerning sorrow. The distinction we must make between appropriate and inappropriate feelings reminds one of Paul's distinction in his second letter to the Corinthians, "sorrow for God's sake produces a repentance without regrets, leading to salvation, whereas worldly sorrow brings death" (7:10). Paul speaks in the verses following about the fruit of appropriate sorrow, and he tells the Corinthians that their sorrow gave them the energy to make things right, and to defend themselves; it created in them the ardent desire to restore the balance of justice and it gave them the energy to activate their desire. On the other hand, worldly sorrow (perhaps depression, despair, shame), locks one up in oneself, drains one of energy, and causes one to give up trying to restore any balance of justice. In fact, nothing at all is accomplished except to wallow in self-pity. In a word, worldly sorrow leads to death. Appropriate sorrow helps us to follow Christ more ardently. Inappropriate sorrow and depression help us to wallow in ourselves.

Paul discerns the type of sorrow among the Corinthians according to the effect it had in their lives. A feeling of sorrow was appropriate, or for God's sake, when it motivated them to do the right things even though they weren't pleasant things to do. Such sorrow gave them energy to make things right, to clarify the truth, and to restore the balance of justice. It produced a repentance without regrets that led to salvation. It supported them in living in the truth. In contrast, Paul mentions that an inappropriate sorrow, or a worldly one, brings death. It undermines our motivation to do the right thing. Instead, it will encourage us to wallow in self-pity and do nothing.

In terms of the psychological insight of A-B-C-D, Paul's discernment criteria here focuses on whether C (our consequent emotions) motivates us and supports us to do the right D (our decision on what to do). If the feelings we have support us doing the right thing, then they are appropriate or "Godly;" if they do the opposite, then they are inappropriate or worldly. Paul's advice is to "just look at the fruit" (2 Cor 7:11). This classic approach of telling a tree by its fruit is a good way to discern whether feelings are appropriate or inappropriate, presuming, of course, that you know what the right *D*ecision is.

When it is not clear what the loving *D*ecision is, then another approach for discernment has to be used that focuses on the connection between B (belief-system or thoughts) and C (consequent emotions). Also, we may successfully determine that sorrow, or any other emotion, is inappropriate, but it might not be at all clear what to do about it. If we realize that we are stuck in inappropriate sorrow, what then? How do we change our state? In short, we can successfully judge our feelings by considering our actions (D) when the right action is known. But this analysis is not helpful when we do not know the right action. It is also of limited help in knowing how to deal with our condition.

We then turn to the second area: discerning our feelings by being familiar with our good gifts and their bad sides. This area concentrates on the B-C connection—the link between our belief-system and our emotions. Consider a situation in which someone gives me a suggestion about a change in our community life. There are many good reasons on both sides of the issue, yet I don't feel good about the suggestion. Why? It is not clear that the suggestion is wrong. How do I discern the nature of my feeling when the action (D) is unknown? We do so by focusing on the B-C connection. B is my belief system or thoughts about the suggestion; we are frequently not in touch with this unless we stop to reflect. C is my consequent emotion of unpeacefulness which is caused by B.

We might note here that the Lord can give a person a spiritual "sense" about the correct decision totally apart from any reflective thoughts about the event. However, this is rare. Usually what a person considers as such a spiritual sense is simply his emotions flowing from his hidden thoughts. It is certainly much easier (though often inaccurate) to call such a feeling a spiritual "sense" than to investigate the matter ourselves or to enter into a dialogue with someone who has come to a different concluson.

Coming back to our example, how do I discern the appropriateness of my feeling of unpeacefulness by focusing on the B-C connection? I already know what C is—a feeling of unpeacefulness about the suggestion. I can find many good reasons to feel unpeaceful about actually implementing the suggestion, but I can also find many equally good reasons why the change should happen. And so I have to find out what B is—the thoughts, insights, and beliefs that cause unpeacefulness.

In one case, I might reflect and pray about the situation and discover that the unpeacefulness really doesn't stem from the anticipated consequences of implementing the suggestion, but from thought patterns I am prone to. For example: the suggestion might inspire the thought that change would drastically alter the status quo in the community and would involve much hard work on my part. Or I might discover a tendency in myself to be so invested in the status quo that I am not receptive to the thought that a change might be good. Becoming aware of such thoughts doesn't mean they are necessarily true. It puts me in a position to think them through and determine if they are correct.

In this case, the cause of my unpeacefulness (C) is the thought (B) that change would be a terrible mess entailing lots of hard work. I need to be freed from these thoughts. Sometimes freedom comes by my own reflection. Other times I must talk with another about the thoughts to see the truth. The truth in this case is that while the suggestion may or may not be the right thing to do, it certainly won't be a terrible mess nor will it destroy or undermine what we have already accomplished. Change might even improve things. When I am freed from the irrational ideas of the B level that cause unpeacefulness, I can then reconsider the suggestion with a clear, unprejudiced, mind. The feelings that now come, and the thoughts that cause them, usually provide a sound basis for a decision.

Unless we are familiar with our good gifts and their bad sides, it will be difficult to get in touch with the deeper thought patterns that are causing our feelings of unpeacefulness. Usually we would feel so threatened by the prospect of contemplating our weaknesses that someone who is really willing to lay down his life must help us overcome our great resistance. "What do you mean you think I'm closed? I hear what you are saying and I understand it. I just don't think it's right. No, I'm not scared of what it might mean." And so forth. A pattern in our reactions usually shows up in our relationships with others. Others might see it more clearly than we do; thus we must invite them to help us.

The pattern in our reactions usually turns out to be the bad side of our good gift. If our gift is to govern and direct things, the bad side is a tendency to be closed to change and to be in control for its own sake. If our gift is to balance viewpoints and events, the bad side is a tendency to water down an urgent word. If our gift is to surrender ourselves to an ideal in a way that inspires others to follow, the bad side is a tendency to be undiscerning about some aspects of the ideals we devote ourselves to. If our gift is a prophetic sensitivity to change, the bad side is anxiety that undermines patience and is prone to discouragement because it gives up on people who are not quickly responsive. One could go on for a long time describing different gifts and their bad sides. There are as many possibilities as people, though many are similar.

The bad side of a gift does not have to have a hold on us. The bad side only exists when our tendency converges with a short, willful step to give into it. Although our particular response flows from the nature of the gift, it must first be activated by the short, willful step that gives in to something. Perhaps we have taken this short, willful step so frequently that we're not even conscious of it. Nevertheless, it is our responsibility to deal with it. Seeing the B-C connection not only helps us see what the decision ought to be, but also provides a means to get in touch with the short, willful step so that we can deal with it once and for all. This doesn't mean that the tendency goes away, but the semiconscious surrender to it comes into the light and can be consistently rejected. As we share about this with others, they can help us see when we are taking the short, willful step. Without an awareness of the bad sides of our good gifts, it will be difficult to effectively use the B-C connection to discern our feelings.

The third approach to discernment of feelings is the approach of traditional spirituality which sees the need for deliverance, repentance, and compunction. In terms of the A-B-C-D progression—*A*ctivating event, *B*elief system or thoughts, *C*onsequent emotions, *D*ecision and action—this traditional approach seeks to get at the source of the irrational thoughts in order to be freed of them.

The Desert Fathers associated different evil thoughts with different demons that caused them.[109] In Evagrius, one of the fourth century Desert Fathers, we read:

> We must take care to recognize the different types of demons and take note of the circumstances of their coming. We shall know these from our thoughts. We ought to consider which of the demons are less frequent in their assaults, which are the more vexatious, which are the ones that yield the field more readily and which the more resistant . . . . Now it is essential to understand these matters so that when these various evil thoughts set their own proper forces to work, we are in a position to address effective words to them, that is to say, those words which correctly characterize the one present . . . . In this manner we shall make ready progress, by the grace of God. We shall pack them off chafing with chagrin and marvelling at our perspicacity.[110]

Here we see that the Desert Fathers' insight into dealing with "irrational" or "evil" thoughts closely resembles Ellis' insight. Both say that we need to speak the truth according to what the thought is. Thus we need to know accurately which thoughts we are most prone to. Evagrius also calls demons the *source* of evil thoughts. Of course, this is spiritual knowledge which lies outside the field of psychology. Evagrius says that we need to be delivered from these demons. He acknowledges that there are personal evil forces at work in the universe which bring to our minds evil thoughts and aggravate the ones that naturally arise. We are really talking about spiritual warfare, with our thoughts (the B-level) as the battleground.

Evagrius also speaks of the classic eight kinds of evil thoughts. (1) "The thought of gluttony . . . brings to his mind concern for his stomach . . . the thought of a long illness . . ." In Ellis' words, "It would be terrible if I got sick." (2) "The demon of impurity . . . (causes us) . . . to speak and hear certain words almost as if the reality were actually present to be seen." (3) "Avarice suggests to the mind . . . the pinch of poverty, the great shame that comes from accepting the necessities of life from others." (4) "Sadness tends to come up at times because of the deprivation of one's desires." (5) "Anger . . . constantly irritates the soul . . . and flashes the picture of the offensive person before one's eyes." (6) Restlessness "... leads him to reflect that charity has departed from among the brethren, that there is no one to give encouragement ... this demon drives him along to desire other sites where he can more easily procure life's necessities, more readily find work and make a real success of himself." (7) "Vainglory ... leads them to desire to make their struggles known publicly, to hunt after the praise of men." (8) "The demon of pride ... induces the monk to deny that God is his helper and to consider that he himself is the cause of virtuous actions. Further, he gets a big head in regard to the brethren, considering them stupid because they do not all have this same opinion of him."[111]

Evagrius' list shows how thoughts of "It is terrible that ..." cause inappropriate feelings. We can also draw much reassurance from this list. People who have gone before us have experienced these thoughts. Like us, they have found such thoughts destructive. They also show us how to protect ourselves by the expedient of guarding our thoughts. The Desert Fathers felt an urgency to deal with these thoughts immediately because they saw demons as their source. Their solution was to "speak the truth" to the evil thought. This is surprisingly similar to Ellis' advice to undermine the irrational idea by speaking the rational idea. The Fathers' testing ground and goal was prayer and the praise of God, which frequently brought to the light the thoughts that needed to be dealt with.

Traditional spirituality helps us deal with an important obstacle on our journey to God. This obstacle is the problem of deep-seated unconscious thought patterns which create an illusory self-concept and which separate us from reality.

As Ellis affirms, the real source of most of our anxiety, hostility, depression, guilt, despair, stress, etc. is *our* judgment not to accept reality. We base this judgment on *our* irrational expectations of ourselves and others. It is usually not a person's lack of loving that upsets us. The cause lies in *our* judgmental response to it ("It is horrible that ...")—an unconscious thought pattern. We think that we would be happy if only the event A changed: if only I was freed from sickness, if I was rich, if I could only have that thing or person, if only he or she would be more sensitive and accepting, if only I was in a better community or marriage, or if only people would recognize and respect me.

Traditional spirituality affirms that living in such illusions and self-justification makes "me" and "my desires" the center and focal point of the universe. This illusion always works against us. The notion that things *ought* to happen the way *we* want them to is an illusion. When things work against us, when we do not succeed in being God, we feel guilty, angry, or depressed. Instead of rooting out the illusion which is the source of our self-condemning feelings, we try to hide from them by building a facade, a false ego to protect ourselves from ourselves. "The problem isn't me, everything would be fine if only ..." In a word, we enter into death.

The solution offered by traditional spirituality boils down to being purified of our false self, our illusions, and our lack of responsibility for our lives in order to enter our true self, to know God, and to accept responsibility for our lives. The way this purification happens is through the gift of compunction—a sudden insight of repentance frequently accompanied by tears, where we see through our facade and false self based on an illusion and suddenly realize the effects our sinfulness has had and the extent of the disorder of our actions. Whereas an atheist like Ellis doesn't believe anything is horrible, for a Christian there is one thing that is terribly catastrophic—hardening our hearts to such an extent that we permanently lose God. And so, "before all else, pray to be given tears, that weeping may soften the savage hardness which is in your soul ..."[112] These tears of compunction that bring us into the great joy of redemption are not meant to be a one-time experience, but something which continues and opens the door to union with God. Traditional spirituality affirms that there is no other way to be deeply united with Jesus except by going through the center of our sinfulness with compunction.[113] This spirit of compunction builds our compassion, for as one modern spiritual writer has put it:

> If you are severe in your judgments, exacting with others, if you easily bring up the faults of your brethren, compunction does not dwell in you.[114]

Hence, traditional spirituality gives us some guidelines to discern the nature of our feelings (C-level). Is their source an evil thought (B-level)? If so, then we need to be delivered, freed from the thought by speaking the truth to it and to guard our hearts so it cannot enter us more deeply. This will free us to base a decision on more solid grounds. Yet we can frequently be blind to these evil thoughts, because we are unable to penetrate our illusions and the facade of a false self. Unless we experience compunction, which softens our hearts and clears our sight, we are on shaky ground in accurately discerning our feelings. We'll wind up being severe in our judgments and exacting with others.

## *Healing of Thought Patterns*

In this concluding section on psychological insights, we will consider their application to the process of healing. Here we will focus on interior healing that sets us free, not physical healing of our bodies. There are many approaches to interior healing. Perhaps the two most popular approaches are "the power of positive thinking," and the approach of "inner healing" that recalls early memories of painful experiences in order to receive Jesus' healing. A third approach to interior healing, the one that flows from the psychological insights of this chapter, is a "healing of thought patterns." In this section we will contrast these three approaches to healing to determine their weaknesses, strengths, and the ways they might complement one another. The purpose of this discussion is not to clarify theory but to gain practical wisdom about what approach might be most valuable in our own healing and that of others we minister to.

First, the "power of positive thinking" approach says we should think positively when we run into obstacles. When we feel afraid, angry, or frustrated, we shouldn't give up but should rather say to ourselves, "I can do it!" An example from my own life illustrates this approach. Once I was in charge of arrangements for a large conference. A few weeks before the conference, I received a phone call from the person responsible for the conference center where our meeting was to be held. He was upset about some arrangements which he felt needed to be changed, and he started yelling at me. I tried to be cool, calm, and collected, but it was difficult not to feel intimidated. I found myself very capable of externally dealing with the problems rightly, but it agitated me so much internally that I was distracted from my duties. In this situation "the power of positive thinking" approach would have me say to myself, "I might feel distracted and preoccupied, but this doesn't have to interfere with my work. I should just carry on despite my agitation."

This approach often works in functional terms, when we are presented with an immediate duty or task to perform. If we focus on the task, we can concentrate, plow through it, and complete it. However, this approach has a few drawbacks. The power of positive thinking does nothing to deal with the underlying agitation which is still present. It does not definitively deal with the difficulty and free me from it.

The psychologist Ellis points out that his approach—actively undermining the irrational idea and taking on a more rational thought pattern—is different from "the power of positive thinking." Ellis found in his clinical experience that simply repeating a positive thought to oneself ("I *can* do it!") in the hopes of being convinced often does not work. It is similar to putting a band-aid on a festering wound. In the long run, the festering wound must be painfully cleaned out. Only then does the band-aid do its job.

The weakness of the "power of positive thinking" approach is that it does nothing to undermine the irrational expectations or judgments. To do this, we must be in touch with these thoughts, experience the feelings they cause, and *simultaneously* be aware of what we are experiencing. In other words, we must realize the dynamic of what is going on according to the A-B-C-D process explained earlier. This enables us to actively undermine the irrational expectations by analyzing them and seeing if they are consistent with reality, with compassion, with love. Only after we have energetically shed the false mental attitude will we be able to put on a more positive rational mentality, far more successfully than we can with "the power of positive thinking."

The second approach to interior healing is that of "inner healing." This is a practice of recalling the earliest memory of painful or troublesome feelings and imagining it again with Jesus at your side. We will take the same example as above to illustrate this approach. A few weeks before the scheduled conference I was responsible for, someone in authority was upset and began yelling at me. I worked out all specific problems and tasks successfully, but I was left with a certain inner agitation which preoccupied me and distracted me from my other duties. The "inner healing" approach would have me focus on the feeling of agitation caused by someone in authority yelling at me. I would try to recall similar incidents in my life—an authority figure was upset with me and I felt agitated. I would go back as far as possible to find the earliest experience in my memory. Then I would vividly relive that experience, but this time with Jesus present at my side, conscious of my security in him. The "inner healing" will be completed when I can recall that early experience without experiencing any agitation. The expectation is that this healing of the past will free me from the present agitation.

In my experience, "inner healing" usually works well and powerfully. However, its effects do not always persist for some people. It seems to have little effect for some. For others, it works well initially but the effects do not "stick." Our repeated prayers for these people are only occasionally successful. However, "inner healing" has proven to be a powerful tool.

We can gain some insight into the reasons for the weakness of inner healing by contrasting it with the A-B-C-D schema. Ellis' rational-emotive psychotherapy differs greatly from orthodox Freudian psychotherapy in its view of the immediate source of emotional problems. Ellis and his school pinpoint the present thought pattern as the source of trouble. The Freudian seeks the source in past childhood experience which initiated the thought pattern. While Ellis would agree that the source is frequently an experience in early childhood, he would not focus on it as something of immense interest or value. Rather, Ellis focuses on our *response* to the childhood experience. This is usually the formation of a self-sabotaging thought pattern ("I can't be responsible;" "I'm worthless;" "This is terrible;" etc.) which now has a life of its own apart from the childhood experience. This present thought pattern is now directly maintaining the emotional disturbance. Childhood experiences are only indirectly its source.

Thus, Ellis feels that awareness of the initiating source in childhood experience—whether described in Freudian terms or as "inner healing"—is of limited value. One could be aware of the source and still be subject to emotional problems caused by strong self-sabotaging thought patterns. These now have a life of their own independent of the childhood experiences, although these experiences may have originally catalyzed the patterns. Hence, Ellis' therapy is to actively undermine the present self-sabotaging thought patterns which are maintaining the emotional disturbance, not to root out the original, initiating experiences which are no longer the root of the problem. Ellis does see a value in a person, at times, understanding how the self-sabotaging thought patterns were formed in order to effectively undermine them, but he does not consider this absolutely essential to undermining them. He believes that returning to and understanding such childhood experiences helps people because the present thought patterns are undermined as a side effect of the process. However, he feels that the thought patterns can be undermined more effectively by directly attacking them.

From this we can draw a few insights into "inner healing." We are presuming here that the Holy Spirit is working through these dynamics. At least a good part of the success of inner healing comes from indirectly undermining the present thought pattern as we apply our imagination to the past. Inner healing should work when the present thought pattern is similar to the initial one in the earliest experience. For those who are symbolically and imaginatively responsive, inner healing may work better than Ellis' more analytic approach. Yet when the present destructive thought pattern is distinctly different than the earliest memory, even though the consequent feelings are the same, "inner healing" either won't work or won't "stick." In the example, my early experience might be of my father yelling at me, feeling agitated, and thinking how terrible it is not to be loved. The present experience is an authority figure yelling at me, feeling agitated, and thinking that this is terrible, that all our planning is being threatened. Even though the feelings are similar, if the thought patterns are different, then "inner healing" may prove to be a temporary relief or none at all. It will be limited to soothing our feelings for a while without dealing with the relevant thought pattern in the process.

For those who are not symbolically and imaginatively responsive, "inner healing" may not be a useful approach in general. For those cases in which the present and past thought patterns are distinct, even though the consequent feelings and circumstances are similar, "inner healing" may be ineffective. For those with enough experience, it may simply be a matter of being familiar enough with the relevant thought patterns that are the source of difficulties so that we are not sidetracked by a memory with similar feelings but a different, real problem.

The third approach to interior healing is "healing of thought patterns." We have seen this in Ellis and in the parallel in traditional spirituality of a transformed mind. We will recall Ellis' approach by quoting from *Christotherapy* by Fr. Bernard Tyrell, S.J.:

> From a purely secular perspective, Dr. Albert Ellis, in his rational-emotive psychotherapy, agrees with the religious thinkers on the importance of mental transformation in the healing process. The key insight in Ellis' therapy is that a person's emotional states are largely dependent on his thinking, and that emotional disturbances arise when individuals either consciously or unconsciously reiterate to themselves negative, unrealistic, illogical, self-defeating thoughts . . . (A person must come) to an understanding of the irrationality of ideas such as these that he may be reiterating to himself, so that he can be helped to dislodge these ideas from his consciousness and affirm internally more positive, rational ideas about life. In this way, emotional disturbances may be healed.[115]

Traditional spirituality, which focuses on our need to be freed from our illusions (irrational ideas), finds its scriptural roots in Paul's words to the Corinthians, "we likewise bring every thought into captivity to make it obedient to Christ (2 Cor 10:5), and to the Romans, "be transformed by the renewal of your mind, so that you may judge what is God's will, what is good, pleasing and perfect" (Rom 12:2).

Here again let us take the same example of the conference. Someone in authority is upset, yelling at me. I am feeling agitated and distracted. The "healing of thought patterns" approach would have me get in touch with the hidden thoughts I am saying to myself (B-level), the thoughts which are causing the agitations. These irrational ideas might include, "how horrible if this messes up the conference;" "there must be something wrong with me for him to get upset." I can begin to undermine these thoughts by acknowledging their irrationality. "It doesn't seem too likely that this can mess up the conference at all. At most, this will be nothing more than a big inconvenience." Or, "this man's upset is pretty clearly a sign of his own emotional state, not an indication of something being wrong with me—even though he would like me to think so." As I undermine the irrational ideas and affirm the truth, I find myself freed from the underlying agitation and distraction.

Our own experience with this approach is that it is simple and works amazingly well for many people. Some may have trouble grasping the process. Their obstacle seems to be unfamiliarity with the analytical approach required. "Inner healing" might be more valuable for them. We also find that when a major irrational thought pattern is being uncovered, the person needs help from others to overcome his resistance, to see the irrationality of the beliefs, and to be reminded later as he begins to forget the truth.

Of these three approaches to interior healing, "inner healing" and the "healing of thought patterns" seem to be the most effective and seem to do similar things in different ways. "Healing of thought patterns" may be more theoretically direct, and "inner healing" more indirect. Nevertheless, the best approach depends on the person.[116] Certainly the two approaches to healing can be used in a complementary way to fill each other's weaknesses.

CHAPTER 9

# JUDGMENTS: THEOLOGICAL INSIGHTS

The narrow path we journey along in our struggle for proper expectations and judgments in relationships has been traveled many times before. As we have seen, scripture has a wealth of wisdom on thought patterns, on expectations, and on judgments of others. Different sources of Christian tradition—the Desert Fathers, St. Thomas Aquinas, and official Church decisions—have clarified our reflections on scripture. Here in Part Three, we have turned to some modern sources that can give us added insight for our journey. We have explored some modern psychological insights about the transformed mind, notably Ellis' rational-emotive psychology. Our reflection on these insights in the light of scripture and tradition has yielded much practical wisdom about the transformed mind—the basis of good personal relationships. This chapter will explore some modern theological insights on judgments. We will ground these insights about a transformed mind in modern epistemology, primarily by considering some aspects of Bernard Lonergan's work.

Father Bernard J. F. Lonergan, a Canadian Jesuit, is a leading proponent of Transcendental Thomism, one of the strongest modern theological movements in the Roman Catholic Church.[117] Born in 1904, his work in philosophy and method in theology has won him the respect of secular as well as religious scholars. His work focuses on the question of "knowing." What does it mean to "know?" How do we "know" what we "know?" This is a crucial question in our discussion of relationships. For example, how do we "know" that our brother or sister has a fault that needs to be pointed out? This may appear to be obvious. But by studying the process of coming to know we can learn much. Lonergan's investigation of this process provides a means of carefully understanding the dynamics of our thinking and judging, the ways they can be distorted, and the means of correcting these distortions.

Lonergan's work is not aimed at establishing abstract principles, but at helping the reader understand what is going on in the reader's own thinking as he reads Lonergan's explanation of the process of coming to know. In the words of Langdon Gilkey, the Protestant theologian of the University of Chicago, "Lonergan is one of the greatest minds of Christendom. I used to read Jacques Maritain or Etienne Gilson to find out what Roman Catholic intellectuals were thinking. Now I read Father Lonergan to find out what *I* am thinking."[118]

In this chapter we want to consider a few aspects of Lonergan's work that are relevant to our questions about judgments and fraternal correction. First, if the process of coming to know is not obvious, then what does it consist of and how can we tell if it is off? Second, how does sin distort our judgments and how can we correct this? Third, how do we form ourselves by the very judgments we make and by our faithfulness to following through on their implications? In conclusion we will consider what implications these insights have for guidelines for making judgments. This topic will be developed further in Chapter Ten.

## *The Process of Coming to Know*

We seldom think about what it means to come to know something, just as we seldom think about how we walk. We think and come to know continually, habitually. We presume that the process of coming to know something is obvious: We look at something and then we know it. However, there is considerable value in carefully understanding the process of coming to know. The question is of theoretical interest, but there is also a very significant practical value in it. Namely, if there is something distorted or erroneous about the way we come to know, then our judgments about others will be distorted or erroneous. If we want to judge correctly, then we must carefully understand the true process of coming to know. When we achieve this understanding we will be able to make any necessary corrections.

To use an analogy, we would not hesitate to correct the way we walk if our gait was causing us to have sore feet. If necessary, we would carefully analyze the way we walk. In the same way, we would correct our way of coming to know if we were making poor judgments in relationships—rash judgments, unfair judgments, false judgments. This is the purpose of this chapter.

Coming to know something is a process, a pattern of operations. It begins with our experiences, continues to our understanding of our experiences, and concludes with our decision to live in accord with what we now know. In Lonergan's words, "Operations in the pattern are seeing, hearing, touching, smelling, tasting, inquiring, imagining, understanding, conceiving, formulating, reflecting, marshalling and weighing the evidence, judging, deliberating, evaluating, deciding, speaking, writing."[119] In Lonergan's schema, judgment occurs in the midst of a process. We must consider judgment in the context of what goes on before it and after it in the process of coming to know.

Let us outline Lonergan's four-fold process of how we come to know:

1. *The level of experiencing.* We have a spontaneous urge to be attentive to things. We experience data either from our senses or our consciousness. Some people are more sensitive than others and so perceive data that others are blind to.
2. *The level of understanding.* We have a spontaneous urge to ask "What is it?" concerning the data perceived. The answer, if it comes at all, is an insight which "comes as a release to the tension of inquiry ... suddenly and unexpectedly."[120] Some are more intelligent than others and to them insights come more frequently and more quickly. The insight is formulated in concepts so that we can communicate our understanding to others.
3. *The level of judgment.* Once we understand something, we have a spontaneous urge to ask "Is it so?" This is

judgment. Judging is answering "yes" or "no" to the question of whether my understanding is correct. As we reflect on our understanding, we realize that it is true if certain conditions are fulfilled. We raise further questions to see whether those conditions are in fact fulfilled. As new answers lead to still further questions, we become aware of the "law of diminishing returns," concluding at some point that there are no further relevant questions. Some people are more reasonable than others and can more easily make the right judgments which others find difficult because of rashness or indecision.

4. *The level of responsibility.* Once we make a judgment, we have a spontaneous urge to ask "What does this mean for me?" We need to evaluate the implications of living in accord with our judgments that our understanding of something is correct. Our decision to live out the implications of our judgments affects our whole being. Those who are more responsible can more consistently opt to live out the implications of their judgments even at great personal expense.

Let us see how Lonergan's four-fold process of coming to know applies to a practical example in our relationships and fraternal correction. Consider a prayer meeting where people come together to pray weekly. A good number of people are committed to coming regularly. Mike, a mature Christian, is the prayer group leader. Tony, a new member of the group, is a very gifted person who is a natural leader, though he is not yet familiar with the ways the Holy Spirit works at prayer meetings. After the first few meetings, Tony begins to prophesy regularly. The prophecies contain nothing questionable doctrinally, yet Mike senses that Tony's utterances are not prophecies. He thinks that they are merely good ideas phrased in prophetic first-person language. Let us use Lonergan's four-fold development to analyze Mike's process of coming to know.

First, there is the level of experience. Mike, through his senses, experiences Tony's prophecies, other people's reaction to them, and their overall effect on the prayer meeting. Good as the content of the prophecies are, Mike notices that they are not consistent with the direction of the Lord's word at the prayer meeting. People at the prayer meeting seem more distracted by the prophecies than helped by them. Mike is conscious of an inner disturbance whenever Tony prophesies.

Second, there is the level of understanding. After considering the situation for a few weeks, Mike has an insight into what is going on: Tony wants to contribute to the prayer meeting and be accepted by people. Being a gifted individual, Tony has recognized that others value prophecy highly and that those who prophesy are well accepted. Since Tony has many good thoughts and doesn't know that much about prophecy, he mistakes his thoughts for prophecy and shares them as such.

Third, there is the level of judgment. Mike reflects and weighs the evidence. He has come to *an* understanding. Now he needs to make a judgment as to whether it is *the right* understanding. He checks with a few other members of the prayer group's core team and they confirm that the prophecies seem off somehow, and that they seem to distract people at the prayer meeting. Mike comes to the judgment that his initial insight into what's going on with Tony is the right understanding.

Fourth, there is the level of responsibility. Once Mike has made the judgment that he has the correct understanding of what is going on with Tony, he experiences the need to live out the implications of his judgment. Mike realizes he has to make a decision. He can do nothing. Or he can attack Tony by gossip, negative humor, slander, harsh criticism, etc. Or he can open himself to Tony by going directly to him with a vulnerable and compassionate posture to talk with him about what is going on. Mike opts for this approach. He has some anxiety in anticipation of talking to Tony, but their talk bears good fruit. It corrects the non-prophecies, and also draws Tony into the core group of the prayer meeting.

It is often difficult to tell when a person's process of coming to know is distorted. Applying Lonergan's four-fold analysis of the process to a practical example can help us realize the source of some of the common problems that we encounter in ourselves and others.

The first level of experience needs to be given the proper attention. We need to experience the data, let it penetrate, and seek an insight *into* the data. Prejudice works in the opposite direction. The insight comes first. Then we seek the data which fits the insight. For example, if Mike had a tendency to always see people trying to steal his leadership, he could be prejudiced against Tony's behavior, and simply ignore data, such as Tony's evident sincerity, that indicate otherwise. A prejudiced Mike might then warn Tony about the need to curb his pride and be more submissive. This would probably do Tony more harm than good and push him out of the prayer group. In other words, we need to be sure that our prejudices do not blind us to the data.

Sometimes we are insensitive to the data because we fear the tensions that are part of coming to an understanding of the process. Before receiving an insight into our experience, we are often in an ambiguous area where data is confusing. If we demand instant clarity, we are bypassing an essential part of the process of coming to know. The result will be a pattern of poor judgments.

Another common problem is entirely skipping the third level—judging whether our understanding is correct. As we mull over experience and suddenly receive an insight that gives us an understanding of it, we often forget to check if it's the correct one. Just because an understanding helps us to make some sense out of our experience does not mean that it is necessarily the correct understanding or that there are no other understandings. We need to double-check and evaluate the understandings we come to no matter how good they seem. In other words, we need to judge.

In Lonergan's schema, we complete the process of coming to know by living out the implications that our judgment is correct. This is, perhaps, the level of the most widespread problems and failures. If, for example, we judge that our brother has a fault that needs to be pointed out, we need to point it out. We also need to point it out correctly—with a vulnerable and compassionate posture. At first, acting on our judgments may not seem to be integral to the process of coming to know. Yet if we do not want to live out the implications of a good judgment, we will resist everything necessary on all the previous levels to arrive at it. If Mike never really intends to confront Tony in love, but rather intends to complain, he will be insensitive to data, prejudiced for a particular insight, and distorted in his judgment. In the end, he will be able to self-righteously avoid confronting Tony in love.

These are a few of the common problems that need to be corrected in our own process of coming to know. We will expand on them both in this chapter and the next. First, though, it is helpful to identify the source of bias in the process of coming to know. This source is sin.

## *Sin Distorting Our Judgments*

As beings made in the image and likeness of God, we have a natural desire to know and a natural capability to come to know correctly. However, our natural bent is distorted by sin, original sin and the sin of the world. Because we have sinned, our desire to know is not pure and our capability to know is damaged. The depth of our resistance to God is so shocking that those occasional graced moments when we fully experience our resistance in the light of God's love can transform our lives. Sin distorts our judgments by distorting something in our process of coming to know.

For example, in making a judgment about whether our understanding is correct, a critical moment arises when there are no more relevant questions to ask. We have looked at all the data, considered the different ways of understanding it, and answered the different questions that have been raised. This is the moment for judgment, the point where we say "yes" or "no" to our understanding. But sin exists and within our hearts is an impurity. Have we truly asked all relevant questions? Is our desire to know the truth being stifled by other interests, such as our eagerness to satisfy other drives like resentment, envy, or wanting to be in control? Drives such as these can prevent the really relevant questions from even emerging in our minds. We often make a judgment without even looking at the most significant questions that would change the whole picture. The source of the problem is sin, the hardness of heart that refuses to be totally open to God.

Sin's effect is self-deception. Genesis tells us that sin finds its root in our refusal to be utterly dependent on God, and it leads us to be committed to the illusion that we do not need God. Instead of starting with our experience of life and coming to the correct understanding that we utterly depend on God, we start with a biased judgment that we can live in some way without God and then cumulatively misinterpret our experience to fit our illusion.

Spiritual reality and spiritual fantasy have a psychological effect. A person may be living a spiritual illusion so intensely that he requires psychological help as he becomes trapped in cumulatively misinterpreted experience. His psychological trouble is precisely his committed and unconscious flight from insight. His psychic recovery depends on insight into the correct interpretation of the misinterpreted experience.[121] With this understanding of how sin distorts the process of coming to know, Lonergan grounds different psychological approaches in epistemology: "It makes no difference whether the patient be led to the insight by an active method or left to discover it for himself by a passive method."[122] Hence active methods such as Albert Ellis' and passive ones such as Freud's all serve to correct the process of coming to know, even though this may not be the way that the psychologists themselves perceive their purpose. Either directly or indirectly they bring to consciousness the misinterpretation of experience that bolsters such irrational ideas as "I absolutely *must* have something my way." These therapeutic methods have an insight into the correct interpretation of the experience: not having it my way is merely unfortunate, not terrible. They can help us to follow through when we achieve the insight that we are caught in a whole pattern of misinterpretation. In spiritual language, this insight is freedom from living an illusion.

Let us return to the example of the previous section and see where sin might distort Mike's judgment of Tony. Mike is the prayer meeting leader and Tony, though a new person, is a natural leader. Anyone in a position of honor and respect, such as the leader of a prayer meeting, must guard against the temptation to place a certain kind of security in the position instead of in God alone. Let us imagine that this has subtly happened to Mike. He has begun to cherish his position as leader in a way he is not even in touch with.

This disorder of Mike's, unconscious though it is, creates an unconscious desire to remain in control and to protect his "power" by putting down those who might "take over." Since

Tony is a gifted natural leader, he is a threat to Mike. So far all of this is not at all in Mike's conscious thoughts. What Mike consciously experiences is a disturbance within himself whenever Tony prophesies. Now comes the crucial question: Is Mike's discomfort really discernment that Tony is giving non-prophecies, or is it a disorder that wants to stay in control and get rid of a threat? Or is it both?

This very relevant question was not even asked by Mike! If we have experienced the depth of sinfulness in our own hearts, then we know the relevance of this question. Does this question propose too much disorder on Mike's part? What if the other core leaders and members of the prayer group agree? We have only to recall who stoned the prophets: not only the king and high priest, but also the council of elders and the entire assembly of Israel. They accused the prophets of uttering false prophecies. Instead of being lovingly related to, they were murdered.

Thus we see the importance of knowing the extent to which sin can distort judgment. If Mike knows this what can he do? Here we will zero in on the third level of knowing—his judgment that his understanding of his experience is correct. Mike feels disturbed whenever Tony prophesies. His initial understanding is that Tony is giving non-prophecies. In the process of making a judgment about whether that is correct, Mike needs to consider other possibilities. Even though he is not in touch with his unconscious sinful desires, nevertheless he needs to realize that he is not completely free from those kinds of things. Mike needs to seriously ask whether his disturbance is caused by the fear of Tony taking over his position. He needs to consider this more than superficially. He needs to seriously reflect on and pray about it. We need to give the Spirit an opportunity to put us in touch with sin and the extent to which it affects our understanding. Once this area has come into the light, we can more confidently make the right judgment.

Finally, we should consider the fourth level—responsibility for living out the implications of our judgments. If sin has pervaded the first three levels, it sometimes becomes most obvious in this fourth level of our action, especially in our posture as we act. In Mike's case, for example, if sin has pervaded the first three levels, he will be strongly tempted to act wrongly on the fourth—to gossip, slander, harshly criticize, etc. But even if he takes the right action—to go to Tony directly and speak with him—he might do it in a posture that is hard, rigid, and condemning. Such a posture is an indication that sin is distorting our judgments without our even realizing it. This might mean that we need an inner healing which could free us to relate more lovingly. Or it could mean that we need to repent and let go of a disordered attachment. Only when sin is not the motivating source of our judgments is it possible to both do the right action and do it in a posture of vulnerability and compassion.

## *We Form Ourselves By Our Decisions*

Sin can distort our judgments in the process of coming to know. God's word about our problem is hard for us to hear: we sin and rebel against him. God's word about the solution is even harder for us to hear because we want to earn our salvation or deserve it: "My Son Jesus, he will save you!" We have been redeemed from sin and our judgments can reflect our redemption. While we cannot earn salvation, which is a free gift of God, we do need to cooperate with it. For our judgments to be free from distortion, we need to experience both aspects of salvation—God's free gift of grace, and our decision to cooperate with grace. In this section we will discuss how the mystery of grace and cooperating with grace operates in our judgments. Then, on the level of our responsibility, we will begin to discover how we form ourselves by our decisions.

On the level of our judgments, sin does not need to exercise power over us as long as we bring sin into the light and allow Jesus to deal with it. In the example we have been using, sin exercises power over Mike by distorting his judgment of Tony only when Mike presumes that such sinful thoughts and desires do not exist within him. This is a bad presumption because sinful desires always exist in our hearts to some extent, even if we are not aware of them. Freedom from the *existence* of sin only happens after we die and fully enter the kingdom. Yet such sinful desires shouldn't exercise any *power* over us if we are living in grace; that is, they don't need to be the motivating source or the foundational reason for our judgments or attitudes. One of the ways to insure that sin doesn't have power over us in a judgment is to bring into the light and clearly acknowledge the existence of sin within us which can affect a particular judgment. A protection for Mike, for example, would be to seriously ponder how sin might distort his judgment. Superficially dismissing the idea because we are not aware of sin affecting us is clearly unwise. Rather, we should strive to be in touch with the forces influencing us so we can make a clearer decision to cooperate with grace and yield to the Spirit.

After we have judged that our understanding is correct, we enter the level of responsibility and values. The question arises, "What does this mean for me?" This fourth level involves our decision of whether we will cooperate with grace by being committed to the truth that is known. If Mike knows Tony is giving non-prophecies then he needs to decide to go to him directly and share the truth in love. Whereas on the first three levels we are led from ignorance to truth, on the fourth level we make a decision about whether to go from selfishness to love. Knowing that Tony gives non-prophecies is a matter of the truth. Deciding to go to him directly about it in a posture of vulnerability and compassion is speaking the truth in love.

The kind of decisions we make form us. In the long run, they determine the kind of person we become. If selfishness and sin are allowed to dominate our decisions even semi-consciously, then more and more we become selfish and sinful persons. If love and God's will become the criteria of our decisions then increasingly we become loving, Spirit-filled persons. Our "external" decisions permeate our whole being and begin to shape and form who we are. If Mike continually decides in favor of gossip, slander, and harsh criticism, he not only acts wrongly but his personality gets shaped toward selfishness and sin. This trap, which St. Paul calls being slaves to sin, makes it harder to choose loving the next time. If Mike decides in favor of going to the person directly, then not only does the objectively right thing happen, but also Mike's personality gets shaped toward loving and the Spirit. This freedom, which St. Paul calls living in the Spirit instead of the flesh, makes it easier to choose loving the next time. The decisions we make make us!

When we make the right decision because we want to do the right things we are living by the law, not the Spirit. When we live according to the law we might be able to do the right things, but we won't necessarily be able to do them in a posture of vulnerability and compassion. When we live in the Spirit, which also has the effect of directing us to the right things, our posture is freed for vulnerability and compassion. Obeying the law is an inadequate solution to the danger of yielding to the flesh. The only adequate solution is yielding to the Spirit. Each time we decide to yield to the flesh, our posture and personality get shaped to selfishness and sin. Obeying the law only makes our approach rigid. Deciding to yield to the Spirit forms us into more loving, Spirit-filled persons as our postures become more vulnerable and compassionate.

Something happens within us when we realize the extent to which we form ourselves by our decisions. I realized this recently when I talked with Alice, a woman who is a regular member of a prayer group. Alice told me that for the first few years of association with the prayer group she would always find it very difficult to go to a person directly about a problem in their relationship. She did her best to avoid gossip and slander. Sometimes, with great anxiety, she would go and talk to a person. But usually she would just try to ignore what was going on. Then one day she began to see the effect this behavior was having on her. She was becoming a bitter person who couldn't be happy with anyone. She was becoming cold and rigid. And she saw that the reason was her decision not to go to people directly and work out unity in the relationships. Her decisions were forming her. When she realized this, something changed inside of her. The very thing that was so hard for her—going directly to people—was now something she was impelled to do. It still wasn't easy, but now she had the strength and motivation which continually overrode any reluctance. The very thing that was so easy for her before—trying to ignore what was happening—now became intolerable. She experienced a change in her values, in what she wanted to do. She became aware of the importance of her decisions in shaping her into a loving, Spirit-filled person, and this awareness allowed her to freely enter into a much deeper cooperation with grace. Alice had learned the meaning of personal responsibility. It changed her life.

Realizing the extent to which we form ourselves by our decisions is what Lonergan calls "the existential discovery." We begin to gain a capacity for it around the age of seven when the ability to make responsible decisions which can form us first begins to emerge in an elementary and inconsistent way. Yet it is usually many, many years until we fully learn what is involved in becoming a loving, Spirit-filled, vulnerable and compassionate person (in Lonergan's language: an authentic human person). To summarize this section in Lonergan's words:

> Finally, the development of knowledge and the development of moral feeling head to the existential discovery, the discovery of oneself as a moral being, the realization that one not only chooses between courses of action but also thereby makes oneself an authentic human being or an unauthentic one. With that discovery, there emerges in consciousness the significance of personal value and the meaning of personal responsibility. One's judgments of value are revealed as the door to one's fulfillment or to one's loss.[123]
>
> In fact, the emergence of the fourth level of deliberation, evaluation, choice is a slow process that occurs between the ages of three and six . . . the child gradually enters the world mediated by meaning and regulated by values and, by the age of seven years, is thought to have attained the use of reason. Still, this is only the beginning of human authenticity. One has to have passed well beyond the turmoil of puberty before becoming fully responsible in the eyes of the law. One has to have found out for oneself that one has to decide for oneself what one is to make of oneself; one has to have proved oneself equal to that moment of existential decision; and one has to have kept on proving it in all subsequent decisions, if one is to be an authentic human person.[124]

## *Guidelines for Making Judgments*

Lonergan's theological insights on judgments clarify the fourfold process of coming to know, show how sin distorts our judgments, and reveals how Christ redeems them. We have also seen how our judgments form us. All of this yields some very practical advice on determing whether there is bias, resulting in a pattern of poor judgments, in our process of coming to know. This advice can be formulated in six guidelines for making judgments. We will present these guidelines along with some questions to reflect on when we have a judgment to make. We will expand upon these guidelines in the next chapter.

The first four guidelines for making judgments are drawn from the four levels of the process of coming to know.

1. *Be sensitive.* Good judgments are based on our being in touch with the full spectrum of our experience. Is the judgment I am making rooted in the total experience or am I basing my judgments on hearsay, half-truths, and one side of the story?
2. *Be understanding.* Our experience and data are meaningless until we have an insight into them which gives us an understanding of what they mean. Am I free to receive the Spirit's insight into my experience or do I read my prejudiced understandings into the experience? Good judgments are based on a freedom to understand that isn't limited by our previous understandings.
3. *Be reasonable.* Our understanding is only one of many possible understandings until we make the judgment that it is the correct one. In reflecting on the adequacy of an understanding, do I give further questions a chance to arise regardless of where they might lead or am I threatened by some possiblities? Am I free from a rash or indecisive temperament that is always too sure or too hesitant? Am I able to compensate for my rashness or indecision? Good judgments are based on a realization that a good understanding isn't always the right one. Thus, much reflective double checking needs to be completed until we achieve the right understanding.
4. *Be responsible.* We must complete the journey from ignorance to truth on the first three levels living out the implications of our judgments and going from selfishness to love. Otherwise we will manage to distort the first three levels in

order to live peacefully with our selfishness on the fourth level. Also, we'll find that this boomerangs, for the decisions we make make us! Am I willing to fully follow through on the implications of the judgments I make even at great personal expense? Do I realize how this judgment will form me? Good judgments can be consistently made only when there is a personal responsibility which is committed to following through on their implications.

The last two guidelines guard against sin's distortion of our judgments and open us to the redemptive process of God's gift of his grace, particularly the love which sent his Son into the world.

5. *Become aware of and acknowledge the existence of sin.* We protect ourselves from hidden forces that would control us when we realize where we are insensitive, misunderstanding, unreasonable, and irresponsible, especially where we have a pattern of such response. Where am I most likely to misjudge my brother, in what circumstances, and why? Where do I need to be especially cautious when judging others? Good judgments presume that sinful tendencies are out in the light where they can be dealt with.
6. *Where sin abounds, grace abounds even more.* Jesus can redeem all of our sinfulness and mistaken judgments if we yield to the Spirit and open ourselves to unity with our brothers and sisters. Is the judgment I am making an attempt to live the law as a way of dealing with the flesh, instead of yielding to the Spirit? Good judgments need to be the fruit of yielding to the Spirit. Otherwise their tone and our posture become harsh and rigid.

CHAPTER TEN

# TRANSFORMATION IN OUR RELATIONSHIPS

We have reflected on scripture, tradition, and some modern sources. What does all this mean for judgments in our personal relationships? In this chapter we will consider the implications for our relationships by taking the specific example of relationships in a prayer group. What we will talk about can also be easily applied to our families, our religious communities, our friends, co-workers, and others.

Prayer groups have sprung up throughout the world in the last decade. Most have been formed in the environment of the charismatic renewal, a movement in the Church witnessing to the rediscovery of the power of the Holy Spirit in the daily life of a Christian.[125] As people experience this empowering of the Holy Spirit, there is not only an outpouring of charismatic gifts, but also a hunger for prayer, a desire to have their lives under the Lordship of Jesus, and an attraction to come together with others to share their life in the Lord. Frequently, people come together weekly to share an evening of prayer, and the relationships among them gradually deepen. As this prayer group develops, needs arise: How are new people to be introduced to this rediscovered life of the Spirit? Who will set up the chairs and organize a meeting now that many people are coming? What ought to be done about the person who is giving a disruptive half-hour sermon every week?

These needs usually lead to the formation of a core group of leaders who pastorally care for the group and come to the right judgments about key areas. At first these leaders might be in the background, but as time goes on the leaders are identified and are affirmed in one way or another. This core group then has to meet another time during the week to prepare for the prayer meeting and to make the necessary decisions to care for it. Often this core group meeting expands in purpose and the members share their lives together more intensely. Eventually, they may make a commitment to support one another's whole lives, not just the spiritual part of it. Occasionally this may evolve into community where people live together, but this is not generally the case.

It is in the context of this network of relationships in a prayer group that we want to apply the wisdom we have gained so far. What should our posture be for expectations and judgments in relationships?

First we will consider what it means to preserve the unity of the Spirit in our relationships and some practical helps to do that. Then we will see how being members of a body gives a context to our judgments. When we are aware of the context, we make better judgments and communicate them in a better way. Lastly, we will continue to develop guidelines for making judgments in our relationships which we touched on briefly at the end of Chapter Nine.

## *Preserving the Unity of the Spirit*

In writing to the Ephesians, St. Paul pleads, "make every effort to preserve the unity which has the Spirit as its origin and peace as its binding force" (Eph 4:3). This same plea can be applied to a local prayer group and its leaders. In this section we want to consider what it means to preserve the unity of the Spirit in our relationships.

The wording of Paul's plea in Ephesians is significant. Our role is to preserve unity, not create it. Only the Spirit can create unity and, in the midst of our sinfulness, make us one. Unity is not a matter of doing all the right things or learning all the techniques of communication in relationships. Unity, like physical healing, is a matter of the Spirit where we open ourselves and trust God to make us one, to make us whole. While we need to do everything we can to be open to and cooperate with the Spirit, unity does not depend on our effort. It depends on God's Spirit.

As we try to preserve unity in a relationship, we can have an experience of poverty where we come to realize that being one is beyond our efforts and capability. This is a time to actively trust in the Spirit and expect God's strength to be made manifest in the midst of our weakness. It is a time of grace where we come to know our need for God. Discouragement only comes when we think unity is up to us and our power. When we know it is up to God and his power, we can place our faith in him and be encouraged. In reflecting on practical ways to preserve unity, we must avoid falling into the trap of thinking that the test depends on us mastering the "how to's." Unity is pure grace.

The unity which is important to preserve is the unity of the Spirit, a unity of common love, openness, vulnerability, and compassion. It is also a unity of truth, vision, and doctrine that recognizes Jesus as Lord and submits to the proper understanding of Jesus as discerned by the Church which has been given his Spirit. While this unity is intense, it is not uniformity. Nor does it imply agreement on matters of strategy or those doctrines about which there can be an authentic pluralism.[126] Rather, the focus of the unity which has the Spirit as its origin is love (Eph 4:32) and the freedom to "profess the truth in love" (Eph 4:15).

When a prayer group or its leaders are not in unity, it rarely involves disputes about doctrine, such as rebaptism, the Virgin birth, etc. When this is the cause, the solution is easy enough—submission to the teaching of the Church, and perhaps some helpful study of how the Church came to that judgment and what she means by it.

The unity that is more difficult to work out in relationships involves a lack of love. It usually starts by a thought or temptation that can, if we give in to it, bring something between us and our brother or sister. Frequently it has to do with something trivial. These are some examples in a typical prayer group:

> A group of leaders meets to talk about beginning a Life in the Spirit Seminar. Louise strongly suggests that she should lead it and lists others who she feels ought to be on the team. While the conclusion might be right, the way she "pushes" the dis-

cussion leaves others feeling like they can have little to say about it. The thought or temptation comes to mind that Louise likes to be in charge of things and wants power.

We notice that Jim rarely sets up chairs or lends a hand when any kind of manual work needs to be done. Rather, he is usually talking intensely with someone else at the very moment when work needs to be done. The thought or temptation comes to mind that Jim is lazy and isn't willing to serve.

Marjorie comes to the prayer meetings regularly. Every week she shares at great length about the way God wants people to respond more. Her sharings tend to discourage and bore the prayer group rather than build it up. The thought or temptation comes to mind that Marjorie is a critical person who only wants to use the prayer group for her own needs.

Thoughts such as these have the potential to destroy unity in relationships if we give in to them wrongly. This can happen in two ways. We can try to ignore the thought or we can act on it unlovingly. Either approach will damage the bond of peace in our relationship. If we ignore the thought, we will be unsuccessful. The thought will remain, though hidden, and will gradually grow into a monster that divides our heart from the other person. We will begin to mistrust the other and be isolated from him. If we act on the thought unlovingly—yelling at the person, telling them they are no good, demanding that they stop, etc.—that will damage the bond of peace in an obvious way.

Both approaches destroy unity because in both courses of action we never come to a clear judgment as to whether the thought is the right understanding of what is going on. We can safely ignore the thought only when we have clearly come to see that the understanding is a wrong one. Even trying to correct a person won't work until both of us have come to the same understanding.

The right solution which guards peace, the binding force of unity in a relationship, could be to go directly to the person as quickly as possible and share with him or her the thought or temptation that has come into your mind. Only by dealing with it in love can unity be preserved. It means going to the person and saying something like this:

> "Louise, I know your suggestion about the Life in the Spirit team might be the right one, but I'm having a problem about the process. I've felt excluded and have the thought that you just like to be in charge of things and want power. Maybe it is just some miscommunication. Maybe I'm too sensitive about these things, or maybe I'm sensing something in you that the Lord wants to deal with. Could we talk about it to see what is going on?"

As we talk to people we can sort out misunderstandings from real difficulties that need to be dealt with. No one is perfect, and so we all need one another's support. While it is important for us to bring things out into the light like this, we can't force something down people's throats. If a person resists what we are saying, we still need to say what is on our mind but then drop it, encourage them to pray about it, and leave the rest up to the Holy Spirit. Sometimes we must forbear. We must remember that while is it easy for the Holy Spirit to convict someone, we often wind up condemning them.

For example, if we talk to Jim about our feelings when he never lends a hand in setting up the chairs, he may reply that he sees no problem but feels that talking to other people and ministering to them is more important. Instead of trying to convince him there is a problem with it we could say something like this:

> "Jim, I don't want to argue about whether you're right or wrong, I just want to bring to light what I'm sensing. I think it's important to lend a hand when the chairs have to be set up, but maybe I'm wrong. Why don't we take the situation to prayer and each ask the Lord about it this coming week. Then we can get together next week and try to see what common understanding the Lord wants us to have. It's so important to be one and love one another in the process, not just get the right answer."

It is important to share with people in this way, not only to support one another in correcting what might be off, but also to preserve our unity in the bond of peace. Thoughts or temptations will distance us from others unless they are dealt with correctly. A focus on our unity together makes judgments in relationships much more open to a vulnerable and compassionate posture. A goal of correcting the other will make us prey to rigidity and hardness.

When we don't deal with a temptation right away, it gives evil a foothold in the bond of peace and undermines unity. The next time something similar happens, the thought or temptation comes more strongly and quickly. The tendancy to handle it wrongly becomes stronger. Each time it gets worse. An animosity and hostility grows in the relationship like a cancer. Instead of being one as Jesus and the Father are one, a unity which would witness to the world (Jn 17:21), the prayer group becomes a witness to the ineffectiveness of watered-down Christianity.

John mentions in his first letter (1 Jn 1:5f) that God is light and in him there is no darkness at all. To have fellowship with him we must live in the light, being honest, open and trusting. When we live in the light, we have fellowship with one another and are gradually purified from sin and temptations against one another. The Trinity is an example of community life with nothing hidden in the darkness by any of the three Persons. And so they are one, with their unity having great power. We are called to experience that same unity in them (Jn 17:21).

Personal relationships must be lived in the light where we can share with one another our thoughts about one another. Unless we are able to regularly talk about our emotions, our temptations, and any tensions in a relationship, they are in the dark and darkness gradually overcomes us. We need to exert ourselves to name and share what we are conscious of. When we fail to do this, we slip away from living in the light. Once the thought is in the darkness, even though we are dimly conscious of it, it grows into a monster that is not able to be checked.

A classic case of a thought growing to destructive evil is described in Tolstoy's novel, *Anna Karenina.* For only a moment Anna experiences a fleeting but exciting attraction to another man during a trip. After arriving home she considers whether to tell her husband about it but she rationalizes and decides this would be unnecessary. But evil has a foothold in Anna's mind. Her first choice not to live in the light borders on the trivial—it was a fleeting experience, nothing objectively "happened," so what could it matter? But given this foothold in the darkness, a monster eventually emerges and the outcome a hundred steps later is adultery and disaster. The plot is too complicated to outline, but the relevant aspects are easy to imagine—the uneasy conscience about the trivial attraction which, hidden in the dark, makes the conscience less sensitive. Not having shared the first movement with her husband, Anna experiences a growing distance from her husband and becomes aware of all his faults. Her judgments against him become biased and she passes from an innocent insensitivity to spiritual adultery to adultery. The conscience tolerates the hundred steps to adultery one-by-one because the prior ones never came into the light.

Certainly relationships in a prayer group cannot have the same intensity as the relationship in marriage. Yet the implications for our relationships are clear: for unity to be maintained, every tension must come into the light.

Anger, resentment, frustration, depression, fear, lust, jealousy, and greed all disturb the bond of peace in much the same way, different as these feelings may be. Some act quickly; and some disorder our relationships only after time. First, the temptation is appealing because of an inner vacuum in our emotional tone. This is why it is important for us to know ourselves, to know the bad side of our gifts and the situations where we can easily go wrong. Second, a passing trivial thought gains a foothold if it remains in the dark. Our conscience becomes less sensitive. Third, in a step-by-step process we come to a biased judgment in the heart (what Aquinas calls basing a judgment on suspicion and condemning another) which sooner or later is manifested in action (see Mk 7:21, 22). By being aware of this pattern, we can recognize it in ourselves and stop it by bringing it into the light.

## *Practical Helps to Preserve Unity*

When negative thoughts are hidden inside, evil has a foothold that can gradually divide and conquer us. The evil one frequently uses the foothold like a trump card which he plays at a later critical moment. It is important for the whole context of our daily life—our emotional tone, the ways we experience the Spirit, our temptations—to be lived in the light. Being in touch with ourselves in this way and sharing appropriately with others is a great protection against the foothold the evil one would like to get.

This does not always mean sharing everything we feel in a large group or even with a few friends. Many people are greatly helped to live in the light by careful use of the traditional examin, a journal, or by days of prayer and retreats.[127] Yet most people also need the help of regularly sharing with another. This might mean spiritual direction or counseling or simply regularly sharing with a mature friend. Another help is small group sharing and witnessing to the entire prayer group about what God has been doing in our lives. Appropriately and wisely used, all these channels protect us by keeping us in touch with ourselves.

While this kind of protection is valuable, it does not eliminate the need to go to a person directly when there is a tension. The question frequently comes down to this: If I am having a problem with someone, do I have to go to that person directly to share with them about it? Are there other alternatives, other practical helps to preserve unity?

Our experience is that there is a whole variety of alternatives depending on the situation. We need to make a key distinction about different kinds of problems to determine which approach we should take to preserve unity. Understanding this distinction and applying it to our lives gives us much insight into what the practical helps are to preserve unity.

The distinction is this. When we have difficulty with another person, is it a matter of another person doing something wrong? Or is it a matter of the person doing the right thing badly? Or is it a matter of the person doing the right thing well, but catalyzing negative feelings on our part which we have to cope with anyway? Depending on our answer—wrongdoing, a flawed performance, or our own reaction—we preserve unity in different ways.

It is usually easy to tell when people are clearly doing something wrong, such as teaching a false doctrine, relating in hatred and bitterness, not fulfilling a specific commitment, or not leading a moral life. In such cases, we need to go to the person directly and immediately and point it out to him. We shouldn't blame or condemn. We don't know how conscious they are that their action is wrong or even how aware they are of doing it. Even if it is obvious to us, it may not be to them. There may be many extenuating circumstances—which does not make the matter less wrong, but does lessen people's guilt. Yet people need to take the responsibility for righting what they have done wrong regardless of extenuating circumstances. Thus we need to speak directly to people about their wrongdoing and we need to do it in love free from condemnation. This is fraternal correction in the strict sense of the word. If a person doesn't listen to us, then we need to take the advice of Mt 18:15-17 and ask another, perhaps the leader of the prayer group, to come with us to share with the person. If that fails, we need to go to the pastor of the congregation or parish. The basic solution to such wrongdoing is admitting it, repenting, asking forgiveness, and repairing whatever damage we can.

Sometimes a brother or sister is not doing something wrong, but is doing something poorly or at least not in the best possible way. Marjorie, who regularly dominates the prayer meetings with lengthy exhortations, is probably in this category. She is not doing something wrong as much as she is doing something poorly. She may be doing the right thing in exhorting people to respond to God, but is doing it in a way that makes people less likely to respond to her words. If this is the case, she needs help to do what she is already doing in a more constructive way. This might also be true of Louise who dominates discussion of forming the Life in the Spirit Seminar team. Perhaps it is merely a matter of insensitivity and miscommunication, not pride that needs repentance. If a person is doing something poorly, it is important to help the person grow and be aware of how to do it better. Usually this approach improves the external situation—Marjorie's exhortations at prayer meetings are likely to improve—and also helps the personal growth of the person and their relationships.

In these situations the person who is aware of another doing poorly is the best one to talk with him about it. Since the point of talking with another is to help him to understand how to do something better, a person who is gifted with this kind of practical wisdom is often the one who should speak with them. If we do not have such gifts, perhaps we need to point the problems out to the prayer group leader or someone who has the gifts to support the person. Yet if we experience a division in our hearts against the person, we may need to also personally share with him to insure that there are no footholds of disunity in our relationship.

In this situation there are a couple of practical helps to preserve unity. Repentance isn't exactly what is called for when we approach someone who has done something poorly. If we ask such a person to repent as if he had done something wrong, then tension will grow in the relationship. We will insist and the other person will feel condemned and confused. For example, Louise may need help in being more sensitive and communicating better, but this is part of the unending process of personal growth, not repentance from wrongdoing. What Louise should do is to talk to those affected by her in order to work out any damaged relationships and to invite others in to support her more in sensitivity and communication.

After someone has talked with a person to help him be able to do better the right thing he is already doing, it might be useful for us to tell him frankly how he came across and how he affected us. We can usually tell when this is a helpful thing to do by seeing whether or not there is a residue of negative thoughts that divide us from the person. If there is, we need to see that they get dealt with. If talking to a third person doesn't do it, then we probably need to speak to the person directly.

The final distinction about different kinds of problems we have with people is coping with our own negative feelings about someone who is doing the right thing well. Here, the *last* step is to speak with the person directly. Take the example of Jim who rarely sets up chairs because he is usually occupied in talking and ministering to people. It could be that listening and counseling is the way Jim is called to serve. Perhaps Jim does not deliberately avoid manual work but is simply always called to counsel people when it is time to take down chairs. If this is the case, then Jim is doing the right thing and doing it well enough, and it is a matter of us coping with our own problem.

The problem is in us, not in the objective situation. Maybe we need to write down what is going on in a journal so we can get a perspective on our feelings. Do we think that service equals hard, manual work? Do we resent the work we are doing? Do we resent Jim? It might be useful to talk this over with a third party—that is, talking over *our* problem, not Jim's. Some kind of inner healing or healing of our thoughts may be called for. Some of these ways of dealing with our feelings ought to work. Only as a final step is it usually good to share with Jim, making clear the problem is ours, not his, and asking him to share about his experience so we can get a better feel for being in his shoes.

The distinction we need to make when there is disunity and division between ourselves and others is to determine what is going on. Is the person doing something wrong? Or is the person doing the right thing poorly? Or is the person both doing the right thing and doing it well enough, yet we have negative feelings to cope with anyway? Knowing what is going on helps to guide us in the practical steps to preserving unity.

Disunity begins with feelings and thoughts that create a difficulty between ourselves and another. The key question is this: Am I in touch with my feelings and thoughts, and do I understand them enough to draw the right conclusion about what is going on?

When, for example, I see Louise wanting to lead the Life in the Spirit Seminars and "bulldozing" the decision through, I might feel angry, unneeded, passed over, etc. However, there might be nothing externally wrong in what happened. Louise may have spoken strongly and lovingly about what she felt should happen, no one else said much, and the decision was made. Yet if I experience disunity in my feelings and thoughts, it has to be dealt with. The way of dealing with it is different depending upon what is going on. How do I decide if it is wrongdoing, need for growth, or my own problem? Does Louise have power ambitions and need to repent of basing her actions on pride? Or is Louise doing the right thing but doing it insensitively? Or is what Louise did fine, and the problem is my oversensitivity, my failure to speak out even though there was adequate freedom, or whatever?

It is often difficult to sort through the answer to these questions. First of all we need to be in touch with our feelings and be able to face the facts of what they are and where they are coming from. We should know how to discern our feelings (see pp. 154-162). If our feelings are intense, it may be hard to see what is going on. Then we should usually talk things out with an impartial third party who can help us get some perspective on our feelings.

The easiest way to see the answers to these questions is by a regular habit of sharing and keeping in touch with ourselves. This protects us. If we keep aware of our strengths and weaknesses this way, we will be better able to see how our feelings of the present moment fit into the broader pattern of our lives. Perhaps our problem is pride and we know we have a tendency to project this weakness onto others' actions. Perhaps we are very oriented to getting things done and easily overlook the importance of good communications with people in the process. Perhaps we are very sensitive and mistakenly read a lack of support into others' actions. If we know the shape of our life, our strengths and our weaknesses, it will be easier to interpret our feelings and thoughts of disunity as indicating wrongdoing, need for growth, or our own problem.

As we try to preserve unity in a relationship with someone, the crucial part is loving them in the process of working it out. We must let go of all resentment, bitterness, rigidity, and desire to dump our feelings—by making a decision to love. We must avoid cooperating with evil which wants to gain every foothold. If we hold something against our brother or sister, it has a hold on us. Loving means forgiving, being vulnerable and compassionate in the process, being concerned first about our brother or sister and how to support him or her. Loving not only sets the goal of where to go, but also directs the process on the way there. Love must be Spirit-empowered and filled.

> Love is patient; love is kind. Love is not jealous, it does not put on airs, it is not snobbish. Love is never rude, it is not self-seeking, it is not prone to anger; neither does it brood over injuries. Love does not rejoice in what is wrong but rejoices with the truth. There is no limit to love's forbearance, to its truth, its hope, its power to endure (1 Cor 13:4-7).

We can't love like this on our own power. But if we make a decision to love, and to trust in God, he can fill our decision with his Spirit, with power to love as he does. Only then is it possible to preserve the unity of the Spirit in the bond of peace.

## *Members of a Body*

We have been considering how to preserve the unity of the Spirit in the context of the network of relationships in a prayer group. While there are many practical helps to preserving unity, the basis is a loving posture for expectations and judgments in relationships. The right mental perspective, which realizes that we are members of a body, frees us from many misguided expectations and judgments.

St. Paul told the Corinthians, "I do not want to leave you in ignorance about spiritual gifts" (1 Cor 12:1). He explained that "there are different gifts but the same Spirit" (1 Cor 12:4) and used the analogy of the body: "The body is one and has many members, but all the members, many though they are, are one body; and so it is with Christ" (1 Cor 12:12). In practical terms, how does the realization that we are members of a body shape and affect our expectations and judgments?

Some people in a prayer group or community will have a special grace to deeply know what it means to be a body. They will be caught up in the vision and purpose of being together as part of the body of Christ to praise and worship God and be his presence to others. This is a gift of leadership or authority. Those who have this gift have a role of service in keeping the common vision and purpose clear, central, and evolving to a greater depth. When we understand this, we are freed from many misguided expectations and mistaken judgments.

For example, consider the job of setting up a book ministry for the prayer group. There are many things that will need to be done: investigating supplies, selecting stock, organizing a staff, deciding what books to recommend at prayer meetings and how to do that, etc. Different people will have different gifts to do these jobs effectively. Yet things will go amuck unless all the gifts work together in unison under the gift of leadership or authority.

The point about the role of authority and leadership is not simply the practical job of working together in unison. Practical communications and coordination is important for the book ministry. Otherwise someone might order books that are not pastorally sound while another might recommend books that are not even in stock. Yet there is a deeper need for the members of a body to work together in unison. It is the need to continually keep in mind that the purpose of setting up a book ministry—or any other common enterprise—is to respond to Jesus more fully, to understand more deeply how to live a life in the Spirit, and to receive more support in being brothers and sisters.

The point might seem trite at first: don't get distracted from your main purpose. But we should never lose sight of it. We don't come together to run a book ministry, but to praise God, to love one another, and to serve. Consequently, groups need someone to function as an authority to keep our purpose before us. Yet our experience is that these simple principles, which most people accept intellectually, are difficult to live out in practice.

For example, the person ordering the stock may feel that he or she is being "checked up on" instead of supported when the prayer group leaders ask to see and approve a tentative list of titles. The person organizing people to help with the book ministry may feel angry when someone he would like to have help is asked by the prayer meeting leaders to serve elsewhere.

We frequently respond emotionally as if we are not members of a body, even though we intellectually accept the fact that we are. We need the service of those who have a leadership gift which keeps the common vision and purpose clear, and lets that fully affect the whole process of how each project happens. For what sense does it make to have a wonderfully efficient book ministry which provides books which can help people love one another more if in the process of setting it up people have come to resent one another?

A role of leadership is to constantly refer the present projects of the prayer group to the whole purpose of being together in the first place. This role is not simply a matter of memory, but it should actively affect how things are done. For example, leaders may need to function as a team rather than as individuals, even though group action is often less efficient. Perhaps the leaders may need to be frequently communicating with everyone about the steps along the way, asking their views, even though this will slow things down. Normally, our goal should not simply be to get things done quickly.

Constantly keeping in mind our main purpose provides the opportunity for continual reflection on our vision of what we are all about. Each time we reflect on our purpose in light of some new project, we might see an aspect where we misunderstand why we are together and what we are all about. Gradually the common vision and purpose is purified and evolves to a greater depth. The vision serves as a protection for the prayer group as well as a solid foundation upon which to build whatever God has in mind for that group.

Because we are members of a body, some members have a special gift to clearly see its purpose and vision and know how it should affect everything. This fact has important implications for our judgments and expectations in relationships. If we recognize that we have an imperfect grasp of the common vision, we know that some judgments should be deferred to others who have a better grasp of the common vision. The key point is this: the context for judgments in a prayer group is the common vision and purpose which constitutes the prayer group. Our expectations and the judgments which follow from the expectations flow from the common vision.

Not everyone in the group has the same grasp of this common vision. All members do have *some* sense of the common vision or they would not be part of the group. But their sense of the common vision may be very general and unrefined. They might try to insert inappropriate purposes into the prayer group setting. For example, Harold, a very good businessman who knows how to get things done, might want to run an efficient, profitable book ministry based on consumer demand. But is this an appropriate purpose and vision for the prayer group book ministry? Perhaps the leaders want the book ministry to be primarily a service to people, and secondarily an efficient, profitable operation. This might mean that it must stock some "unpopular" titles, and that its staff must spend considerable time talking to customers about what they should be reading. The solution is not for the prayer group leaders to run the book ministry themselves. Rather,

Harold ought to do it, but under the direction of the leaders. However, for this kind of submission to work out smoothly, all must realize that we are all only members of a body and we need one another.

Here the role of authority in preserving and developing the common vision becomes clearer. People have different gifts. Some have a gift to be aware of and articulate the common vision; others need to submit or defer within the scope of their gift. Those who have been in a prayer group or community longest and especially those in authority are more likely to be caught up in the vision. Those who have been in a prayer group for a short period should presume that they do not understand the common vision fully yet and should defer certain decisions to those with other gifts.

Our grasp of the common vision is the context of our judgments. If we see this context as a common vision which we share in incompletely, we will have a submissive posture. Those who have gifts other than leadership and those who are new in a prayer group should be cautious making the kinds of judgments which direct or implement the call and vision of the prayer group. They should not ignore their own judgment in such areas, yet they should not weigh it as heavily as the judgments of others.

New people who come to a prayer group—or any other group—especially need to realize this. Often new people tend to want to share all their ideas about what should happen as soon as they become part of the group. There are times when their perspective is right and very valuable. Much more frequently, however, the newer people have not yet absorbed the common vision and their judgments are off. The new person should not ignore what he is sensing, but rather should be careful about drawing firm conclusions and judgments on the basis of what he is sensing. He is not yet sensitive to the common vision in the particular group and so will not usually be sensitive to the things which ought to be the basis for conclusions and judgments in the group.

For example, consider Harry, a man who has a gift to preach and evangelize. Harry goes to a large prayer meeting one night for the first time. This particular prayer group has met for four years and has been formed in the vision of witnessing through loving relationships among the members. Of course, Harry knows the importance of loving relationships and the prayer group goes out to preach and evangelize. But Harry and the prayer group differ in emphasis and focus. Harry concludes that the group is weak in evangelism. During his first visit, he tries to help the prayer group get straightened out and go out to preach and evangelize. Harry is not totally wrong, but he misses the point because he is not sensitive to the common vision within the prayer group. Harry should not ignore what he is sensing; he could talk to one of the prayer group leaders. Yet neither should he judge that the group is off track and "help" redirect it. A judgment rarely works well if made by a person not sensitive to the context, the common vision.

At the same time, those who clearly are caught up in the common vision and are a full part of the prayer group must be sensitive to the context of judgments. All of us are imperfect. Awareness of our sinfulness, weakness, and incomplete conversion should temper our judgments. The foundational posture for our judgments should be respect for the persons involved, and the Church's understanding of due process is helpful here.

Recall from Chapter Seven the four guidelines of due process: (1) who is responsible for what needs to be clear; (2) the criteria by which the person responsible will discern what ought to happen needs to be clear; (3) reasons for decisions that adversely affect a person's life needs to be clear; (4) people affected by a decision should be asked for their input during the process of decision-making and be aware of what is going on. While these guidelines are designed for a more institutional setting, the principles are helpful for prayer group leaders.

For example, they can help the leader know how to relate to Harry. The prayer group leader should make clear to Harry that the leaders' group is responsible for discerning the direction of the prayer group, even though everyone's input is important, including Harry's. He should tell Harry that the leaders place great weight on the consistency of the Lord's word over a period of time, a criterion that Harry, present for his first meeting, would not be familiar with. The leader should sit down with Harry, taking the time to sift through the wheat and the chaff, and lovingly support Harry. He should show Harry how to integrate his gifts into the prayer group in a better way. This might also mean getting back in touch with Harry to let him know how the leaders' group feels about his insights.

Being in touch with our own limitations and weaknesses should give us a non-dogmatic posture. We should "feel in our bones" that we are only one part of the body and that the whole body is necessary for a more definitive judgment. If I know myself well enough, I should know what I tend to miss and what I tend to over-emphasize. I can compensate for these tendencies by consulting with others who have complementary gifts before I make a judgment. So even when my judgments are definite and clear, my posture is not rigid or harsh. For example, if Harry was in touch with his limitations and weaknesses, he would not share in a self-righteously directive way, but rather as input to help the leaders reach a conclusion.

## *Guidelines for Making Judgments*

In this chapter, the network of relationships in a prayer group has been the context for applying the wisdom of scripture, tradition, and some modern sources. Transformation in our relationships depends upon our preserving the unity of the Spirit and realizing the implications of being members of a body. In this section we will apply the six guidelines for making judgments (Chapter Nine) to judgments in the context of relationships in a prayer group.

1. *Be sensitive.* Good judgments are based on our being in touch with the full spectrum of our experience. Is the judgment I am making rooted in the total experience, or am I basing my judgments on hearsay, half-truths, and one side of the story?

Take the example of Jim who rarely sets up chairs because he is always occupied "ministering" to people. The thought or temptation might easily come that Jim is lazy or is not willing to serve. We should apply the first guideline for making judgments: be sensitive. Even though Jim rarely sets up chairs, are our thoughts based on half-truths and one side of the story? Are we noticing how Jim serves by ministering to people? How does this happen? Do people call upon Jim to serve them? Or does Jim just try to find anybody to talk to when there is work to be done? In this way, we can determine whether the thoughts that divide our hearts from a brother or sister are based on half-truths and one side of the story. Reorienting our thoughts to be in touch with the full spectrum of our experience provides a solid foundation for making a judgment consistent with both truth and love.

2. *Be understanding.* Our experience and data are meaningless until we have an understanding of what they mean. Am I free to receive the Spirit's insight into my experience or do I read my prejudiced understandings into the experience? Good judgments are based on a freedom to understand that isn't limited by our previous understandings.

Consider Marjorie who comes to the prayer meetings regularly and every week shares at great length about the way God wants people to respond more. Because the effect of her exhortations is to discourage others, the thought comes that Marjorie is a critical person who wants to use the prayer group for her own needs. How do we apply this second guideline—be understanding? With respect to Marjorie herself, we may need to understand that she simply needs to grow in learning how to participate in the prayer group and how to share constructively. Instead of labeling her as a crank and telling her not to share at prayer meetings (or even worse, not talking to her about it at all and gossiping), we should help her learn what she does not know. Perhaps this means putting her in touch with the right person who has the gifts of practical wisdom to help her.

We also need to be understanding with respect to what Marjorie is saying. Do we trust that there is something valuable and true in what she is saying, even if it is mixed up with questionable elements and perhaps the wrong conclusions? It is precisely when Marjorie realizes that she is trusted in this way that she will be freed to hear about her need for growth. This is what it means to respect Marjorie as a person. There is usually something true and valuable in what a person shares. Trusting people in this way and understanding what is being said paves the way for a judgment that speaks the truth in love.

Frequently, we must exert energy to understand another, for our busy daily life absorbs all of our available energy. In a large prayer group, for example, leaders tend to be busy. It is easy to become over-committed in a way that causes us to mistrust people; we may find ourselves not bothering to understand complex situations. To understand properly, we must have a climate conducive to understanding. We need enough time-space to be free to creatively understand, to allow what others say to touch us, to enter in, to reach out to understand it. This climate of proper space and pace in turn means very practical decisions about priorities, life-styles, and values.

3. *Be reasonable.* Our understanding is only one of many possible understandings until we make the judgment that it is the correct one. In reflecting on the adequacy of an understanding, do I give further questions a chance to arise regardless of where they might lead or am I threatened by some of the possibilities? Am I free from a rash or indecisive temperment that is always too sure or too hesitant? Am I able to compensate for my rashness or indecision? Good judgments are based on a realization that a good understanding isn't always the right one. Thus, much reflective double-checking needs to be completed until we achieve the right understanding.

Recall the instance of the group of leaders who are trying to decide upon how to begin a Life in the Spirit Seminar. Louise strongly suggests that she should lead it, and names the others who should be on the team. People are left feeling that they had little to say about this decision and the thought comes to mind that Louise likes to be in charge of things and wants power. What does it mean to apply the third guideline for making judgments—be reasonable?

To be reasonable means that it has dawned on us that it is one thing to have an understanding that makes sense of the data (Louise wants power), but it is another thing to verify that understanding to insure that it is correct. We must think more clearly about our own thought patterns so that we are free to evaluate our understanding. We should not just presume it is the right one.

For example, perhaps Louise has touched the other leaders' insecurities and they begin thinking "Oh, how horrible this is. Aren't we really needed? Are we worthless? No, it is just that Louise wants power." Thought patterns like these will not allow a person to reasonably evaluate the truth of an understanding. In Ellis' terms, the thought "how horrible this is" is an irrational idea. Realizing this should protect us from judgments in relationships based on a wrong understanding. A different thought pattern would free the other leaders to evaluate their understanding, an approach like this: "Perhaps Louise just wants power, or perhaps this is playing on our insecurities. Maybe we just need to coordinate our gifts in a better way, or maybe we need to think and share and evaluate what is going on."

This guideline of reasonableness in making judgments integrates sensitivity and understanding without violating either of them. Hence, we must be careful not to cut short understanding by demanding verification too early in the process. For example, a concern over whether an idea will work or is valid inhibits creative brainstorming sessions which focus on generating understandings.[128] Some people in a prayer group or community will have a gift on the level of understanding—they are creative. Others will have a gift on the level of judgment—they are good at weighing and balancing in perspective and discerning understandings.

Perhaps Louise has a governmental gift for good decisive judgments, though perhaps she makes them too rashly, while the other leaders have more creative/prophetic gifts, making them appear indecisive. If this is the case, then the right understanding probably isn't one of pride and power, but one of how leaders with a variety of leadership gifts can work together. Louise might often be annoyed because she thinks the other leaders slow things down or raise irrelevant issues. For their part, the other leaders might see Louise as insensitive and closed to understanding what they sense. They both may be partly right since there is a natural tension between such gifts. They must take care to insure that the gifts can properly complete one another, not clash and compete. No one has a totally complete leadership gift. Realizing that we are members of a body and loving one another in the process can certainly (if not easily!) relieve a multitude of creative tensions.

4. *Be responsible.* We must complete the journey from ignorance to truth on the first three levels by living out the implications of our judgments and going from selfishness to love. Otherwise we will manage to distort the first three levels in order to live peacefully with our selfishness on the fourth level. Also, we'll find that this boomerangs, for the decisions we make make us! Am I willing to fully follow through on the implications of the judgments I make, even at great personal expense? Do I realize how this judgment will form me? Good judgments can be consistently made only when there is a personal responsibility which is committed to following through on their implications.

Let us again consider Marjorie, the woman who regularly gives long sharings at the prayer meetings about the need for everyone to respond more to God. Being responsible—the fourth guideline for making judgments—means that we need to take the initiative to live out what we know to be loving. If I have come to a judgment—an understanding of a person or situation which I have verified as correct—then I am responsible to properly act on it.

With Marjorie, the judgment I have come to may be relatively complex. She needs support in growing in a healthy relationship with the prayer group; she must learn how to share constructively. And yet, there is something valid in what she says, even if it is not being communicated effectively. In light of that judgment it would be irresponsible to ignore it or to gossip. The responsible thing to do is to help her by pointing out that what she is sharing is coming across poorly, listening to what she is trying to say, and either helping her to grow or putting her in contact with someone who can.

If we choose not to follow through with our judgment of Marjorie responsibly and lovingly, then we will semi-consciously distort our judgment so as to live peacefully with our selfishness. If we ignore it, the problem will not go away and division will gain a foothold. If we want to gossip, we will convince ourselves that others must know what we think. The only real solution is to fully follow through on the judgments I come to even if this is difficult.

If we live irresponsibly and selfishly by not following through on the implications of our judgments, then we begin to be formed into irresponsible and selfish people. Our decisions permeate our whole being, shaping and forming who we are. When we realize this, then the love of Christ that calls us to be authentic impells us. It is no longer a matter of how we *ought* to share with Marjorie based on external laws imposed on us or the pressure of other's expectations.

5. *Become aware of and acknowledge the existence of sin.* We protect ourselves from hidden forces that would control us when we realize where we are insensitive, misunderstanding, unreasonable, and irresponsible, especially where we have a pattern of such response. Where am I most likely to misjudge my brother, in what circumstances, and why? Where do I need to be especially cautious when judging others? Good judgments presume that sinful tendencies are out in the light where they can be dealt with.

In coming to a judgment about Jim, Louise, or Marjorie, it is important to know the particular way we are most likely to judge or act wrongly. For myself, the weak spot is understanding deeply enough so that the other person feels understood and loved. I can speak the truth without enough love, so that it isn't really the truth anymore. This tendency is even more pronounced when I am busy and rushed. Just being aware of this is a protection for me. Whenever I am busy and rushed I can compensate by being especially careful and even asking people if they are picking up coldness in our relationships.

This fifth guideline for making judgments—being aware of sin—means that we realize that everyone has missed the mark (Rom 3:23) and that to say otherwise is to deceive ourselves (1 Jn 1:8). The continued experience of sin interfering with our judgments, especially at the fourth step of decision, makes clear the cleavage between knowing and doing. "I do not do what I want to do, but what I hate . . . Even though I want to do what is right, a law that leads to wrongdoing is always ready at hand" (Rom 7:15, 21). With Paul we realize we are prisoners to this law of sin (Rom 7:23).

This continual experience of weakness, of our judgments being tainted with sin, brings the fruit of compassion into our posture when we judge others. Our expectation of others includes a knowledge of human frailties and their inevitable effects on our relationships and community life. We can experience being passionately with (compassion) others in our lack of perfect sensitivity, understanding, reasonableness, and especially responsibility. Our very weakness not only gives us patience with another's weakness and with communal weakness, but also leads us to our concluding guideline.

6. *Where sin abounds, grace abounds even more.* Jesus can redeem all of our sinfulness and mistaken judgments if we yield to the Spirit and open ourselves to unity with our brothers and sisters. Is the judgment I am making an attempt to live the law as a way of dealing with the flesh, instead of yielding to the Spirit? Good judgments need to be the fruit of surrender to the Spirit. Otherwise their tone and our posture become harsh and rigid.

What does this sixth guideline for making judgments mean when it is applied to our relationships? Knowing our lack of perfection in making and following through on our judgments, we know our need for God's power to redeem the process. The overriding concern in coming to a judgment about Jim, Louise, or Marjorie must be love for them and a desire for unity with our brothers and sisters. Yet love without truth isn't really love, just as truth without love isn't really truth. Our love and unity must be integrated with the truth, yet love and unity should be the focus. A focus on truth can lead us into the trap of living the law which hardens our posture in judging. Focusing on love forces us to receive God's power which relaxes our posture and makes us vulnerable.

Our expectation of human frailties and their inevitable effects is not one of pessimistic resignation. Rather, knowing that God mysteriously uses even our failures in his plan (Rom 8:28), we experience hope. While being able to honestly face sin in ourselves and others, we experience the grace whereby mercy triumphs over judgment (Jas 2:13).

The experience of sin being redeemed by God's love empowers us to make ourselves vulnerable in loving others. This mediates that same grace even further. In the process of pointing out another's fault we can make ourselves vulnerable in our own weakness. Our purpose is always unity, to win our brother or sister back and be with him or her. Our purpose is not to blame or dump our feelings. In faith, we can relax. We can trust that misjudgments or failure to follow through on them in love can be redeemed. In fact, redeemed imperfection is better than perfection in no need of redemption, for where sin abounds, grace abounds even more. In the words of the liturgy, "O happy fault, that merited for us such a Redeemer!" As God pointed out to Paul, his power reaches perfection in our weakness (2 Cor 12:9) and it is much better than our power could ever be. Only out of this context comes thought patterns of praise.

In summary, the expectations and guidelines for judgments in relationships are to be sensitive, understanding, reasonable, responsible, patient with the lack of these, and redeemed by vulnerably loving. Unless at least one of these is being served by a prospective judgment, we should refrain from making it.

## *Conclusions*

In light of Part Three of this book—reflections on contemporary authorities—let us again consider the questions: What does it mean to be pure of heart as we call one another to holiness? How should I approach my brother or sister when there is a fault to be pointed out? What should my posture be? How can I authentically support instead of condemn or discourage?

The introductory chapter pointed out the importance of a vulnerable posture in approaching our brothers and sisters. Part One on scripture revealed the background for this posture in a mind-set that acknowledges God's plan and is secure in our identity as sons and daughters of God. Such a mind-set frees us from judging according to the law, from competing with others to gain an identity, from imposing our vision on others, from letting the bad side of our gift get out of control, and from condemning or attacking others when there is a charism clash. While this paves the way to approach people in the posture of vulnerability and compassion, there is also the need to approach people differently depending on where they are at. Through Matthew 18 we were directed to encourage our brethern, actively care for those who have begun to stray, intensely desire unity, and limitlessly forgive as means of authentically supporting others.

Part Two on Christian tradition expanded our answers to the critical questions above. The Desert Fathers' practical helps to purity of heart, the freedom from penetration by worldly ways of thinking, included guarding our thoughts and being caught up in the apocalyptic vision. St. Thomas Aquinas' insight into guiding our knowing power by love shows us how to support others and to avoid rash judgments based on suspicions. He explained how to use the guiding principle of love in giving people the benefit of the doubt, and he explained the need for authority in order to make a judgment that would be definitively enforced. The Church's wisdom spoke of the need to respect freedom in the process of vulnerably sharing our hearts, a supportative way of approaching others when there is a fault to be pointed out. The Vatican Council's concern for respecting persons is practically applied in the four due process guidelines which, while originally meant for a more institutional setting, have valuable applications for interpersonal relationships and prayer groups.

Part Three consists of reflections on contemporary authorities about what is involved in becoming vulnerable and compassionate in our posture in fraternal correction. The psychological insights about a transformed mind revealed that our thought patterns are responsible for the way we feel, and we must be freed of irrational ideas if we are to be pure of heart in approaching our brothers and sisters. A process of discernment that uses our feelings was a great help to knowing how to interpret our negative feelings. Is something wrong in the situation or is something wrong with me? This knowledge is crucial to know how to authentically support instead of condemn or discourage. The chapter concluded with a description of how to experience a healing of our thought patterns so as to be freed to relate more lovingly.

Chapter Nine centered on theological insights on judgments that underlie coming to know the answers to the critical questions above, namely, what is involved in the process of coming to know? There are four levels that build upon one another and end in knowing: experiencing, understanding our experience, judging if our understanding of our experience is correct, and deciding to responsibly follow through with the implications of the judgment. We saw the role of sin in distorting our judgments, yet realized the redemptive power of Christ to overcome sin. We also come to see that we form ourselves by the judgments we make. The chapter concluded with all this theological advice formulated as six guidelines for making judgments.

This chapter applies much of the wisdom we have been learning to the network of relationships in a prayer group. The unity of the Spirit which we must eagerly preserve is a unity of love in a posture of vulnerability and compassion. When we experience thoughts and temptations that divide us from another it must be dealt with correctly or else evil gains a foothold. Depending on whether the situation concerns another's wrongdoing, immaturity, or our own negative feelings, there are different ways of dealing with it. Yet always the focus is loving. Realizing we are members of a body is also a great aid to transformation in our relationships. It clarifies the role of authority and gives us a less absolutist posture in our judgments. We concluded with an application of the six guidelines for making judgments to relationships in a prayer group.

CHAPTER ELEVEN

# FREEDOM FOR COMPASSION

We have covered a great deal of material in our reflections on our posture in relationships: the freedom to be vulnerable to others; scriptural teaching on our thought patterns, expectations, and judgments; tradition's reflections on purity of heart; how to judge others and respecting freedom; and what modern psychology and epistomology can tell us about transformation in our relationships. The preceeding section summarized many of our reflections. This chapter will spell out what this material should mean for our lives, our relationships, and our prayer groups.

Our central topic—judgments, expectations, and fraternal correction—might seem complex at times. Yet the simple point of our reflections is not the topic itself but our posture, the state of our heart, with respect to the topic. Vulnerability and compassion are the two central qualities of a Christian's posture. They are very noticeably absent or present in our judgments and expectations of others.

The fruit of our reflections can be measured by the new insights we have into the questions at the beginning of the book. What does it mean to be pure of heart as we call one another to holiness? How should I approach my brother or sister when there is a fault to be pointed out? What should my posture be? How can I authentically support instead of condemn or discourage? These are crucial questions as our relationships with other Christians deepen and as we take seriously the call we have to love one another as Christ Jesus has loved us. We have discussed much practical wisdom about our posture in fraternal correction, yet practical help is not the final answer.

The answer is our posture of love, more than the truth of what we are saying. We need to communicate the truth, but a warm truth that is *with* the other person, not a cold truth that chops him down. A classic example of the difference is in Dostoyevsky's novel *The Brothers Karamazov.* The cold, young ascetic Therapont is contrasted to the warm old monk Zossima. Therapont wants to exclude others in order to purify, to live the truth without compromise, to exercise all the self-control needed to become "perfect." Zossima wants to embrace in order to redeem, to live the gospel without compromise, to yield to all the grace needed to become loving. Both men speak the truth. The difference is their postures. Therapont's posture is hard and distant. Zossima's posture is vulnerable and compassionate—a posture of love.

We can see the same contrast in our prayer groups and churches. Some people are focused on being "perfect"—their concern is fulfilling the law, being well-ordered and disciplined. Others are focused on being loving and are concerned about the person and the quality of relationships. Ideally we know there is no conflict between being perfect and being loving, and we shouldn't oppose these tendencies too sharply in our thinking. Yet there is a real difference. For example, there is a real difference between a prayer group leader who loves the ideal which he is shepherding the prayer group to, and the leader who shepherds the group to the ideal because he loves the people in the prayer group.

Which kind of person are we? Being "perfect" is easy. Not because it doesn't involve sacrifice, hardship, discipline, and self-control, but because it means being secure in earning salvation. Being loving is harder. It requires what for us is a struggle—security in God's love. Our posture in fraternal correction depends to a large extent on our underlying focus. Are we focused on being "perfect" or on being loving? Not the distorted loving which ignores the truth. But nevertheless—are our lives focused on being loving and receiving the grace to be loving?

## *Compassion*

When our focus and posture is love, it expresses itself in certain characteristics. "Love is patient; love is kind. Love is not jealous, it does not put on airs, it is not snobbish. Love is never rude, it is not self-seeking, it is not prone to anger; neither does it brood over injuries. Love does not rejoice in what is wrong but rejoices with the truth. There is no limit to love's forbearance, to its trust, its hope, its power to endure" (1 Cor 13:4-7). The bases of a Christian's love posture are vulnerability and compassion. In the first chapter we considered one basis—vulnerability. Now let us turn to the other.

"Compassion" means being passionately *with* another. The Oxford English Dictionary defines it as "(1) suffering together with another, participation in suffering; fellow feeling, sympathy. (2) the feeling or emotion, when a person is moved by the suffering or distress of another, and by the desire to relieve it."[129] The English word "compassion" finds its source in the Latin *compati,* to suffer with another. *Pati* means to suffer, to endure, to be patient; *com* means with, together, in union. The original meaning of compassion, then, is closer to the first dictionary sense: joining to another in suffering. This is far from the second definition: feeling moved by the suffering of a person who is apart from us.

However, the dictionary classifies the first and original sense as obsolete! This shows the extent to which relationships have become less personal in our age. The dictionary says that "the compassion of sense one was between equals or fellow-sufferers; the second is shown to a person in distress by one who is free from it, who is, in this respect, his superior."[130] Modern people have largely lost the sense of being in the same boat of human frailty together, of being passionately with one another in our common brokenness. Compassion flowers when we realize "that the brotherhood of believers is undergoing the same sufferings throughout the world" (1 Pt 5:9).

For myself, I experience this separation from others in my tendency to withdraw at times, especially when I am caught up in being busy. It took me a while to realize the effect this tendency had on my relationships. I always thought I was consistent since I was faithful in keeping commitments and good at getting things done well. Yet through other people's feedback I began to realize that I wasn't being consistent at all when it came to being fully present to other people. My heart would be absent though my mind remained present. I would hear what people were saying on the surface and talk with them about it, but I sometimes failed to give any deeper wholehearted support. My sharings with people would become superficial, focused on the *things* I was doing instead of how *I* was doing. I also could not tell whether I was present or whether I was withdrawn; I had no ability to judge this in myself. I was solely tuned in to the task at hand and doing the function well.

This had serious consequences in my relationships. Others would feel excluded from my life, pushed out, forgotten, or disrespected. They would feel unneeded, as if they were interfering in my life. At times people would say to me, "I feel I can't get beyond your periphery," "I don't think I really know who you are," or "Sometimes you seem so cold and distant." At first I would disagree with such remarks. But then I began to react differently toward them. Disagreement and denial changed to toleration, and I gradually learned to accept and even appreciate such feedback. I saw that if my withdrawal was caught immediately, it was easy to overcome.

Although I was oblivious to whether I was fully present or withdrawn, some of the people around me could tell in minutes. I had to stop treating others' perceptions of this weakness as an attack or misunderstanding and learn to trust them. When they pointed out my inner withdrawal, I could correct it in minutes. If they were afraid to share it with me because they feared how I would react, it would be many weeks or months before I realized something was wrong. Then it would take a painful, confusing struggle to correct my withdrawal and be fully present to people. I realized I needed my brothers and sisters, and it was a very specific need. Through this I became close to my brothers and sisters, known by them, and freed for compassion. I came to see how deeply I suffer along with others, even if we are weak in different ways.

This experience is a good example of how the right posture in approaching a difficulty can immeasurably free our relationships. Others were free to share openly with me; I was free to receive and trust their support. Not only was my specific weakness corrected, but the process deepened the relationships of unity with my brothers and sisters. I need them and feel close to them; they know me more deeply and are invited in to permanently support me. A bond of unity developed. The weakness brought deeper relationships and unity.

In Hebrew the word for compassion is a plural form of the word for "womb" and it "signifies yearning love, like that of a mother for the babe within her womb."[131] Compassion is what a pregnant mother experiences—the love that is with, suffers with, and is yearning to bring forth birth. It means waiting, being patient, never forcing, yet always being intimately involved with the child because it is part of her. The gospels often describe Jesus being moved with compassion by using a Greek word that literally means "to be moved in one's bowels."[132] The Greeks regarded the bowels as we would the heart—the seat of our deeper emotions. Thus, Jesus was often deeply moved, filled with compassion, suffering *with* the other. He suffered *with* the sheep without a shepherd, with the people without food, with the widow whose son had died.

The Pharisees and Scribes complained that Jesus was too close to sinners, "This man welcomes sinners and eats with them" (Lk 15:2). Jesus responded to their complaints by telling three parables about God's compassion for those who are distant and his happiness when they are close again: the parables of the lost sheep, the lost coin, and the prodigal son. Recall the father's response to the prodigal son coming home. What was his posture? What kind of judgment and expectation did he have? "While still a long way off, his father caught sight of him and was deeply moved. He ran out to meet him, threw his arms around his neck, and kissed him" (Lk 15:20). The father was deeply moved, filled with compassion. He was always with his son, suffering with his son, and yearning to bring his son forth to new birth. It is like the love of a mother for her about-to-be-born baby, only greater, since there are no prodigal fetuses. And when the birth happens there is a great rejoicing. " 'Let us eat and celebrate because this son of mine was dead and has come back to life. He was lost and is found.' Then the celebration began" (Lk 15:32).

This is the compassionate posture for judgments and expectations in relationships. Compassion, while based in suffering with one another, is the source of deep joy and happiness in our love and unity with one another and with God. The freedom God gives us is for tender compassion, for being *with* one another as much as God was with us in Christ. As God has said, "My grace is enough for you, for in weakness power reaches perfection" (2 Cor 12:9).

## *Becoming Vulnerable and Compassionate*

In the struggle to become vulnerable and compassionate, it gradually dawns on us that we can deeply experience union with one another in the very weaknesses we try to hide in order to be accepted. When we first get in touch with our unique weakness or brokenness, our response is to deny it, to refuse to face it, to make excuses. We become angry, guilty, or depressed. What will happen if people find out what we're really like? They will never love us or accept us. A huge amount of our psychic energy goes into creating a false self that will be accepted. More energy goes into maintaining it, with all the defense mechanisms necessary for protection.[133]

I recall the experience of Jack, one of the brothers in our community. After being with us for a while it became evident that Jack had particular difficulty expressing his negative feelings in a constructive and loving way. He expressed them indirectly, through negative humor, being late for meetings, and withdrawal. The problem was rather obvious and many people tried to help Jack express his negative feelings in a more useful way. Yet every time someone talked to him about it, Jack denied he had any negative feelings. He would have elaborate explanations for his negative jokes, his absences, and other behavior. He refused to face his weakness. The effect was to make Jack more and more isolated.

All of us are like Jack, not so much in his negative feelings, but in our refusal to face our weakness, admit it, and invite the needed support. We wonder why we're tired, why it is hard to relax, why our security is so easily shaken, why we don't feel confident that anyone *really* loves us, why we're frustrated in relationships, why we don't feel close to people, or why we can't understand what it means to experience needing others. The problem is our desperate effort to maintain a facade. This masks a semiconscious refusal to let God be God and accept that we are creatures loved by him. If we never grow out of this stage, then our personalities become distorted: a proud and tyrannical parent, a tearful and demanding martyr parent, a sadistic and overbearing boss, an anxious and depressed spouse, a nagging perfectionist, an ineffectual worker, a self-righteous religious, a busybody and tale-teller, a cynic and judge of everyone, a bossy and demanding friend, a misunderstood prophet, a self-pitying idealist, or even a pseudo saint. Our brother Jack was becoming a fearful, withdrawn, and somewhat embittered man.

If we have the courage to continue the journey, the truth about our false self begins to dawn. Even when people accept our imitation identity, we still do not feel loved because our false self is not us. We can be accepted and loved only by putting our real self forward. When others accept our false self, we are left with a fragile peace, with anxiety, anger, pride, or depression ever ready to surface. It creates a worse problem than the one we were trying to solve. It suddenly dawns on us that the false self we are presenting is in fact the very thing that is preventing us from being fully accepted and loved.

As the journey continues we need to be sustained by our relationship with God. We need to risk and trust, to have faith and step out of the false self we've created. God is with us; in Jesus he has suffered with us; in the Spirit he is with us now. And so we can risk and trust, we can reveal to other people our weaknesses and our brokenness. Sometimes others seem to know about it already and we get defensive again. Sometimes we feel free to share about our weaknesses only if other people deny them, or say that we're exaggerating. But gradually we feel more comfortable sharing about our weak points. And then we need to make a decision about continuing the journey. It's easy to get stuck in bargaining with others about our weak points.

Jack experienced a breakthrough one day. He got tired of being isolated and complaining that everyone misunderstood him. As he shared with one of the pastoral leaders in the group he began to get in touch with the extent of his negative feelings. He was scared because he didn't know what to do with them. Jack didn't want to hurt anyone by acting hostile, nor did he want to manipulate anyone through his anger. The only alternative he saw was not to have negative feelings. Since he could not get rid of his feelings by an act of will, he got out of touch with them and denied that they were part of him. Jack went to one of the pastoral leaders because he realized that whatever he was doing was isolating him from others. In fact, denying his negative feelings only intensified them. In the course of his talk Jack began to realize what was going on and started to admit his weakness to himself and others.

This seemed to bring real freedom to Jack's relationships for a while. He could admit he had negative feelings and worked at expressing them in a constructive way. Yet he sometimes bargained about his weakness instead of dealing with it. Sometimes subtly and sometimes more openly, Jack would try to make a deal: "I'm feeling angry about the music at the prayer meetings, but you feel resentful that Neil gave the teaching. If you leave my anger alone, I'll leave your resentment alone." Jack's temptation points out a pitfall for all of us. It is possible to merely adapt to one another's weaknesses, and to avoid them, without really accepting them and supporting one another in overcoming them.

We need to go further. We need to invite people to support us in our weaknesses. Not to avoid our weakness, not to learn to live with it, and not to coerce us, but to complement, support and compensate for our weaknesses.

Jack, for example, finds the strength of God and Christian community most operative when he is angry and most in need of support. Jack's negative feelings will probably never disappear because he is a sensitive person with sensitive gifts. Yet he never needs to express them in an unloving or useless way as long as he receives support in the area of his weakness. What's more, as we let others support us, and as we cooperate with their support, we suddenly realize that other things have happened in the process. We are close to people, one of them. This would not be possible without our weaknesses and brokenness—the anchor points of our identity.[134] The very thing we thought would bring death brings life and we are accepted and loved for who we are. We are freed for tenderness and compassion. Our posture has changed.

The journey to be freed for compassion is a life-long struggle and is always precarious. When we stop exercising, our muscles turn to fat. It doesn't matter whether we used to exercise a lot and were in wonderful shape. If we stop, our muscles soon turn to fat. When we stop risking and being vulnerable, our unity disappears. It never works to limit our reaching out, risking, sharing ourselves and inviting others in to support us. Unless we do it with a wider circle of people and do it more and more deeply with those we're closest to, our unity disappears. We regress to being distant; we don't feel accepted and loved; our posture hardens; we withdraw.

Becoming vulnerable and compassionate leads to unity and the deep joy and peace that unity brings. The Lord wants us to become one. As we share our lives with each other we are doing exactly what he wants us to do. And so we must be vulnerable and compassionate and open our lives to others if we are to grow as Christians. We cannot live our Christian lives alone. In our journey to the Lord, we must open ourselves to other people. The gospel will be compromised in our lives unless we become vulnerable and compassionate. Does our treasure lie in self-protection and achievements? Or does it lie in becoming vulnerable and compassionate as Jesus was and is today? "Wherever your treasure lies, there your heart will be" (Lk 12:34).

How can we cultivate loving personal relationships where we can grow in becoming vulnerable and compassionate? The brief pastoral advice offered here is in the context of the network of relationships in a prayer group. Supporting one another in our weaknesses requires that we are secure in love—both God's love and one another's love. A loose relationship rarely provides the opportunity for such security. To give and receive support in becoming vulnerable and compassionate needs a committed relationship where people are committed to work things through in love, not to leave when the going gets rough.

In the context of a prayer group, here are three useful ways of cooperating with grace. First, see what committed relationships you are already in and see how they can become explicitly supportative of your whole lives together. Second, consider whether the prayer group should have small sharing groups for this purpose alone. Third, explore what ways the prayer group can support such smaller groups. Let us go over each briefly.

First, what committed relationships are you already in? A leaders group? A music group? A bookstore team? These groups involve a commitment to be together for the purpose of the ministry. Should some of these groups also explicitly have a second purpose of supporting one another in becoming vulnerable and compassionate? This may already be happening to some extent implicitly. Perhaps the group should explicitly discuss supporting one another in this way, and agree to do it if everyone wants it. Then such sharing can happen more deeply, more regularly, and as a central goal instead of a possible interference.

Second, consider whether the prayer group should have small sharing groups exclusively devoted to supporting one another in becoming vulnerable and compassionate. Such small sharing groups form an environment where people can draw closer to each other. Such a group of four to eight people might gather weekly to share what the Lord has been doing in their lives, especially focusing on our relationships with others, whether we are becoming vulnerable and compassionate, and why. We all need to learn how to share our lives in a healthy way.

Third, explore what ways the prayer group can support such smaller groups. The leaders of a prayer group need to discern if they ought to move toward forming small sharing groups for some, most, or all the members of the prayer group. This should happen slowly so that the groups can learn from experience. The leaders also need to exercise a role in forming these groups. Sharing groups should include people of different gifts and personalities; natural attractions are not always the best criteria for putting groups together. The leaders also need to offer regular teaching about healthy relationships, and to help those sharing groups which experience difficulty. The leaders should grow in the needed wisdom themselves by their own personal commitment to sharing, by visiting larger prayer groups or communities where this is happening, and learning from those experienced in handling relationship problems.

## *Union With God*

Yet the journey continues regardless of pitfalls or the practical details. If we get off track, there is always grace to get back on. The process is painful at times, with new idols and false selves to be exposed, yet it is well worth the effort. The process brings us to the Lord who is faithful and good to us. As we enter the unity of the Trinity, we grow increasingly intimate with Jesus: "I pray that they may be one in us . . . that they may be one as we are one—I living in them, you living in me—that their unity may be complete" (Jn 17:21-23).

Our closeness with people is a sharing in God's closeness to us in Jesus. Our experience of others loving and accepting us for who we are is only a reflection of our security in the Father's love for us. Our freedom for compassion is a sharing in Jesus' ministry of compassion. We are vulnerable to others to the extent of our union with Jesus. He was vulnerable even to the point of his Passion, which, by the power of his Spirit with us, empowers our ministry of compassion.

Prayer is crucial to staying on track in this process. We are prey to many temptations and deceptions in order to avoid pain, hurt, suffering. It hurts to be vulnerable when others are not sensitive. It is painful to reach out and suffer with another when they are not ready to let us in. The journey leads to the center of suffering, not away from it. The mystery revealed by Jesus Christ is that we can be free from suffering only by entering into the core of suffering in unity with him who went first. As we do so, we embrace others in the process so as to redeem them through the power of Christ. Without prayer, without a total abandonment to God by uniting ourselves to Jesus, the journey gets compromised. We try to avoid suffering, to intersperse the process with vacations, or at least to keep it to a reasonable limit. It is only in a prayerful union with Jesus that we can slip into the core of suffering with him and rise to be free for boundless compassion.

We must remember that the foundation of prayer, the heart of it, is an apocalyptic urgency about coming to God more deeply and living the gospel more intensely. I use the word "apocalyptic," not in the end-time sense, but in the visionary sense that sees to the spiritual heart of the matter. Apocalyptic refers to revelation, in the way a stage is revealed by the opening of the curtain. Our apocalyptic vision perceives the battle between God and the evil one which underlies our struggles. When we are intensely living the gospel, the day of the Lord is at hand for us and we know the urgency of it. It is a matter of vision, not prediction.

The foundation of prayer is to resist the tendency to water down the gospel in order to be respectable or sensible. The heart of prayer is living the gospel intensely, with the apocalyptic urgency that catapults us into a deeper response to God. As we earnestly desire to be fully responsive to the Lord, the Holy Spirit will lead us into closer communion with him.

The journey is in freedom, and in order to be free we have to let go and simply live the present moment. We can't be in control of our freedom to be vulnerable, our freedom for compassion, and insure it for all areas simultaneously. It is possible to hoard our freedom, to try to be in control of it and be able to manipulate it, to force it to be there instead of trusting in the Spirit moment by moment. Control rots freedom. It closes vulnerability and hardens compassion. It makes others feel distant and condemned. It makes us isolated. Our lack of ability to be in control is part of our incompleteness. As we accept our utter inability to be in control, and trust in the Spirit's ability to guide and lead us, vulnerability and compassion flourish.

The more we journey and realize we cannot be in control, the more we rejoice in it and celebrate the Spirit's control, guidance, and direction. We always have plans to bring about the kingdom of God through hard work that involves easy suffering. These plans make us lose the way on the journey. Intellectual knowledge about fraternal correction, judgments, and expectations in relationships is necessary, but is catastrophically inadequate. Our critical need is for prayer that makes us one with Christ. In the journey to God, there is a crucial question involved in becoming vulnerable and compassionate, in experiencing relationships in the Lord. Will we follow these words of Christ that brought Peter into the core of suffering so that he could rise with great joy?

"I tell you solemnly:
as a young man
you fastened your belt
and went about as you pleased;

but when you are older
you will stretch out your hands,
and another will tie you fast
and carry you off against your will."
When Jesus had finished speaking
he said to him, "Follow me." (Jn 21:18, 19)

CHAPTER TWELVE

# THE POSTURE FOR HOPE IN JUDGMENTS

In this book we have explored what is at the heart of experiencing relationships in the Lord—our posture of love. By now we also realize that achieving this posture is not simply a matter of understanding and mastering practical wisdom, but of yielding to grace. If we depend on our own power, we will be hopeless. The posture for hope in judgments only comes as we depend on God and his love. "And this hope will not leave us disappointed, because the love of God has been poured out in our hearts through the Holy Spirit who has been given to us" (Rom 5:5). We become vulnerable and compassionate as we experience our own weakness and sinfulness in the light of the Lord's love. It softens and purifies our hearts, bringing a posture for hope in judgments.

Many of us are shocked when we first experience sin deep within our hearts. Yet this experience of sin leads to a broken heart and spirit. A broken spirit allows God's Holy Spirit to purify our hearts and to draw us into his love. We stop trying to earn our salvation. We stop trying to make all our weaknesses into strengths, and instead we open up our weaknesses so that the power of God can be made manifest through them.

The freedom of the Spirit is then released as we rely on God's power. God's love floods our hearts through the Holy Spirit. In his love, God pierces our hearts so that all fears are drained out, and with gratefulness and joy we enter into the life of God anew.

The journey is not easy, because to seek God means to leave this world although we remain in it. We leave our selves and begin to live for others. When we relinquish our self-assertion and self-seeking, we begin to experience the life of Jesus. To renounce the pleasure of our illusions about ourselves is to die more effectively than we could ever do by martyrdom. God will not spare our illusions if we are seeking him. And when illusions of the self die, they give place to the reality of God's love which purifies our hearts and makes us a new creation.

Purity of heart means renouncing the struggle to resist the desires of others; the desire to assert ourselves against others' wills; the rebellion against any restraints on us; the desire to impose ourself as distinct and superior; the effort to hide our limitations from ourselves; the tendency to disguise our faults as virtues. The inner pride and security of fallen man must be crucified. We need to be poor—emptied of the false self we have erected and our own "light" which is darkness in the eyes of Jesus.

> Jesus said: "I came into this world to divide it, to make the sightless see and the seeing blind." Some of the Pharisees around him picked this up saying, "You are not calling us blind, are you?" To which Jesus replied: "If you were blind there would be no sin in that. 'But we see,' you say, and your sin remains." (Jn 9:39-41)

The Pharisees did not want to understand deeply enough; they were more concerned with self-righteous seeing than with the source of their sight. These words of Jesus to the Pharisees apply to us also. There is impurity and sin deep within our hearts.

I saw this in myself one day as I was praying in a chapel. While I was kneeling, I began to daydream, slouch down, and fall half asleep. Suddenly I heard noise outside and the doors opened. I quickly knelt and tried to pray again, so as to appear to be in prayer. I was more concerned with pleasing men than serving God from the heart.

From this experience, I began to see the limitations of my heart and accept that that is the way my heart is right now. This insight ended my illusion of my own sanctity by showing me myself. It was a purifying work of the Holy Spirit and it resulted in new freedom. Self-deception no longer had the same power over me. I was grateful to see my blindness.

It is a gift to see the darkness, an opportunity for those of us without sight to know that we are blind. Jesus can then remove our guilt. He gives his own light as we accept the truth about ourselves. We recognize the darkness we have been saved from, and see what we have been saved for—a pure heart.

Purity of heart is the beginning of unity within ourselves. Freed from the necessity to serve our own unyielding, relentless will, we begin to know the freedom and love of God's life. We see ourselves and others as we are. No longer bound to serve our own appetites first, we find that all things bring us joy because we experience in them the glorious freedom of the sons and daughters of God—owning everything because we have nothing; having no fear because perfect love is here; having no frustrations because we accept our limitations as creatures; living in the peace and joy that comes from falling in love with God; being happy and grateful because once we were lost and now we are found; counting our own "light" as darkness because of the value of knowing the light of Christ Jesus our Lord.

The path to glory is through our weakness and brokenness redeemed by God. As we take this path, we also become vulnerable and compassionate, as Jesus was.

It is in this context that we desperately need to pray. Wisdom and knowledge are valuable: "It is better—much better—to have wisdom and knowledge than gold and silver" (Prv 16:16). Yet it is so easy for the posture of vulnerability and compassion to ebb away into pride and arrogance. As we all know only too well, "Pride leads to destruction, and arrogance to down-fall" (Prv. 16:18). As mentioned in the last chapter, prayer is pivotal.

## *Psalm 51*

In this chapter, Psalm 51 is presented as a paradigm of a prayer for purity of heart because in it we can see our sinfulness in the light of God's love. The psalm itself is a penitential prayer of supplication. The brief commentaries on each verse bring out the original meaning of the psalm. As we come to experience and understand the psalm, praying it becomes a life-giving protection of the incarnation of God's vulnerability and compassion in us.

> Have mercy upon me, O God, according to your loyal love;
> according to the abundance of your compassion, blot out my transgressions.
>
> (Psalm 51:1)[135]

In the first line there is an interesting interplay between "mercy" and "loyal love," or in the Hebrew between *hen* and *hesed.* The verb *hen* (mercy) has as its fundamental sense the bestowal of a kindness which cannot be claimed. It could be thought of as grace in the way that a person might say that something was pure grace. The opening words, then, are asking for the mercy to which we have no right. *Hesed* (loyal love) is the covenant love of God. It is the proved loyalty of God in his covenant relationships.[136] The psalmist knows he is in a covenant relationship with God, and so he has a claim on God's covenant love, his loyal love. He is saying, "Because of the relationship we have, I can claim your mercy which, by its very nature, no one can claim." In the same way that we "deserve" undeserved mercy from God because of the new relationship we have with him in Christ, so others "deserve" our mercy merely because we are brothers and sisters in Christ. "Have mercy upon me, O God, according to your loyal love."

The second line also has this interesting interplay: the psalmist confidently asks for something undeserved because of a relationship. The relationship is "compassion," for which the Hebrew word is the plural form of the word for "womb." It signifies a yearning love, like that of a mother for the babe within her womb. Thus God has a relationship with us similar to the relationship a pregnant mother has with her unborn baby. The fruit of the relationship is compassion, a yearning love which wants to give birth so that a new level of presence to one another will be possible.

In light of this relationship, the psalmist asks, "blot out my transgressions." He is asking for an undeserved pardon. The Hebrew word used here for "transgressions" means political rebellion against constituted authority. Isaiah employs it to describe the rebellion of children against their father, an analogy to the revolt of Israel against Yahweh. "Transgressions" suggests a willful, self-assertive defiance of God, a conscious perversion of our free-will choice in rebellion against God. Of all the Hebrew terms for sin, this is the strongest; it represents sin under its most active aspect. This is the grave offense the psalmist is asking God to blot out! The psalmist had an image of God keeping track of all sins in a record book. He prays that God would remember the sin no more, no matter how bad it was.

We too are in a relationship with our brothers and sisters in which we desire to bring them to birth more fully. Because of this relationship, we must pardon them so fully that we even forget what they did wrong. "According to the abundance of your compassion, blot out my transgressions."

Psalm 51 is a prayer for purity of heart. Its opening lines tell us how we ought to see our sinfulness in the light of God's love relationship with us. We need to be in touch with the depths of our sin and our desperate need for mercy, but always in the light of God's love, confident that we can ask even what is undeserved because of his relationship of love with us.

> Wash me thoroughly from my iniquity,
> and from my sin cleanse me. (2)

The first verse is reverently confident of God's mercy and forgiveness because of the relationship of loyal love and compassion God has with us. This second introductory verse completes our reverent confidence by making clear that although God's mercy is always available, receiving it is not an easy process. Our very being must be purified.

Hebrew contains a number of words that signify different kinds of washing. There is the ceremonial washing, the washing of one's face and hands, the washing of one's whole body, and the washing of clothes. Clothes were washed by bringing them to the river, putting them on rocks in the stream, and beating them clean. This is the word the psalmist uses when he cries out, "wash me thoroughly." He prays that God will make him clean and soft by treading, kneading, and beating in cold water. It is a vigorous term that makes clear the depth of the process involved in receiving mercy and forgiveness.

The word "iniquity" comes from a root that has two meanings. One of the root meanings is to "bend or twist." It signifies the moral perversion of a personality which is deeply warped and twisted. The other root meaning is to "err or go astray," signifying a deviation from the right track. What needs to be thoroughly washed is the core of our being that has a deep stain. This is why the washing must be such a depth-process. We need to be washed as clothes would be in order to receive a soft heart, repentant and open to God. "Wash me thoroughly from my iniquity!"

"And from my sin cleanse me." "Sin" in Hebrew means literally "missing the mark," and is used, for example, of slingers who sling stones at a target. A slinger who misses the mark has "sinned" (Jgs 20:16). The idea comes into the Greek as *hamartia* with the same meaning of missing the mark: "All men have sinned (missed the mark) and are deprived of the glory of God" (Rom 3:23). The psalmist is asking to be cleansed from missing the mark. The word for "cleanse" used here means to cleanse "physically, ceremonially or morally," or to "pronounce clean ceremonially." The root of the word is largely a cultic term, yet here carries the connotation of not being guilty of passing a contagious disease to others. The community or family aspect is emphasized. The psalmist has been put outside of the community because he missed the mark. He is asking to be reinstated, to be cleansed of sin and freed to be with God,

> For my transgressions I know,
> and my sin is before me continually. (3)

After the first two introductory verses, the psalm has three parts: The confession (vv. 3-6), the prayer (vv. 7-12), and the vow (vv. 13-17). We can learn much about how to pray for purity of heart by reflecting on the flow of prayer in this psalm—from confession to prayer to vow.

In this opening verse of the confession, the psalmist makes explicit his consciousness of sin. The consciousness of sin is intensely personal; it is not expressed vaguely. In the first three verses he refers to his sin five times as my "transgressions," "iniquity," and "sin." True sorrow is a vivid, ever-present, intensely personal consciousness of sin. His wrongdoing is something the psalmist knows, or as the Jerusalem Bible translates it, "I am well aware of." His transgression is an oppressive burden which is continually weighing on him. However, this knowledge does not depress the psalmist. To the contrary, it motivates him to seek mercy, forgiveness, washing, and cleansing: "For my transgressions I know."

"And my sin is before me continually." As Dalglish comments, "This oppressive consciousness of sin is not an intermittent obtrusion, but rather perpetual obsession which fixes his guilt conspicuously and continually before him. Such unrelieved pressure urges him here to find relief in the catharsis of audible self-disclosure and to move on toward the realm of divine forgiveness, the sole solution of his problem, through confession of his sin."[137]

> Against you, you only, have I sinned,
> and that which is evil in your sight have I done.
> that you may be justified when you speak,
> and be blameless when you judge. (4)

The confession progresses from the consciousness of sin to a full confession and frank admission that the psalmist totally deserves God's judgment. The confession of guilt has gotten down to the primary fact: his sin is an attack against God. "Against, you, you only, have I sinned."

To understand the spirit in which the psalmist confesses, one cannot underestimate the "For" which introduces the confession of verses 3-6. He asks for mercy and forgiveness, washing and cleansing *because* he is confessing. The whole spirit underlying the confession is not despair, but faith. It is based on the Hebrew belief summed up in Proverbs 28:13, "You will never succeed in life if you try to hide your sins. Confess them and give them up; then God will show mercy to you" (TEV).

True confession is always made in a spirit of faith. It means acknowledging our sinfulness in the light of God's love. It strips itself of all facades and sees through to the basic reality of our sinful struggle against God. It finally recognizes the fact, "That which is evil in your sight have I done." In utter sincerity it hands in a guilty plea before the righteous judge, not compromising it with any excuses, "That you may be justified when you speak, and be blameless when you judge." The psalmist lets go of any imaginary control over God that would allow him to blame God if mercy is not granted.

> Behold, I was brought forth in iniquity,
>   and in sin did my mother conceive me.
> Behold, truth you desire in the inward being,
>   and in the secret part, wisdom you teach me. (5-6)

These concluding verses of the confession are a confession of moral powerlessness. The Hebrew interjection, translated as "behold," is used to announce a new fact, declaration, or discovery. This new item, which completes the confession, is the admission of the psalmist's complicity with human sinfulness from the very inception of his being. The psalmist does not merely confess one sinful action but rather he acknowledges congenital sinfulness. His guilty plea extends to the full extent of his sinfulness, to a world marked by selfishness and sin. He is more conscious of sharing in the sin of the world than in what we call original sin.

These two verses, as can be seen from the common introduction of "behold," contain an important contrast. "I" (the psalmist) of verse five is contrasted with "you" (God) of verse six. The "iniquity" and "sin" which belongs to "I" is contrasted with the "truth" and "wisdom" that belongs to "you." The confession of sin includes the radical acceptance of what it means to be a creature separated from God.

The psalmist wants no loopholes in his guilty plea. The modern mind seeks a way out of a guilty plea. However, a Hebrew would realize that a way out would only interfere with the granting of mercy. In the last line, the psalmist deals with the loophole that would blame sin on ignorance (from having been born in sin). The psalmist knew wisdom even in "the secret part," meaning "the closed chamber of the womb." That is, the psalmist knows not only that he was in sin since the moment of his conception, but also that God taught him wisdom even before birth, that is, while still in the womb. Thus, he is not wholly evil and he is not ignorant of what is right. The psalmist's knowledge—and ours—makes us even more culpable for sin. Even though his sinfulness reaches to the moment of conception, he has sinned with some degree of knowledge of right and wrong, not merely out of ignorance. The confession is total, with no loopholes, because total mercy is being asked for.

> Purge me with hyssop, and I shall be clean
> wash me, and I shall be whiter than snow.
> Cause me to hear joy and gladness
> and the bones which you have crushed will rejoice.
> Hide your face from my sins,
> and all my iniquities blot out. (7-9)

After the confession of verses 3-6 comes the prayer of verses 7-12. There are two prayers, one for forgiveness (vv. 7-9) and one for renewal (vv. 10-12). The prayer for forgiveness asks for cleansing and is the psalmist's response to the first part of the confession (vv. 3-4) in which he admits sin. The prayer for renewal will ask for spiritual renewal and is a response to the second part of the confession (vv. 5-6) where he admits the extent of his inner lack of response and confusion.

The prayer for forgiveness asks to be purified from uncleanness, which to the Hebrew mind prevented one from being in the presence of God. The request for cleansing with hyssop echoes the purifying of a leper's house (Lv 14:49, 52) and the cleansing of a person defiled by death (Nm 19:18-19). Seven of the ten uses of the term "hyssop" in the Old Testament are in connection with these two rituals. This underscores the freedom being asked for, freedom to enter the presence of God. The word for "wash" here is again the word for washing of clothes, as the psalmist prays, "wash me, and I shall be whiter than snow." The purpose of the plea to "wash me" comes through clearly. It is not a masochistic prayer of a religious fanatic, but a realistic prayer of hope by one who knows the ways of God.

"Cause me to hear" is a typical introduction to a divine oracle. Here it becomes a prayer that asks for a divine word of forgiveness which would bring about "joy and gladness" to the one praying. The fruit of this forgiveness is that "The bones which you have crushed will rejoice." The word "bones" refers to the person himself and as Dalglish puts it, "The meaning would seem to be that by the oppressive context of conscious rebellion against God, by the mental depression of guilt, the psalmist has been broken."[138] He has asked to be washed as clothes would be, beaten by sticks while on the rocks in a stream. This will crush the sinner, but the broken bones will rejoice as the word of forgiveness comes.

"Hide your face from my sins" is a graphic petition for forgiveness, coupled with the request that all iniquities be blotted out of the divine record book. This powerful three-verse prayer for forgiveness sets the stage for the prayer for renewal. The psalmist realizes that unless the inner core of his personal life is transformed, the future will simply repeat the past. He needs purity of heart even more than forgiveness.

> A clean heart, O God, create for me,
> and a steadfast spirit make new within me.
> Cast me not away from your presence,
> and your holy spirit take not from me.
> Restore unto me the joy of your salvation,
> and uphold me with a willing spirit. (10-12)

This prayer for spiritual renewal is a response to the second part of the confession (vv. 5-6) where the extent of our inner lack of response and confusion is admitted. Purity of heart is needed in order to be sustained in truth and wisdom.

The psalmist prays for "a clean heart" because he realizes that the noxious pollution of sin has infected the deep sanctuary of his being. As a result he is essentially defiled. The "heart" refers to the inner life, the personality, in contrast with the outer life or actions of a person. It is not limited to the emotions or even focused on them. It is a prayer for new, clean thought patterns and choice patterns that spontaneously are attracted to God (see 1 Sm 10:6, 9; Ez 11:19, 36:26; Jer 32:39). He is asking God to create this for him. This imperative form of "create" is used only with reference to God; only God can create a clean heart; only God can save.

"And a steadfast spirit make new within me." Heart and spirit are generally synonymous in these instances. The basic thought is that sin has brought more than defilement; it has also brought a disintegration of willpower. Hence there is need of a new spirit (inner personality, heart, disposition) which is steadfast. What is needed is a transformed, firm, stable, settled personality, inclined to God and faithful to him. It is beyond the reach of the psalmist to achieve this; only God can, and the psalmist earnestly asks God to do it.

The psalmist's concern with "a clean heart" and "a steadfast spirit" has a purpose: he wants to be close to God, to be in his presence. His prayer to God is "Cast me not away from your presence and your holy spirit take not from me." His goal is to be with God continually. When he prays, "Restore unto me the joy of your salvation," he has gone beyond the request of verse 8 to be momentarily joyful at hearing a word of forgiveness. He asks for a new strata of life, the normative and continuing joy in abiding salvation, not merely the "on the spot" rejoicing from a word of forgiveness. Knowing himself and his capacity for falling away again, he prays "uphold me with a willing spirit," a spirit that wants to continue in the joy of God's salvation and that is continually upheld by him.

> Let me teach transgressors your ways,
>   and sinners shall return to you.
> Deliver me from bloodguiltiness, O God, my saviour,
>   and my tongue will sing aloud of your righteousness.
> O Lord, open my lips,
>   and my mouth will declare your praise. (13-15)

After the introductory verses, the confession, and the prayer comes the vow. The first part of the vow is a psalm of thanksgiving (vv. 13-15) and the second part concerns the sacrifical offering (vv. 16, 17).

The vow naturally flows from the confession and prayer for forgiveness and purity of heart. The psalmist makes a commitment to God that expresses the things he desires to do. Because he is a wounded healer, he can teach transgressors God's ways and lead them back to God. His ministry to sinners and transgressors is empowered by his personal testimony: he is in the same boat as they, but he has been reconciled to God. He is able to be compassionate.

The bloodguiltiness the psalmist prays to be delivered from is not death, as some translations have it, but the moral inhibition of bloodguilt that presently prohibits him from thanksgiving, and that has ruptured the blood bonds between him and members of his family and community. His guilt, his awareness of it, and his awareness of his need for forgiveness prevent him from praising God. As God delivers him from his guilt, he is freed to "sing aloud." This means to give a ringing cry in joy or exultation. It is the uttering of a shrill, piercing cry, expressive of emotional excitement. The petitions made in the psalm thus far indicated that the psalmist has not been able to open his lips because of a silence caused by moral inability. The realization of his guilt and his need of God's forgiveness in order to be able to praise him is gathered together in the words "O Lord, open my lips" and released in "and my mouth shall declare your praise."

> Yes, you delight not in sacrifice,
> were I to give a burnt offering, you would not be pleased.
> My sacrifice, O God, is a broken spirit;
> a broken and contrite heart, O God, you will not despise.
> (16-17)

In the second part of the vow, the psalmist promises the gift of himself to God, and makes clear that nothing else will do. The value of any external solution such as a sacrifice is not found in mere external ceremony. (Verses 18-19, not quoted here, are a latter liturgical addition made during the exile.[139] They interpret the meaning of verses 16-17 as only a relative denial of the worth of sacrifice in the context of being without Jerusalem; and point to the great need for liturgy when properly reformed. The original meaning of verses 16-17, though, is a clear rejection of empty sacrifice as a solution.)

No external solution exists for a problem that is so deeply internal. Rather, the notion of sacrifice must become metaphorical because the only appropriate sacrifice must coincide with the spiritual nature of the problem. The solution must be in terms of the depths of personality—a broken spirit and a crushed heart. As we experience what in English we call contrition, we should remember that the word comes from the Latin *contritio* meaning "grinding, bruising, crushing." This is what the psalmist means by a contrite heart which he is vowing to the Lord, yet he does so with great hope. For while the pulverization of the psalmist's heart brings him to realize his utter dependence upon God, he has unshaken confidence in God's response. "A broken and contrite heart, O God, you will not despise."

# NOTES

## Chapter One

1. Community of God's Love (formerly called Ignatius House Community) is a Catholic Charismatic Community in Rutherford, N.J. The Community publishes a quarterly newsletter for its friends which can support people in growing in radical love for one another in deeper relationships. It is available free of charge by writing to Community of God's Love, 70 West Passaic Avenue, Rutherford, N.J. 07070, and requesting your name be put on the mailing list for it.
2. The charismatic renewal is the fastest growing movement in the churches today. It is a movement of spiritual renewal in faith and people touched by it often form prayer groups where they gather together for shared prayer. The story of the beginnings of the movement are well documented in the following books: Edward O'Connor, *The Pentecostal Movement in the Catholic Church,* 1971; Kevin and Dorothy Ranaghan, *Catholic Pentecostals,* 1969; and *As the Spirit Leads Us,* 1971. These books and others on the Charismatic Renewal are available from Charismatic Renewal Services, 237 North Michigan, South Bend, Ind. 46601.
3. For this example I am indebted to Harry J. Cargas, "Love is Vulnerable," *Desert Call* 11, no. 4 (Fall 1976): 9.
4. Msgr. Robert J. Fox, Argus Communication poster. Copyright © by Robert J. Fox. Used by permission.

## Chapter Two

5. For a listing of the scriptural passages which show this and an exegesis of them, see James Dunn, *Jesus and the Spirit* (Philadelphia: Westminster Press, 1975), pp. 14-40. The following paragraph also relies principally upon Dunn.

6. See note 5, p. 26.
7. For a list of scripture passages where mind *(nous)* means thought pattern, attitude, way of thinking, consult Felix W. Gingrich, *Shorter Lexicon of the Greek New Testament* (Chicago: University of Chicago Press, 1965), p. 144. Also see J. Behm, "Nous in the New Testament," in *Theological Dictionary of the New Testament*, ed. Gerhard Kittel (Grand Rapids, Mich.: Eerdmans, 1967), vol. 4, p. 958.
8. Joseph Fitzmyer notes that "*Nous* for Paul seems to describe man as a knowing and judging subject; it designates his capacity for intelligent understanding, planning and decision. . . . It is this capacity of man that recognizes what can be known about God from his creation (Rom 1:20). . . . There is really little difference in Paul's use of *nous* and *kardia* (heart), which, as in the Old Testament, often means 'mind.' If anything, *kardia* would connote the more responsive and emotional reactions of the intelligent, planning self." "Pauline Theology" in *The Jerome Biblical Commentary*, ed. Raymond E. Brown, Joseph A. Fitzmyer and Roland E. Murphy (Englewood Cliffs, N.J.: Prentice-Hall, 1968), vol. 2, section 79:122, p. 821. Another scripture scholar, J. Behm, reminds us that "In the *nous* of Christians, that is, in the inner direction of their thoughts and will and the orientation of their moral consciousness there should be constant renewal (Rom 12:2, Eph 4:23)." "Nous in the New Testament," *Theological Dictionary of the New Testament* (see note 7), vol. 4, p. 958. Dunn writes, "It is not something accomplished once and for all at any one time; Paul understands it rather as a process." See note 5, p. 223.
9. Lucien Cerfaux, *The Christian in the Theology of St. Paul* (New York: Herder and Herder, 1967), p. 311.
10. Merlin R. Çarothers, *Prison to Praise* (Plainfield, N.J.: Logos, 1970), p. 92.
11. Job actively praising God instead of complaining about disasters is an archetypal praise response. Actively praising God, blessing him and giving thanks can be seen as being at the heart of a Christian's life and the community's life in the Eucharist. A valuable book that helps to see this is Robert J.

Ledogar, *Acknowledgment: Praise-verbs in the Early Greek Anaphora* (Rome: Casa Editrice Herder, 1968). In the chapter on praise-verbs in the New Testament he notes that "public thanksgiving in the New Testament is aimed at stimulating and increasing the faith of those in whose presence it is uttered" (p. 125). That is to say that actively praising is aimed at stimulating our faith, not merely giving God his due. In commenting on Hebrews 13:15 ("through him let us continually offer God a sacrifice of praise, that is, the fruit of lips which acknowledge his name"), Ledogar claims that "this praise-confession is understood not only as a vocal act, but as a commitment of one's life to Christ" (p. 135). Again, actively praising is seen as revealing an inner decision that opts for a faith perspective.

12. Paul Hinnebusch, *Praise: A Way of Life* (Ann Arbor, Mich.: Servant, 1976), pp. 197, 198, 200.
13. Although the end of the world is an apocalyptic time, it is not the only one; any time of crisis which is bringing to birth a new era is also an apocalyptic time. For a better understanding of this see John Randall, *Revelation: What Does the Book of Revelation Say?* (Locust Valley, N.Y.: Living Flame Press, 1976).
14. Pope Paul VI, "Let not your hearts be troubled," *L'Osservatore Romano* (English edition), February 3, 1977, p. 1.
15. Raymond E. Brown, *The Gospel According to John (XIII-XXI)*, The Anchor Bible, vol. 29A (Garden City, N.Y.: Doubleday, 1970), pp. 653, 733.
16. Michel Bouttier, *Christianity According to Paul*, Studies in Biblical Theology #49 (Naperville, Ill.: Alec R. Allenson, 1966), p. 77.
17. See note 5, p. 316.

## Chapter Three

18. See Kevin Perrotta, "Agreeing to Make Agreements: How to Take Some of the Tension Out of Our Service and Personal Relationships," *Pastoral Renewal* 1, No. 11 (May 1977):86-88.
19. Daniel D. Rhodes, *A Covenant Community: A Study of the Book of Exodus* (Richmond: John Knox Press, 1964), p. 45.

20. George W. Buchanan, *The Consequences of the Covenant* (Leiden: E. J. Brill, 1970), pp. 282-315.
21. Dennis J. McCarthy, *The Old Testament Covenant: A Survey of Current Opinions* (Richmond: John Knox Press, 1972), pp. 10-11.
22. Delbert R. Hillers, *Covenant: The History of a Biblical Idea* (Baltimore: John Hopkins Press, 1969), p. 188.
23. George E. Mendenhall, "Covenant Forms in Israelite Tradition," *The Biblical Archaeologist* 17, no. 2 (May 1954):26-46 and no. 3 (September 1954):49-76.
24. C. H. Kraeling, *John The Baptist* (New York: Scribner, 1951), p. 129. As quoted by Dunn (see note 5), p. 56.
25. See note 5, p. 59.
26. See note 5, p. 79.
27. See note 5, chapters II and III.
28. See *New American Bible* introduction to the Epistle of Paul to the Galatians.
29. William Barclay, *The Revelation of John* (Philadelphia: Westminster Press, 1960), vol. I, pp. 77, 78. Another interesting commentary on the dynamics going on here is given from a psychological point of view by Carl G. Jung, "Psychology in the Classical Age: The Gnostics, Tertullian and Origen," in *Psychological Types,* Bollingen Series XX (Princeton, N.J.: Princeton University Press, 1971), vol. 6, pp. 8-20.
30. See *New American Bible* footnote on Acts 13:13.
31. Edward J. Mally, "The Gospel According to Mark," in *The Jerome Biblical Commentary* (see note 8), vol. 2, section 42:2, p. 21.
32. Richard J. Dillon and Joseph A. Fitzmyer, "Acts of the Apostles," in *The Jerome Biblical Commentary* (see note 8), vol. 2, section 45:78, p. 197.

## Chapter Four

33. F.J. Connell, "Correction, Fraternal," in *New Catholic Encyclopedia*, 15 vols. (New York: McGraw-Hill, 1967), 4:348.
34. The same distinctions are mentioned in Kevin Perrotta, "An Ounce of Correction . . . ," *Pastoral Renewal* 1, no. 10 (April 1977):75.

35. Commenting on Matthew 7:1, John McKenzie writes that "the meaning of 'judge' is not simply to have an opinion—this can scarcely be avoided; the word means to judge harshly, to condemn, and the form in which the saying appears in Luke (6:37-38) makes this explicit .... Men must judge one another, but they can expect to be called to responsibility for their judgments." "The Gospel According to Matthew," in *The Jerome Biblical Commentary* (see note 8), vol. 2, section 43:48, p. 75.
36. A study on the Greek word 'to judge' by F. Buchsel concludes, "From the fact that God's judgment threatens man it is often deduced that no man has the right to judge another (Mt 7:1f; Jn 4:11; Rom 14:4, 10; 1 Cor 4:15). This does not imply flabby indifference to the moral condition of others, nor the blind renunciation of attempts at a true and serious appraisal of those with whom we have to live. What is unconditionally demanded is that such evaluations should be subject to the certainty that God's judgment falls also on those who judge, so that superiority, hardness and blindness to one's own faults are excluded, and a readiness to forgive and to intercede is safeguarded." *Theological Dictionary of the New Testament* (see note 8), vol. 3, p. 939.
37. Xavier Leon-Dufour, ed., *Dictionary of Biblical Theology*, article on "Education" (Montreal: Palm Publishers, 1967), p. 114.
38. For a more detailed description of Paul's tender relationship with the churches see Thomas Dubay, *Caring: A Biblical Theology of Community* (Denville, N.J.: Dimension Books, 1973), p. 200ff.
39. The interconnections of the entire chapter, the structural division of Matthew 18 and the background for a redaction-criticism of it are found in William G. Thompson, *Matthew's Advice to a Divided Community, Mt 17:22–18:35*, Analecta Biblica Series #44 (Rome: Biblical Institute Press, 1970).
40. See note 39, p. 5.
41. See note 39, p. 264.
42. See note 39, p. 153.
43. See note 39, p. 154.

44. See note 39, p. 259.
45. See note 39, p. 159.
46. See note 39, p. 174.
47. On Matthew 18:15a, Thompson notes that "verbal contacts suggest an allusion to the law in Leviticus: 'You shall not hate your brother in your heart, but you shall reason with your neighbor, lest you bear sin because of him' (Lv. 19:17). This regulation may refer to a juridical process, but it seems to have a wider application. One person experiences hostile thoughts and feelings towards another, and may be inclined to nourish them in the secrecy of his own heart. He must, however, bring them out into the open either before a juridical body in a formal process or in a private conversation. For it is a sin to keep such feelings hidden instead of clarifying the issue in open conversation with one's adversary." See note 39, p. 179.
48. See note 39, p. 181.
49. See note 39, p. 185.
50. William Barclay, *The Gospel of Matthew* (Philadelphia: Westminster Press, 1958), vol. 2, p. 209.
51. See note 39, p. 195.
52. See note 50, p. 207.
53. See note 39, p. 207.
54. See note 39, p. 213; the dollar equivalents are from Thompson's book. The *Jerusalem Bible* footnotes indicates the contrast as $9,000,000 to less than $15. The contrast remains unchanged.

## Chapter Five

55. John Cassian, *The Conferences*, in *A Select Library of Nicene and Post-Nicene Fathers of the Christian Church*, Second Series, tr. Edgar C. S. Gibson (Grand Rapids, Mich.: Eerdmans, 1973), Vol. XI, p. 296.
56. See note 55, p. 295.
57. See Cassian's *The Institutes* (in same volume as *Conferences*, note 55) on the eight principal faults (pp. 223-294); *Conferences*, pp. 339-351.

58. For an explanation of the meaning of purity of heart see Joseph Breault, *Seeking Purity of Heart: The Gift of Ourselves to God* (Locust Valley, N.Y.: Living Flame Press, 1975).
59. Thomas Merton, *The Wisdom of the Desert* (New York: New Directions, 1960), p. 37. Pronouns are put into modern English.
60. The understanding of the progression of events has been helped by the perspective of Albert Ellis. See Chapter Eight.
61. See note 59, p. 40.
62. See note 55, pp. 304, 306.
63. See note 55, p. 365.
64. See note 55, p. 534.
65. See note 55, pp. 300, 301.
66. See note 55, p. 441.
67. See note 55, p. 363.

## Chapter Six

68. Herbert Thurston and Donald Attwater, *Butler's Lives of the Saints* (New York: Kenedy, 1963), vol. 1, p. 513.
69. Part 2a, 2ae, Question 60. The Blackfriars edition of *The Summa* notes on Question 60 that "Judgment, judicium, not here a topic for logic or epistemology, but for moral and social science: a decision on what is just, mainly in court, but extending also to private judgment on the probity and character of another." St. Thomas Aquinas, *Summa Theologicae* (Cambridge, England: Blackfriars; New York: McGraw-Hill, 1964 - ), vol. 37, p. 66.
70. For more information on Aquinas' distinction between the theoretical (or speculative) realm and the practical realm see John E. Naus, *The Nature of the Practical Intellect According to Saint Thomas Aquinas*, Analecta Gregoriana, vol. 108 (Rome: Libreria Editrice dell' Universita Gregoriana, 1959); Jacques Maritain, *The Degrees of Knowledge*, tr. Gerald B. Phelan (New York: Charles Scribner's Sons, 1959), pp. 456-464; Jacques Maritain, *The Philosophy of Art (Art and Scholasticism)*, tr. John O'Connor (Sussex: St. Dominic's Press, 1923), pp. 3-5.

71. See note 69, vol. 36, p. 103.
72. See note 69, p. 69.
73. See note 69, p. 71.
74. See note 69, p. 71.
75. See note 69, p. 29.
76. See note 69, p. 21.
77. See note 69, vol. 36, p. 5.
78. See note 69, p. 73.
79. See note 69, p. 73.
80. See note 69, p. 75.
81. See note 69, p. 77.
82. See note 69, p. 79.
83. See note 69, p. 79.
84. See note 69, p. 79.
85. See note 69, pp. 83, 85.

## Chapter Seven

86. Manifestation of conscience is "the revelation of intimate and personal matters made to another in order that the revealer might be guided more efficaciously by his director in the spiritual life." See D. Dee, "Manifestation of Conscience," in *New Catholic Encyclopedia* (see note 33), 9:160. This is the source of much of this section.
87. For a more detailed explanation of this see J. Creusen, *Religious Men and Women in the Code*, tr. A. Ellis (Milwaukee: Bruce Publishing Company, 1953), pp. 92-97. It might also be noted that some people would have a sensitive spiritual gift that sees into the heart. These matters would still be in that inner realm of conscience, however, since most people would not perceive them.
88. A partial text of the decree is as follows:

> As all human things, however good and holy in themselves, may by the abuse of men be turned to an unfit or improper use, so also laws, however wisely they may be drawn up; and therefore it sometimes happens, that they cease to attain their object, and even produce an effect contrary to what was intended.

This, it must be acknowledged with regret, has happened in regard to the laws of many Congregations, Societies, and Institutes, both of women taking simple or solemn vows, and of men who in their profession and government are laymen. Thus, the manifestation of conscience, which was sometimes permitted by their Constitutions, in order that the members might more easily be trained by experienced Superiors, in the difficult way of perfection, has by some Superiors been turned into a searching examination of conscience, such as belongs only to the Sacrament of Penance . . .

The consequence has been that these regulations, which had been wisely laid down for the spiritual advancement of the members, and for the maintenance and increase of peace and concord in the Community, have not unfrequently caused danger to souls, anxiety of conscience, and disturbance of peace, as is clearly proved by the appeals and complaints made by subjects to the Holy See on every side.

Wherefore, Our Holy Father Pope Leo XIII, out of special solicitude for this most chosen portion of his flock, in an audience granted to me, the Cardinal Prefect of the Sacred Congregation of Bishops and Regulars, on the 14th day of December, 1890, after carefully weighing everything, has willed, determined, and decreed as follows:

I. His Holiness annuls, abolishes, and declares of no force in future, all regulations contained in the Constitutions of pious Societies and Institutes, both of women with simple or solemn vows, and also of laymen—even though the aforesaid Constitutions may have been approved by the Holy See and in the form which is called "most special,"—so far as they relate in any way, or under any name, to the manifestation of the inward heart and conscience. He therefore lays upon the Superiors, whether men or women, of such Institutes, Congregations, and Societies, the grave obligation of completely cancelling and erasing in their Constitutions, Directories, and Manuals, the regulations aforesaid. He likewise annuls and cancels all usages and customs whatsoever to the aforesaid effect, even though they may be immemorial.

II. His Holiness, moreover, strictly forbids the Superiors aforesaid, whether men or women, of whatsoever rank or dignity, to endeavour, directly or indirectly, by precept, counsel, fear, threats, or any kind of enticement, to induce their subjects to make such manifestation of conscience to them. He commands all subjects to denounce to their chief Superiors any Superiors of a lower degree who dare to induce them to do this; and if it should be the Superior-General, whether man or woman, the denunciation must be made to this Sacred Congregation.

III. This, however, by no means hinders subjects from opening their minds to their Superiors freely and of their own accord, for the purpose of obtaining from their prudence, in doubt and anxiety, advice and direction for acquiring virtue and making progress in perfection . . .

VIII. Lastly, His Holiness commands that copies of this Decree translated into the vernacular, be inserted in the Constitutions of the aforesaid pious Institutes; and that at least once a year, in each house, at a fixed time, either at the public table or in a Chapter specially called for this purpose, they be read in a loud and clear voice.

Arthur Devine, *Commentary on the Decree Quemadmodum* (New York: Benziger Bros., 1896), pp. 5-8.

89. Timothy L. Bouscaren, Adam C. Ellis, and Francis N. Korth, *Canon Law: A Text and Commentary*, 4th ed. (Milwaukee: Bruce Publishing Company, 1963), p. 254.
90. See note 86, p. 161.
91. See J. T. Catoir, "Internal Forum (Matrimonial Cases)," in *New Catholic Encyclopedia* (see note 33), vol. 16 (Supplement 1967-1974): 224.

92. Walter M. Abbott, ed., *The Documents of Vatican II* (New York: Guild Press, 1966), p. 716.
93. See note 92, pp. 199, 200.
94. See note 92, p. 213.
95. See note 92, p. 222.
96. See note 92, p. 227.
97. *On Due Process,* Revised Edition (National Conference of Catholic Bishops), p. 2.
98. See note 97, p. 3.
99. See note 97, pp. 8, 41.
100. See note 97, pp. 41, 42.
101. See note 97, pp. 34, 47.
102. Pope Paul VI's February 4th, 1977 allocution to the Sacred Roman Rota, *L'Osservatore Romano* (English edition), February 24, 1977, pp. 5, 9.

## Chapter Eight

103. Albert Ellis and Robert Harper, *A New Guide to Rational Living* (North Hollywood, Calif.: Wilshire Book Company, 1976), pp. 11-12.
104. See note 103, p. 25.
105. See note 103, p. 27.
106. See note 103, pp. 207-208.
107. Albert Ellis, *Reason and Emotion in Psychotherapy* (New York: Lyle Stuart, 1962), Chapter Three; and some revisions he has made in the book referred to in note 103.
108. Donald J. Tosi, *Youth: Toward Personal Growth, A Rational Emotive Approach* (Columbus, Ohio: Charles E. Merrill, 1974), pp. 55-56.
109. For a discussion of this understanding see the Introduction by John Eudes Bamberger in Evagrius Ponticus, *The Praktikos* (Spencer, Mass.: Cistercian Publications, 1970), pp. 8-9. Also, Louis Bouyer, *Liturgical Piety* (Notre Dame, Ind.: University of Notre Dame Press, 1955), pp. 257-259.
110. Evagrius Ponticus, *The Praktikos*, p. 28, #43.

111. See Evagrius Ponticus, *The Praktikos*, pp. 16-20, #6-14. Cf. John Cassian, *Institutes* (see note 57, pp. 233-290). Also *Conferences* (see note 55, pp. 339-351).
112. Evagrius Ponticus, translated by George Maloney in his article, "Tears and Enlightenment," *Review for Religious* 33, no. 6 (November 1974): 1398-1399.
113. For example, see John S. Maddux, "When You Pray ... Self-knowledge and Prayer," *The Way* 17, no. 3 (July 1977): 229-238.
114. Columba Marmion, *Christ, The Ideal of the Monk* (London: Sands & Co., 1926), p. 160.
115. Bernard Tyrrell, *Christotherapy: Healing Through Enlightenment* (New York: Seabury, 1975), pp. 75-76.
116. A further understanding of the usefulness of different approaches to healing for different personality types can be seen by considering Carl Jung's *Psychological Types* (see note 29). He distinguishes between those who are primarily perceivers (through either intuition or sensation) and those who are primarily judgers (through either thinking or feeling). Each of these four types can be either extroverted or introverted, and so he arrives at eight personality types. His descriptions of the way they perceive, judge, and are oriented give insight into the appropriateness of a particular approach to healing for a given person.

## Chapter Nine

117. For an explanation and critique of "Transcendental Thomism" see article in *New Catholic Encyclopedia* (see note 33), vol. 16 (Supplement 1967-1974): 449-454.
118. Quoted in *Current Biography Yearbook 1972* (New York: H. W. Wilson), p. 280.
119. Bernard Lonergan, *Method in Theology* (New York: Herder and Herder, 1972), p. 6.
120. Bernard Lonergan, *Insight: A Study of Human Understanding* (New York: Philosophical Library, 1968), p. 4.
121. See note 120, p. 200 and Bernard Lonergan, "Insight Revisited," in *A Second Collection*, ed. William F. J. Ryan and

Bernard J. Tyrrell (Phildelphia: Westminster Press, 1974), p. 271.

122. See note 120, p. 203.
123. See note 119, pp. 38, 39.
124. See note 119, p. 121.

## Chapter Ten

125. See note 2.
126. See Bernard Lonergan, *Doctrinal Pluralism* (Milwaukee: Marquette University Press, 1971).
127. For more information on the examin see Louis J. Puhl, *The Spiritual Exercises of St. Ignatius* (Chicago: Loyola University Press, 1951), #24-43. For journal techniques see Ira Progoff, *At a Journal Workshop, the basic text and guide for using the Intensive Journal* (New York: Dialogue House Library, 1975).
128. See Alex Osborn, *Applied Imagination: Principles and Procedures of Creative Problem Solving*, 3rd rev. ed. (New York: Charles Scribner's Sons, 1963). For creative brainstorming sessions, the first guideline is "Criticism is ruled out. Adverse judgment of ideas must be withheld until later" (p. 156). In speaking of the personnel at brainstorming meetings Osborn says that "probably the most difficult panel members are executives who have been over-trained in the usual kind of non-creative conference ... (as one of these business leaders said to me:) 'It was hard to get through my head what you were trying to do with us. My fifteen years of conference after conference in my company have conditioned me against shooting wild. Almost all of us officers rate each other on the basis of *judgment*—we are far more apt to look up to the other fellow if he makes no mistakes than if he suggests lots of ideas' " (pp. 159-160). Yet there needs to be a creative tension among these gifts both within a leaders group and within an individual. Osborn's suggestion is that "Normally, it is good creative policy to make our imagination shoot wild as long as we still have time to choose our good ideas from our bad" (p. 295).

## Chapter Eleven

129. James A. H. Murray, ed., *The Oxford English Dictionary* (Oxford: Clarendon Press, 1933), vol. II (C), p. 714.
130. See note 129.
131. Edward R. Dalglish, *Psalm Fifty-One in the Light of Ancient Near-Eastern Patternism* (Leiden: E. J. Brill, 1962), p. 85.
132. F. R. Achtemeier, "Mercy," in *The Interpreter's Dictionary of the Bible*, ed. George A. Buttrick, 4 vols. (New York: Abingdon Press, 1962), 3:352. Also see Mt 9:36; 14:14; 15:32; Mk 6:34; 8:2; Lk 7:13; 10:33; 15:20.
133. See the excellent study of defense mechanisms in this context by Arnold Uleyn, *Is it I Lord: Pastoral Psychology and the Recognition of Guilt* (New York: Holt, Rinehart and Winston, 1969).
134. "... the anchor points of our identity are in the common experience of a broken existence." Henri Nouwen with Donald McNeill and Douglas Morrison, "Compassion: The Core of Spiritual Leadership," *Worship Jubilee* 1977, p. 13.

## Chapter Twelve

135. The translation is adapted from Dalglish's, found in *Psalm Fifty-One in the Light of Ancient Near-Eastern Patternism* (see note 131). The chapter depends principally upon Dalglish. Personal correspondence with Rev. Carroll Stuhlmueller was also valuable.
136. See note 131, p. 83. Also see W. F. Lofthouse, "*Hen* and *Hesed* in the Old Testament," *Zeitschrift fur die alttestamentliche Wissenschaft* 51 (1933): 29-35.
137. See note 131, p. 105.
138. See note 131, p. 144.
139. Most modern scholars regard the last two verses (vv. 18-19) as a later liturgical addition during the exile for four reasons: (1) in vv. 1-17 the pronouns are I-Thou; in vv. 18-19 it is third person plural; (2) vv. 1-17 is absorbed in personal spiritual problems, while vv. 18-19 have a communal frame of reference; (3) vv. 1-17 have good poetry, creativity and

metrical regularity; vv. 18-19 do not have the same character; (4) vv. 1-17 indicate sacrifice may be offered but is inadequate, while in vv. 18-19 sacrifice is possible only when Zion's walls are restored. See note 131, p. 20 for more information. In light of the lack of continuity, there was no reason to include vv. 18-19 in the prayer for purity of heart.

# INDEX OF SCRIPTURAL REFERENCES

# INDEX